Hennepin Canal Parkway: History Through the Miles

Barton Jennings

Hennepin Canal Parkway: History Through the Miles
Copyright © 2020 by Barton Jennings

All rights reserved. This book may not be duplicated or transmitted in any way, or stored in an information retrieval system, without the express written consent of the publisher, except in the form of brief excerpts or quotations for the purpose of review. Making copies of this book, or any portion, for any purpose other than your own, is a violation of United States copyright laws.

Publisher's Cataloging-in-Publication Data
Jennings, Barton

Hennepin Canal Parkway: History Through the Miles
404p.; 21cm.
ISBN: 978-1-7327888-4-8

Library of Congress Control Number: 2020935065

First Edition

Front cover photos all by Barton Jennings
From top: Bridge #10; Trail at Milepost 19.1; Lock #22
Back cover photo by Sarah Jennings

Please send comments or corrections to sarah@techscribes.com

TechScribes, Inc.
PO Box 620
Avon, IL 61415
www.techscribes.com

Printed in the United States of America

Contents

Preface 5
Acknowledgments 7
Illinois' Hennepin Canal 9
Traveling the Hennepin Canal 11
History of the Hennepin Canal 15
Hennepin Canal Parkway State Park 61
Main Channel of Hennepin Canal 67
Rock River Pool of Hennepin Canal 279
Milan Section of Hennepin Canal 291
Feeder Canal of Hennepin Canal 323
About the Author 403

Other books by Barton Jennings

<u>History Through the Miles</u>
Arkansas & Missouri Railroad: History Through the Miles
Alaska Railroad: History Through the Miles
Iowa Interstate Railroad: History Through the Miles
Everett Railroad: History Through the Miles
Tennessee Central Railway: History Through the Miles
Whitewater Valley Railroad: History Through the Miles
Oregon's Joseph Branch: History Through the Miles
Missouri & North Arkansas Railroad: History Through the Miles

<u>Textbook</u>
The Basics of Transportation: Policies, Practices and Pricing – An Applied Perspective

Preface

This book began when the author moved to rural western Illinois, and frequently passed the canal on his way to and from Chicago. The canal trail was often used as an excuse for a short walk to break up the long drive. The author learned more about the canal as he researched the nearby Iowa Interstate Railroad, originally the Chicago, Rock Island & Pacific's mainline west of Chicago. The result of the railroad research was the book *Iowa Interstate Railroad: History Through the Miles*.

The histories of the Rock Island Railroad and the Hennepin Canal were closely tied, and the combination of short walks and railroad research led to an interest in the canal, and the Hennepin Canal Parkway State Park. Volumes of notes from walking the trail, access to many of the Corps of Engineers records in the Illinois State Archives, newspaper articles, several books, and other sources quickly formed the basis of a book about the canal and parkway. With an interest in both the history of the canal and what can still be found today, the book changed from a pure walking guide to one that includes "what was once here."

While the Hennepin Canal was never a commercial success, it was a technological step forward. Many of the engineering designs and construction techniques used on the Hennepin Canal later became aceepted practices. In particular, the Hennepin Canal served as a testbed for many concepts that were later put to use in the construction of the Panama Canal.

This book combines the history of the canal, and the communities that it passes through, with a guide for walking the trail. Information on access points, parks and campgrounds, nearby stores, and wildlife that may be seen is included. Also included is the history of what was once at various locations, things like staff housing, warehouses, ice houses, grain elevators, and other structures needed to operate the canal. Particular attention is paid to the locks and other structures that still exist along the 170 miles of hiking, biking, equestrian, and snowmobiling trails in the Hennepin Canal Parkway State Park.

Acknowledgments

A number of people deserve a special thanks for their help in collecting the information necessary for this book, and in getting it written. Jim and Chris get a great deal of credit for their explanation of the Illinois State Archives and their many trips to 9N to provide me with access to the several rooms full of Hennepin Canal documents and photos. A number of people who I don't even know also get thanks for providing information and pointing out features as I met them along the canal. My mother also deserves a thank-you. In her free time, she read the initial draft of this book and provided comments from the point of view of someone who knew nothing about the canal. Finally, my wife Sarah again played a big role in making this book possible. She did everything from helping with the final edit to finding me at some lonely spot along the canal after a day of exploring. Thanks to all.

Illinois' Hennepin Canal

The Hennepin Canal Parkway State Park, also just called the Hennepin Canal, is an abandoned canal waterway in northwest Illinois, located between the Mississippi River at Rock Island and the Great Bend of the Illinois River near Hennepin. The entire canal is listed on the National Register of Historic Places and today serves as a recreational center with trails, fishing, and many other activities. In January 2019, the Hennepin Canal Parkway was designated as part of the national Great American Rail-Trail. This proposed 4000-mile trail has been created by the Rails-to-Trails Conservancy and seeks to connect a number of existing trails with new connecting routes to allow a coast-to-coast network of hiking and biking trails.

Opened in 1907, the Hennepin Canal was abandoned by the early 1950s because of railroad competition and a difference in engineering specifications from connecting waterways. The canal was resurrected in the late 20th century as a recreational waterway. Its formal name was the Illinois & Mississippi Canal, a name used to demonstrate a national importance for the property. The canal included two sections – the 75-mile long Main Channel and the 29-mile long Feeder Canal. Both parts are today the Hennepin Canal Parkway State Park, Illinois' longest multi-use trail. While water still remains in much of the canal, navigation on the waterway is limited, but the towpath is today a popular walking and biking trail across Western Illinois.

The name Hennepin traces back to Father Louis Hennepin, a Roman Catholic priest of the Franciscan Order. Father Hennepin served in several locations before being selected as one of four missionaries to be sent to explore New

France in May 1675. New France was the part of North America claimed by France from 1534 until 1763, and numerous expeditions were sent to attempt to make the lands profitable for France. While settlement was one goal of the French government, trade with the Native Americans and the search for mineral wealth were also important.

The exploration that involved Father Hennepin was under the command of René-Robert Cavelier, Sieur de La Salle, who is generally credited with being the first European to traverse the Ohio River, and the leader of the second trip over the Mississippi River. La Salle was also a major fur trader who worked the Great Lakes region.

During the late 1670s, Hennepin traveled and met with many different Native American tribes. In 1679, he accompanied La Salle on a voyage across the Great Lakes and then down the Illinois River, arriving at Fort Crevecoeur (Peoria, Illinois) in January 1680. While exploring for routes to the Mississippi River, Hennepin was captured by a Sioux war party and taken to today's Minnesota. Hennepin was eventually released and sent back to Europe where he wrote about his travels, including the book *A New Discovery*, printed in 1683 about Niagara Falls. Besides Niagara Falls, Hennepin is also credited with being the first European to see Saint Anthony Falls, the only natural waterfall on the Mississippi River.

Today, a small community alongside the Illinois River carries the name Hennepin, but the attempt to connect the Great Lakes with the Mississippi River and other western waterways is what really ties the name Hennepin to this canal system.

Traveling the Hennepin Canal

The Hennepin Canal is a popular walking and exercise trail in the urban areas of Colona, Milan, Geneseo and Rock Falls, Illinois. At the same time, it is a rural hiking and backpacking route further east and south. Snowmobiling in winter is common, and it is reported that there are 91 miles of snowmobile trails on the towpath, the longest snowmobile trail in Illinois. Additionally, explorers on bike and horse can be found most of the rest of the year. The use of small boats is also possible, supported by a series of boat ramps. However, all along the canal, day trips, picnicking, and fishing are probably the most popular activities.

Along the canal are a number of campgrounds and day use areas, generally located at lock locations where toilets, picnic tables, and other facilities have been built. Most of these locations can be driven to and make good locations to start or finish a trip over part or all of the canal's route. However, it should be noted that except for snowmobiles in winter, motorized vehicles are not allowed on the canal's trail system.

The sign says it all – the trail through the Hennepin Canal Parkway State Park is not for motorized vehicles. Photo by Barton Jennings.

Signs often mark the busiest canal locations, where there may be pavilions, picnic tables, and toilets. Many also have major signs along the highway that help you find them. Photo by Barton Jennings.

A unique activity along the canal is the *Hennepin Hundred*, an event that includes a 100-mile ultramarathon, Illinois' only point-to-point, all-trail ultramarathon. The event, held the first Saturday of October, also includes a 50-mile and a 50-kilometer nighttime run, as well as a 100-mile relay. The 100-mile route is from Sterling, Illinois, south to Feeder Junction, then east to near Wyanett, and then west to near the Rock River at Colona.

When the property was acquired by the State of Illinois, the plan was to provide a recreational corridor between Bureau and the Quad Cities (Moline and Rock Island, Illinois, and Davenport and Bettendorf, Iowa). Because of this, access to the canal property is available at almost one hundred locations, mostly where roads cross the waterway or at parks alongside various locks. Some locations are better than others, and this book provides information about the official and unofficial access points along the canal. Changes do happen, and updated details are available from the Hennepin Canal Parkway State Park.

Wildlife

The Hennepin Canal Parkway State Park passes through miles of rural country with only a few miles of urban area at its west and north ends. Because of this, wildlife is very common along the route. For them, the canal and trail provide a source of water, shelter, and a quick and easy route across the territory. Hikers and bikers who are quiet and observant of their surroundings will likely see plenty to keep them entertained.

While walking the parkway trail, smaller animals such as squirrel, rabbit and raccoon are common sightings. Others such as deer, fox, coyote, muskrat, beaver and otter can be seen, especially early and late in the day. Have little fear, they are far more scared of you than you are of them, and even the smallest sound can send them running. Each year, there is a lottery for archery deer hunting – as well as dove hunting – along the canal, which helps to keep the fear of humans in the wildlife. A drawing is also held for duck blinds at Lake Sinnissippi at the north end of the Feeder Canal.

The canal is also the home of a large number of birds. Basically, if they stay in Illinois for any period of time, they can be seen along the canal. Larger birds such as great blue heron, bald eagle, Canadian geese, and kingfishers are common. Watch as they often fly or paddle away at your approach. Smaller birds such as goldfinches, blue jays, chickadees, purple martins, mourning doves and hundreds of others are everywhere. For bird watchers, the canal is a great place to work on their list.

Since the opening of the canal, fishing has been a popular activity. Many species of fish came naturally to the canal thanks to the water from the Rock River. Others have been and are still stocked by various private and government agencies. Fishing on the canal is allowed 24 hours per day, and ice fishing in winter is common. Large and smallmouth bass, catfish, walleye, crappie, and bluegills are popular. The major pools are regularly stocked. On the first Saturday in April, and the third Saturday in October, the lagoon behind the visitor center is netted off and hundreds of pounds of trout are released.

Views such as this are typical along the canal, so stop and enjoy the wildlife. Photo by Barton Jennings.

While fishing is allowed 24 hours per day, there are a few rules as shown on this sign, found at many of the road crossings along the canal. Photo by Barton Jennings.

History of the Hennepin Canal

The Hennepin Canal is a historic canal that is listed on the National Register of Historic Places. This does not mean that the canal was ever financially a success, because it wasn't. By the time it was built, railroads already dominated the route. The canal was also built to standards that would soon be out of date as newer standards were being established for major waterways. However, it did become known as a successful experiment that led to a number of improvements in canal engineering, standards that were soon adopted in projects such as the Panama Canal.

    One of the best histories and descriptions of the Hennepin Canal can be found in the *National Register of Historic Places Inventory – Nomination Form*, for the Hennepin Canal Historic District, dated 1977. While many of the infrastructure details found in the report are dated – many bridges and buildings have been removed, for example – the 70 pages of the report are still fascinating. Some of that material is included in this volume. Other sources of information include various documents produced by the Illinois Department of Natural Resources, the Friends of the Hennepin Canal, and the U.S. Army Corps of Engineers. The book *A History of the Rock Island District U.S. Army Corps of Engineers 1866-1983* includes a detailed chapter on the canal's history. The book *Voices of the Hennepin Canal: Promoters, Politicians, and the U.S. Army Corps of Engineers*, by Dr. Donald W. Griffin, is also a great read for those interested in the many details of the canal, including its history and political background.

    While the history can be found elsewhere, coverage of the basics is helpful as an introduction to the canal and what can be found while walking or hiking along its route. The National Register of Historic Places breaks the history of the Hennepin Canal into four eras: Promotion and Planning (1834-1890), Construction (1890-1907), Commercial Navigation (1907-1951), and Recreational Use (1951-Current). This analysis will be used here to describe the history of the canal.

Promotion and Planning of the Hennepin Canal (1834-1890)

Talk of a canal between the Illinois River near Hennepin, and the Mississippi River near Rock Island, began in the early 1800s, just as plans for the Illinois & Michigan Canal were being finalized. The Illinois & Michigan Canal was an Illinois project to improve navigation on the Illinois River, and connect it with the Chicago River and Lake Michigan. The first documented promotion of the Hennepin Canal was in the early 1830s, when the canal was suggested as a way to open up this part of Illinois, to lower shipping rates, and to cut more than 400 miles off the water route between the upper Mississippi River and Lake Michigan near today's Chicago. Experienced canal managers and land speculators soon joined in promoting the project. For example, by 1834, Joseph Galer, a former construction superintendent on the Ohio & Erie Canal, and Dr. Augustus A. Langworthy, a local land speculator, were pushing for a canal through a series of speeches and presentations.

Galer went as far as conducting an informal survey of the route west from the Illinois River at Hennepin to the Mississippi River, declaring it to be a natural low pass between the two rivers. Canals were being built at the time across the country, and these and other statements led to interest in the idea. However, a lack of funds in Illinois prevented the construction of the canal, but the route soon became that of a railroad. The Rock Island & La Salle Railroad Company was incorporated on February 27, 1847, and then became the Chicago & Rock Island on February 7, 1851. Construction started on October 1, 1851, and trains were running between Chicago and Rock Island by late February of 1854, along much of the route promoted by Galer.

Even though the railroad greatly lowered rates, farmers, miners, and area businessmen still campaigned for a canal in order to lower freight prices even more. The Civil War provided another reason for the canal as Canada controlled part of the Great Lakes and the St. Lawrence River route east to the Atlantic Ocean. Canada, as a part of the United Kingdom, favored the Confederacy during the first part of the war, leading to concern about water access to the region. However, no construction took place.

Illinois still lacked the funding to build the canal, but other states such as New York and Iowa also began to campaign for the project. The first official survey for a canal took place in 1870, two years after Illinois resident Ulysses S. Grant was elected president. By this time, the Granger movement was in full swing, calling for lower freight rates to move farm products. Graham P. Low, a civil engineer and surveyor with the U.S. Army Corps of Engineers, conducted a survey and created a plan for a canal. His plan called for locks that measured 350 by 70 feet, and a canal that was 160 feet wide and 7 feet deep. This made the canal and locks about four times larger than the original Erie Canal, an early standard for canals. The cost to build the canal was estimated to be about $12.5 million, and a United States Senate committee was created to study the plan.

As with many such studies, little was done, and in 1881, the Hennepin Canal Commission was created by more than four hundred representatives from various industries in seven states. One of the major benefits promoted by the commission was the ability to regulate railroad freight rates in the Chicago area. This push to use the canal as a way to force the railroads to lower their rates was documented for several decades. For example, the July 26, 1907, issue of *Engineering World* had an article on the subject. This article provided some calculations that were being used to show benefits of the canal.

> "According to the report of Capt. Lon Bryson, to the Davenport Commercial Club (Davenport, Ia.), on his recent trip to Washington, D.C., in the interest of Hennepin canal, the capacity of the present canal will permit barges of 600 tons to pass through its locks. A tug boat running at an expense of $50 per day can tow three of these barges and in two days at the most can tow them through from Chicago to the Mississippi river, with 1,800 tons of freight, at a cost, including transfers of cargo, not to exceed $500 for the round trip, leaving a liberal margin to the owners at a cost of not more than 50 cts. per ton to the shipper or consignee. The present rate of freight from Chicago to the Mississippi river, at Moline, Rock Island and Davenport, on the lowest class of freight, is $1.30 per ton. The canal rate will scarcely exceed 50 cts. per ton. Supposing this rate were one-half of the present rate, or 65 cts. per ton, and the canal would be, by passing five boats per day, carrying 9,000 tons for 200 days in the year; that would haul 1,800,000 tons on the low estimate of a haulage of 1,000,000 tons, at a saving in freight of 65 cts. per ton, which would amount to $650,000. The railroad rate

would be reduced on every pound of freight between Chicago and the Mississippi river at least 25%."

The growing regional interest resulted in $30,000 in funding for a second survey, made by Major W. H. H. Benyaurd of the Corps of Engineers. Major Benyard created new plans based upon an eastern origin located about 1.75 miles above Hennepin. The difference in the surveys was the west end at the Mississippi River – the three locations of Marais d'Osier, Watertown, and Rock Island. Later in 1882, The State of Illinois ceded the Illinois & Michigan Canal, located between the upper end of the Illinois River and Lake Michigan, to the Federal government on the condition that the entire canal would be enlarged. This was part of a plan to make the proposed Hennepin Canal a part of a larger canal network.

Major Benyaurd has an interesting history, having graduated sixth in his class at West Point in 1863. He was immediately promoted to the rank of first lieutenant in the Corps of Engineers. He was promoted twice during the Civil War for bravery and heroism, and later awarded the Medal of Honor for his actions. He worked on a number of military and waterway projects across the United States, and was in charge of submarine defenses (mines) at Jacksonville and Tampa Bay, and fortification on the St. John River in Florida, during the Spanish-American War. He died while on active duty in 1900 and is buried at the West Point Cemetery.

Benyuard's study was based upon the assumption that the development of the Upper Mississippi Valley would be a national economic advantage and that the inland waterway system was a unified and viable mode of transport and commerce. His study, as well as the reports of supporters, stated that the construction of the Hennepin Canal was needed to compete with the railroads and would reduce the cost of transportation in the Upper Mississippi Valley.

The year 1886 saw more support for the canal from organizations such as the Knights of Labor. A Board of Engineers was created in 1886 to examine the routes and the Marais d'Osier route, located north of the Quad Cities, was originally selected. However, this was quickly changed to Rock Island to connect to the military base there, today's Rock Island Arsenal. The change was also influenced by the heavy concentration of industry in the Rock Island-Davenport area, potential users of the canal. To gain more support for the canal, the name was changed from the Hennepin Canal to the Illinois & Mississippi Canal in 1889. After another engineering study in 1890, the Corps of Engineers estimated a cost of $6,925,960 to build the canal. However, even after several decades of studies, they did not recommend enlarging the canal's earlier plan. But, funding would soon be available for the start of construction.

Construction of the Hennepin Canal (1890-1907)

The first action to actually build the Hennepin Canal was supported by the *River and Harbors Act of September 19, 1890*. This Act authorized the design and construction of the canal, but with some of the canal's dimensions smaller than the plans from 1870 and 1883. The channel dimensions were the same – 80 feet wide at the water line and 52 feet wide at the canal bottom – but the locks were 170 feet by 30 feet. This lock size was larger than those that already existed on the Illinois & Michigan Canal, but smaller than new plans coming out at the time.

Plans for the canal's construction broke the project into five sections. These were known as the Eastern, Western, Feeder, Rock River Pool, and Milan sections. While the estimated cost of the project was $6,925,900, the first funding was for $500,000 to handle the construction of the Milan section, about five miles of canal just above the mouth of the Rock River near Milan, Illinois. This part of the canal had priority due to the area's population, as well as the need to move coal from mines to the east to the industries around Rock Island. Coal was always a proposed purpose of the canal. Early reports stated that "70,000 tons of coal were annually consumed in the cities on the Rock River, and a material reduction in the price of this coal to the consumer should result from water transportation."

Because of the focus on shippers along the Rock River, some of the earliest plans for the canal actually used many miles of the river. One of the first routes surveyed, and engineering plans created for, had the canal head more northwest from Bureau and connect with the Rock River at Penny's Slough, north of Geneseo. While some estimates said that the route would cost slightly less and serve more customers, a more direct route toward Rock Island was eventually chosen and built.

Many of the Corps of Engineers officers who supervised the construction of the Hennepin Canal were noted military leaders with distinguished careers, and some of their stories will be told throughout this book. The initial construction was supervised by Major William Louis Marshall, commander of the Second Chicago District of the U.S. Army Corps of Engineers. Marshall had served in the Civil War, joining the 10th Kentucky Cavalry, Union Army, at the age of 16. He was later commissioned in the Corps of Engineers after graduating from the United States Military Academy in 1868. He was part of the Wheeler Survey that explored the Southwest during the early 1870s, and then he supervised improvements on the Lower Mississippi River and the Fox-Wisconsin Waterway canal system in Wisconsin. Marshall worked on the 1890 plan for the Hennepin

Canal and then was in charge of its construction until December 31, 1899.

Marshall was well-known for his belief in concrete construction, and was next assigned to New York to help with the Ambrose Channel project (the only shipping channel in and out of the Port of New York and New Jersey), and to develop standardized fortification construction methods. In 1908, he became the Chief of Engineers, the last Chief of Engineers to have served in the Civil War. Marshall retired in 1910 but was immediately appointed a consulting engineer to the Secretary of the Interior on hydroelectric power projects by President William Howard Taft.

Even before construction began on the canal, Major Marshall began to campaign for the use of concrete in locks and other structures. He argued that concrete was stronger and less expensive, even though all locks in that time period were made from cut stone. The Secretary of War approved the use of concrete on May 11, 1891, and the savings were used to widen the locks by five feet, making them 170 feet long and 35 feet wide. Later, it was stated in the book *A History of the Rock Island District Corps of Engineers* by Roald Tweet (1975), that the use of concrete in the Hennepin Canal "revolutionized the construction industry and set a pattern for canal construction, especially at the Panama Canal."

Construction Begins

Construction on the canal began near the Mississippi River during July 1892. The first goal was to build the canal around the shoals of the lower Rock River near Milan, opening up several miles of the river for the movement of coal and other goods. The locks were completed and the canal was tested with water by late 1894. After that winter, the Milan section of the canal opened on April 17, 1895, the first part to handle commercial traffic.

Building the concrete locks required a great deal of planning, and the construction of large wooden forms. Finding labor and the contractors who could do the work was often a challenge for the Corps of Engineers. Illinois and Mississippi (Hennepin) Canal, "Photographic Files," Record Series 497.037, Illinois State Archives.

Limited construction on the 24 miles of the eastern end of the main channel of the Hennepin Canal started in 1894. This part of the canal was considered to be the most difficult to build since it included a 196-foot lift. An article entitled "Canal Workers Strike – Already There Is Trouble at the Hennepin Ditch" may explain some of the delays in construction in this area. Found in the September 12, 1894, issue of the *San Francisco Call*, the article states:

> *The contractors for the eastern terminus of the Hennepin canal had their first strike six days after the first sod was turned. The head mule boss and twenty teamsters quit work last night and drew their time checks. The men claimed that the hours were too long; that the board was not worth $4 per week;*

> *that the beds were no more than blankets, and the late rains came through the holes of the tents, soaking the ground on which they lay, and many had to go to the railroad and sleep in empty boxcars. A reporter visited the camp and found Contractor Callahan eating supper at the same table with his men. The food was good and well cooked. The cause of the strike, he said, was the discharge of the mule boss for refusing to obey orders. The places of the strikers were immediately filled from the horde of waiting men and the work goes merrily on.*

A major challenge with the construction was that funding came in spurts based upon passage of various funding bills. However, the *River and Harbors Act of June 3, 1896*, started regular allocation of construction funding for the period 1897-1902. With this, construction on the western end of the canal began in 1897. The western end had only a 93-foot lift and only half as many locks as the eastern end. Work on the eastern section of the canal was mostly completed by 1899, and the western section was completed several years later, although heavily delayed by very wet weather in 1902 and 1903.

Besides the use of concrete, the construction of the Hennepin Canal was also able to take advantage of more modern construction techniques. Steam-powered dredges were used to dig parts of the canal. The dredges were noted for the early use of the "orange-peel" buckets, the classic four-part bucket that opens fully to work in damp soil. Several portable narrow gauge (3-foot) railroads were used along the canal to move the dirt, concrete, supplies and workers. These railroads and their track and equipment were moved from location to location as needed, generally operating on the planned 16-foot-wide towpath of the canal. Because of the soft ground due to a peat bog found along the route between miles 20 and 23, an overhead cableway was used to dig that section. Cableways with dredge buckets were stretched between wooden towers 500 feet apart, moving the soil to locations where it could be disposed. The September 1921 issue of *The Excavating Engineer* credits several experiments by contractors working on the Hennepin Canal in developing and proving the use of the dragline bucket, today a common device used in excavation. While little used by commercial waterway traffic, the timing of the canal's construction was perfect for testing new construction techniques.

Manpower was sometimes the only source of work. Horses were also used to pull scrapers, digging and moving much of the dirt from the canal's basin. This photo, found in the Corps of Engineers' files of the Illinois State Archive, shows a number of teams posing for their photo somewhere along the canal. Illinois and Mississippi (Hennepin) Canal, "Photographic Files," Record Series 497.037, Illinois State Archives.

The Corps of Engineers used a narrow gauge railroad to help build much of the Hennepin Canal. Small dump cars like these were used to move dirt and other materials all along the line. Note that while some modern equipment was used, manual labor still moved much of the dirt by shovel. Illinois and Mississippi (Hennepin) Canal, "Photographic Files," Record Series 497.037, Illinois State Archives.

The narrow gauge railroad of the Corps of Engineers was designed to operate on rough track and be moved quickly from place to place. This locomotive, the *Davenport*, was one of the largest used on the Hennepin Canal railroad. Illinois and Mississippi (Hennepin) Canal, "Photographic Files," Record Series 497.037, Illinois State Archives.

History of the Hennepin Canal

This photo shows a concrete mixing plant on the railroad of the Corps of Engineers. Using concrete for locks and other structures was new for the Corps, and much of the work was well documented. Illinois and Mississippi (Hennepin) Canal, "Photographic Files," Record Series 497.037, Illinois State Archives.

The narrow gauge railroad of the Corps of Engineers not only moved dirt, but also delivered construction materials to various work sites. This 1905 photo shows sand and gravel being delivered to a concrete mixing plant. Illinois and Mississippi (Hennepin) Canal, "Photographic Files," Record Series 497.037, Illinois State Archives.

Besides the unexpected peat bog, a number of other issues came up that increased the cost of the construction. One of the most significant was that the canal was built long after roads and railroads had already been built through the region. This required the Corps of Engineers to build sixty-seven highway bridges and eight railroad bridges over the canal. During the construction of the canal, Illinois highway standards changed from a strength requirement of 80 pounds per square foot to 100 pounds per square foot, resulting in litigation over the design of the bridges. A change was also made that limited the bridge approach ramp grade to four percent, leading the Corps of Engineers to reduce the bridge clearance on the Feeder Canal from seventeen feet to twelve feet. A final issue is that the canal construction plan was based upon the ten-hour work day, but eight hours became the standard for the contractors before much work took place.

The year 1899 was significant for the Hennepin Canal. Besides the completion of most of the main channel, construction finally started on the Feeder Canal. There was also a major change in management of the construction of the canal as work was taken over by the Corps of Engineers from The Globe Construction Company of Cincinnati, Ohio. The third major change was that on December 31st, Major Marshall was replaced as commander of the Second Chicago District by Major J. H. Willard. Willard had previously been assigned to the Vicksburg office, responsible for improvements of waterways in Louisiana, Texas, Arkansas and Mississippi. Besides the Hennepin Canal, Willard supervised a great deal of work on various canals and rivers in the Chicago area.

Completion of the Canal

The Feeder Canal section of the project was the major delay to opening the Hennepin Canal. While some construction began in 1899, the location of the north end of the canal still wasn't determined. The plan was to obtain water from the Rock River, with Dixon, Illinois, being the initial planned source. However, a political battle between several cities led to new surveys that showed that the Rock Falls-Sterling area would be eleven miles shorter and less expensive than Dixon. This change led to changes on the main channel of the canal as the source of the canal's water would now be lower, meaning the summit elevation would also have to be made lower. The change eliminated three locks from the canal's plans, and lowered the summit as much as nine feet.

The final delay involving the Feeder Canal was the design, approval, and construction of a dam at Rock Falls to supply the water. After several plans were submitted and reviewed, on December 6, 1906, the Sterling Hydraulic Company agreed on the original plan to construct the dam. When built, the dam was 1335 feet long and included twenty-five gates. The dam raised the river level almost twelve feet and backed water up all the way to Dixon, creating Lake Sinnissippi.

On July 31, 1903, Major C. S. Riche assumed command of the project, and some of the bridges have his name on their builders plates. Riche served in this position until the end of the canal's construction, except for a year (April 1905-April 1906) when he was temporarily assigned to several projects along the upper Mississippi River. While gone, Riche was replaced by Major William Herbert Bixby. Bixby had graduated first in the United States Military Academy class of 1873 and later served as Assistant Professor of Engineering at the Military Academy. He worked on both domestic and international projects for several decades, and oversaw improvements on the Ohio River and its tributaries from Pittsburgh to Cincinnati before this assignment. He later served as president of the Mississippi River Commission and as Chief of Engineers. Bixby is also known for overseeing the raising of the battleship *USS Maine*.

Construction on the Hennepin Canal officially ended on October 21, 1907, and water was sent into the canal on October 24, 1907. There was a great deal of concern about this process as parts of the canal had been completed as long as thirteen years earlier. The canal held and the few leaks soon ended as silt filled the cracks. However, the water in the canal raised the area water table, flooding some fields. Most of the area that the Hennepin Canal flowed through was once marsh, and the canal when dry had helped to drain much of the area land. However, once full of water, this stopped, requiring the construction of a series of ditches outside the canal to handle water that was leaking into the water table.

When the canal was opened, the Corps of Engineers wanted to make an inspection voyage of the canal before the winter freeze. On November 8, 1907, the steamer *SS Marion* departed the Illinois River at Bureau and headed west, covering the entire canal system over the next week. The voyage faced two major challenges: ice and water levels. The ice was handled by installing iron guards on the bow of the *SS Marion*, allowing the ship to push through and break up the ice. The second issue was more interesting as the canal wasn't yet full of water. In some places, water had to be held at locks and moved with the *SS Marion* to make sure there was enough to float the boat. However, at other places, the river levels were up and the canal was full, and the boat had to take on additional passengers to get it under bridges.

History of the Hennepin Canal

This photo of the *SS Marion*, found in the Corps of Engineers files of the Illinois State Archive, shows the general look of a paddlewheel canal boat of the early days of the canal. The SS Marion is noted as being the first boat to traverse the Hennepin Canal. Illinois and Mississippi (Hennepin) Canal, "Photographic Files," Record Series 497.037, Illinois State Archives.

Construction Details

A final accounting of the construction costs to June 30, 1908, showed that the cost of the canal was $7,319,563.39. The almost $400,000 in costs above the original estimate of $6,925,900 were blamed on higher labor costs, the need for more bridges over the canal, changes in the design of the Feeder Canal, and the strategy of buying land only as it was needed for construction. Saving money was the use of concrete in the locks and other structures, and the shorter Feeder Canal.

For those who are interested in the details of the construction of the Hennepin Canal, there is no better reading than the *Annual Reports of the War Department*. Each year, the Chief of Engineers included a report on activities of the Corps of Engineers. The construction of the Illinois & Mississippi Canal often took dozens of pages. The reports of L. L. Wheeler, James C. Long, J. H. Willard, and others included enormous detail about costs, the progress of various contractors, the frustrations and successes, weather conditions, and often the maintenance work required even before the canal opened. At times it is easy to see these various officers almost begging for the end of the project. It is also easy to see their celebration when it was done.

When completed, the Hennepin Canal's main canal length was 75.2 miles long, and the Feeder Canal was 29.3 miles long. The system was located in five counties in Illinois, with the canal in Bureau, Henry, Rock Island and Whiteside Counties. The Sinnissippi Lake stretched into a fifth – Lee County. The canal was built to be a minimum of 52 feet wide at the bottom and 80 feet wide at the water line. To allow boats to pass and pause along the waterway, there were turnouts built every 4 or 5 miles. The canal was also wider above and below every lock to allow boats to wait their turn. The right-of-way was at least 300 feet wide, but there are places where the canal is 1000 feet wide. The canal provided seven feet of water depth, reduced to five feet in 1951.

All locks were built 170 feet long and 35 feet wide, and the lock walls are 240 feet long to support the gates. All the gates were manually operated, and only two designs were used. The lower gates on all of the locks were miter gates, while eighteen of them had miter upper gates. Miter gates are the traditional gates consisting of two leaves (gates). Miter gates, also spelled mitre, were invented by Leonardo da Vinci sometime around the late 15th century. When closed, the gates meet at an angle like a chevron pointing upstream. When the upstream water level is higher, even by a small amount, there is pressure on the gates that force them together, sealing the gap between them. Miter gates can only be operated after water levels on each side have been equalized. Even when both gates are miter gates, they are not identical. The lower gates are taller, equaling the upper gate plus the rise of the lock. When the miter gates are open to allow a boat to pass, they are housed in a recess in the lock wall, requiring that the lock wall be longer than the lock itself.

Miter gates are a very traditional type of gate used in locks. They point upstream and are held tight by the water pressure. These gates, located at Lock #22, are open, possible when the water level on each side of the gates is the same. Photo by Barton Jennings.

The second type of lock gate used was the Marshall Gate. The gate was designed by Major William Louis Marshall as a method to create an automatic gate that did not require human power to open or close. As described in several canal and dam engineering manuals, the Marshall Gate "is a single gate extending from one wall to the other and is made to raise and lower on a horizontal axis. The middle third of the gate has a leaf extending out from the axis at right angles to the main part of the gate. The leaf operates in a water tight chamber. This chamber is connected to the lower pool through spillway pipe. To open the gate, a valve is opened in the pipe which, due to the differences in elevation of the pools, makes a pressure on the leaf. When the water levels on the two sides of the gate become nearly equal, the pressure on the leaf causes the gate to sink below the level of the sill. To shut the gate, the valve is closed and the gate raises and closes from its own buoyancy." Locks #8 through #21 originally had Marshall Gates on their upper ends, and Lock #16 has had its Marshall Gate restored.

The Marshall Gate was an attempt to have a one-piece automatic lock gate. The gate would lay on the floor of the lock and raise to block the water only when activated. Photo by Barton Jennings.

To raise and lower each lock it required a lockman (also called lock tenders and lockkeepers) to handle the various tasks. These included opening and closing the gates, as well as adjusting the water levels. The water filled the lock by using two tunnels, one in each lock wall. At the head of each tunnel was a butterfly valve which was operated from the top of the wall by a hand wheel. Because the water flow exceeded what was needed just for the locks, most mainline locks included a spillway around the lock. The spillways were cast iron pipes laid behind the lock wall. The largest spillways were near the summit level and were 48 inches in diameter. Because of evaporation and other water losses, the spillways at the lower locks were only 18 inches in diameter.

While many of the gate mechanisms have been removed along the canal, some parts still remain. This is a maneuvering gear, located at Lock #2, once used to open and close a butterfly valve to fill or empty a lock. A hand-wheel was located on top of the short shaft to turn the gears, and therefore the butterfly valve. Photo by Barton Jennings.

The Hennepin Canal also featured nine aqueducts (a bridge to carry a canal across another waterway or valley). The aqueducts all had an inside width of 39'-6" and were made of structural steel with a reinforced concrete lining. The aqueduct floors featured 20-inch steel I-beams spaced 2'-3" center to center. The piers that supported the aqueducts were 75 feet long, 4 feet wide at the top, 6 feet wide at the foundation, and between 19 feet and 26 feet high. Each pier was built with an upstream batter to serve as icebreakers. Each aqueduct also featured a towpath, even though no animals were ever used to pull boats through the canal. Instead, the towpath was used by canal inspectors and others who used the canal for recreation.

Besides the aqueducts, there were 26 concrete arch culverts and 38 pipe culverts to allow small streams and drainage ditches to pass under the canal. Fourteen of these featured flush ducts that allowed water from the canal to flow into the culvert to clean them out.

The canal included 76 road and railroad bridges with a minimum clearance of 17 feet on the main canal and 12 feet on the Feeder Canal. The Corps of Engineers' telephone wires, and other obstructions such as power lines, had a required clearance of 27 feet on the main canal and 22 feet on the Feeder Canal. To attract employees, there were 14 supervisor (overseer) houses, 13 built by the Corps of Engineers. The standard two-story frame house featured 8 rooms on a foundation 24 feet wide and 30 feet long. Thirty-eight houses were built for lockmen or patrolmen, with thirty of them being a common design featuring two stories with a gambrel roof (symmetrical two-sided roof with two slopes on each side like many barns) and seven rooms on a foundation measuring 22 feet wide and 28 feet long. At many of these houses, the Corps of Engineers also built barns and equipment sheds.

There were a number of maintenance facilities, warehouses, office buildings, ice houses, and other buildings at Lock #19 and Lock #26, and at a few other locations A boat repair facility, or boat ways, was located at mile 17.6, with earlier ones at Rock Falls and Milan.

History of the Hennepin Canal

This photo dates from the construction of the Hennepin Canal, and shows a new office and storage shed, along with several workers. The photo was found in the Corps of Engineers' files of the Illinois State Archive, and is believed to be the office near the swing bridges at Milan. Illinois and Mississippi (Hennepin) Canal, "Photographic Files," Record Series 497.037, Illinois State Archives.

The canal property was lined by a 4-strand fence strung on concrete fence posts. The fence posts were manufactured by the Corps of Engineers at the Post House near Lock #17. Each post weighed 165 pounds. Concrete poles that weighed 750 pounds were used to support parts of a telephone communication line, located along the entire canal. The telephone system was used to alert lockmen about boats moving on the canal, and to report emergencies.

A report by the Corps of Engineers stated that:

> The entire work embraced in the original project for the canal, as modified by subsequent projects and plans as the work has progressed, may be summarized as follows:
>
> Surveys and location upon the ground;
> acquisition of right of way and fencing;
> construction of ninety-five and eight-tenths miles of earthwork;
> sixty-seven highway bridges;
> one farm bridge;
> three pontoon bridges;
> eight railroad bridges;
> nine aqueducts;
> fifty-two culverts (increased to sixty- two);
> thirty-three locks;
> nine sluiceways and gates;
> three dams;
> nineteen houses (increased to thirty-nine);
> outlet to Rock River;
> new highway on mile sixteen;
> improvement of eight and five-tenths miles of Rock River; and
> Moline wagon bridge (not in original estimate).

Canal Contractors

It is worth noting who actually built the canal. While the Corps of Engineers was the party responsible, dozens of contractors and subcontractors actually did much of the work. Initially, the plans were for contractors to do most of the work with the Corps of Engineers doing some of the specialized projects, such as river dredging and some of the lock work. A report from 1903 stated that the following contracts were "in force during fiscal year ending June 30, 1903."

Pound Construction Co.	Earthwork mile 34
T. W. Kinser & Sons	Earthwork miles 50-52
Katz & Callahan	Earthwork mile 49 and new channels, Earthwork mile 31
Callahan Brothers & Katz	Earthwork miles 58 and 59
John J McCuughcy	Earthwork miles 29, 30 and 32
Chicago Bridge & Iron Co.	Superstructures for 21 highway bridges
Wallace Marshall	Superstructures for 6 highway bridges
Cogan & Pound	Pits and foundations for 2 locks and 4 culverts
Charles Stone	Pits and foundations 4 aqueduct bridges
Page & Shnable	Foundations and walls for locks and piers and abutments for bridges western section

These contractors were from places such as Chicago, Illinois; Terre Haute, Indiana; Lafayette, Indiana; Des Moines, Iowa; and Omaha, Nebraska. When originally planned, contracts were let on a per-mile basis, or for special items such as bridges, abutments, foundations, and fencing. Later, contracts were often moved or changed based upon local conditions.

Various reports indicate that some contractors were very successful while others were a problem. In a number of cases, contractors failed and had to be replaced by others. For example, the *Annual Reports of the War Department for the Fiscal Year Ended June 30, 1903*, stated that the "contractor for aqueduct foundations has lost plant and material and the work must be taken up by the bondsmen or else the United States must take hold of it," and that the Corps has been busy "cleaning up the miles abandoned by the Globe Construction Company." Numerous reports also mentioned that a contractor was given another assignment that had not been completed. Weather, supplies, and other conditions often caused the Corps to move contractors from project to project.

Because of these problems, much of the work was actually supervised and conducted by the Corps of Engineers. Many of the locks had the digging and foundation work performed by a contractor, while hired labor reporting directly to the Corps' supervisors and engineers built the locks themselves. Some earthwork, building construction, and other projects were also done that way. This control of much of the construction and labor is shown in an early Corps of Engineers report that stated that the "deep cut at and below Colona and the embankments to Rock River miles 60, 61 and 62 are being executed by hired labor and plant owned by the United States, consisting of steam shovel and railway equipment." Local farmers and town residents could often make a few dollars by hiring on, especially when the canal was damaged by flooding or where projects had to be completed when a contractor failed.

Commercial Navigation on the Hennepin Canal (1895-1951)

The Hennepin, once known as the Illinois & Mississippi Canal, was operated for commercial navigation on the Milan section starting on April 17, 1895, and over its entire length from October 24, 1907, until July 1, 1951, by the Rock Island District of the U.S. Army Corps of Engineers. To operate and maintain the canal, the Corps of Engineers employed fifty men year-round. During the summer, addi-

History of the Hennepin Canal

tional workers were hired to conduct planned maintenance and work on special projects. Lockmen and/or a patrolmen were assigned a section of the canal to operate, inspect, repair breaks, and handle any other operating chores required. Reports indicate that they were initially paid $90 a month.

The Corps of Engineers provided houses for these workers, except for one who was assigned a houseboat. The houses were initially pretty basic; none had electricity or indoor plumbing. The workers also had barns, warehouses, sheds, and workshops. Concrete was commonly used for sidewalks and other structures. One employee house was even built of concrete. Over time, improvements were made to many of the houses, with electricity, furnaces, and bathrooms added.

Concrete was at first an experiment along the Hennepin Canal, and then it became a staple building material. This concrete warehouse at Lock #11 is an example of what could be done using concrete. Photo by Barton Jennings.

To help the workers, employees were allowed to have gardens and a limited amount of livestock on the canal property. Even though there was a technical limit to the number of cows and other livestock, there were frequent reports of excessive animals grazing on the right-of-way. The workers also had trapping rights as a way to discourage embankment damage from beaver, muskrat and other animals. The right-of-way was well fenced for all of these activities. According to the Corps of Engineers, the canal right-of-way was for the purpose of navigation and construction only, and it was for the exclusive use of United States government employees. However, fishing and picnicking quickly became a popular activity along the canal, and public recreation was slowly accepted.

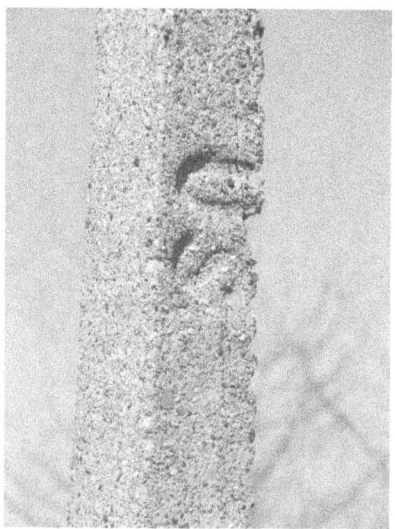

The symbol US was stamped in the posts which were placed at corners or sections to show federal ownership of the property. Photo by Barton Jennings.

The first revenue from the canal came even before it opened. In 1895, the Corps of Engineers began selling ice rights, and even built a large number of ice houses along the canal for their own use and for the buyers of the ice. For example, there were ice houses built in 1908 at Locks #12, #22, #24, #30 and #33. More ice houses were built the next year at Locks #5, #11, #23 and #28, as well as Mile 23 on the Feeder Canal. Reports were that this ice was used in company houses by canal employees. During the winter of 1910-1911, the Milan Section of the canal raised $252 from selling ice rights. However, leasing ice rights and property were about the only revenues created by the canal, as when coal and other freight began to move on the Milan Section, there were no charges for the use of the canal system. This practice was clearly stated in 1911 by the *State of Illinois Rivers and Lakes Commission Bulletin 1* (October 1, 1911), which reported that this "is a Government canal and there are no tolls or lock fees."

Canal Navigation – Opening through World War I

The Milan Section of the Hennepin Canal opened for navigation on April 17, 1895, and until 1908 was the only part of the canal in regular service. During this time, the Milan Section basically served the communities that today form the Quad Cities – Davenport and Bettendorf in Iowa, and Rock Island and Moline in Illinois, plus East Moline, Milan, Silvis, and several others. Shipments that could work their way down the Rock River were also helped as the canal allowed them to bypass the shoals near the mouth of the Rock River. Looking back at the traffic volumes of the late 1890s, these were some of the largest to ever use the canal.

The Hennepin Canal was designed and built to handle 18 million tons of freight a year, a number that was never approached. Although coal was an early commodity moved on the west end of the canal, and a major reason for the canal's support, shipments soon ended. This was because the nearby coal fields, active since the Rock Island

Railroad built through the area in the 1850s, began to close as they depleted their coal supplies.

Because of the projected volume of traffic, the canal was built with numerous places for boats to wait until traffic allowed them to move again. This set of piles is located at Aqueduct #9, and was designed to protect the ends of the aqueduct from accidently being hit by a runaway barge or boat. These piles were also designed to be used by boats to tie up while they waited their turn to move through the narrow aqueduct. Clusters of piles like these are found throughout the canal system, and especially around locks and aqueducts. Photo by Barton Jennings.

An interesting part of the canal's design was that the Corps of Engineers did not build any freight facilities. This was because it was expected that most freight would move through between the Illinois and Mississippi Rivers. There was also the belief that shippers would build their own facilities if they were needed. The design of the canal, which bypassed almost every community on the route, also reduced the need for local freight facilities.

The first full year of operations on the Main Canal was designed to start when the ice broke up enough for the lock gates to work and water to flow reliably from the Rock River. However, because of a break in the canal, it wasn't until May 1908 that there was enough water to operate the entire canal.

Almost immediately, regular canal packet boats began serving the Hennepin Canal. Local newspapers reported that the steam boat *City of Henry* would leave Peoria each Thursday, serving Bureau, Tiskilwa, Wyanet, Geneseo, Rock Falls and Sterling. Princeton was also served by transferring freight at Bureau to the Chicago, Ottawa & Peoria Railway (an electric interurban railway) that once connected Bureau with Princeton to the northwest, and Joliet to the east. The shipping company promoted that goods ordered from Peoria would be delivered to their buyer's place of business by 6:30 Saturday morning. A freight house was built near Geneseo due to the large number of orders.

The December 13, 1907, issue of the *Tampico Tornado* newspaper showed the original promise of the packet business on the canal. The issue reported that the Sterling, Dixon & Rock Falls Packet Company "has operated boats on the Main canal for about six weeks and have carried vast quantities of coal and grain. At a recent meeting of the directors in Sterling, a dividend of more than seven per cent on the stock was declared. The company's boats hauled over 125,000 bushels of corn, oats and other grain down the Illinois River during the six weeks that followed the organization of the packet company and the stockholders have the money in their pockets representing a part of the profits."

The article stated that the company would build more boats as "there is money in canal boating even in these days of railroading." There were also comments about a "string of barges loaded with coal for Sterling lying below Milan" waiting for the canal to open. A great comment about the situation was that the "croakers who howled for a dozen years saying that the canal would never see a boat carry a load of grain or coal will be glad to forget that they have ever been prophets."

However, the croaking prophets may have been more accurate as within two years the service ended, with the packet company stating that it had never turned a profit. The company complained of the difficulty in serving Sterling, and also cited a lack of freight terminals along the canal. The shipping company was shut down, its assets sold, bills paid, and the service ended in 1910. A report on the company's lease of property along the canal showed that the leases ended on September 29, 1910.

With coal and merchandise movements ending, grain became the primary product moving on the canal. The largest shipper was the Smith-Hippen Grain Company of Pekin, Illinois. This firm loaded grain at several locations along the Feeder Canal and moved it to their primary mill at Pekin, or to distilleries at Peoria and Pekin. The October 25, 1910, issue of *The Grain Dealers Journal* stated "Sterling, Ill. – The grain shipping season has opened on the Hennepin Canal and it is estimated that more than 15 cargoes will be shipped from the feeder near this point before navigation closes. The government has granted a permit to the Smith-Hippen Co. to load grain from the bridges along the canal feeder and the firm has planned to establish a terminal elevator here to take advantage of the canal's cheap transportation."

The Smith-Hippen Grain Company was a sister company to the T. & H. Smith Wagon Company of Pekin. Both were owned by the Smith brothers, a family of German immigrants who came from Hamsverum, Germany, in the mid-19th century. They eventually owned a number of businesses in the region, and built or bought several grain elevators on the Feeder Canal. *The Daily Times* of Davenport, Iowa, had a story in their July 6, 1927, issue that carried the news that the "Smith-Hippen Grain Company had been sold to the Turner-Hudnut Grain Company of Pekin."

While grain was the largest volume of product moved on the canal, 55% for the years 1909 through 1913, the volume was only 21,073 tons, far short of the planned 18 million tons a year. By 1920, there were four grain elevators on the Hennepin Canal according to *Water and Transfer Facilities, a Letter from The Secretary of War to the U.S. House of Representatives*, dated January 21, 1920.

The October 1912 *Bulletin of the Atlantic Deeper Waterways Association* had two short articles about the Hennepin Canal. Both articles discussed a break in the canal and how there were plans to build "eleven new locks the size of those on the Hennepin canal" on the Illinois & Michigan Canal to create a through waterway route from Lake Michigan to the Mississippi River. The first article stated:

> *Traffic in the Hennepin Canal was completely stopped by a big break, occurring about the middle of August, which the engineers promised should be repaired during September. One pier of the aqueduct will have to be rebuilt, and there was a long breach between locks 22 and 23. The break is causing much inconvenience, as the salt shipments have been very active this season."*

The second article provided a description of the break and the work involved to repair it.

> *The big break in the Hennepin canal near Mineral, which has caused a complete cessation of traffic since the time it occurred, some*

ten days ago, will be repaired and the canal ready for use in two weeks' time according, to the statement issued by Assistant Engineer L. L. Wheeler, who has the Hennepin waterway in charge.

Mr. Wheeler has been given authority by the government to engage as many men as he can handle, and over 1,000 men are now working day and night in an attempt to repair the damage. One pier of the aqueduct will have to be rebuilt as well as the wing walls and then work of filling in the dirt will commence. Considerable time will be consumed in filling the breach between locks 22 and 23, which is one of the longest on the canal, being 10 miles in all.

The break comes at a very inopportune time, inasmuch as traffic on the I-M canal is now becoming active with the Morton salt shipments, which are now unloaded at La-Salle.

Salt was moved for several years by Morton Salt. In 1912, the company moved 1200 tons, and then 2000 tons in 1913. However the firm soon phased out shipments due to the lack of connectivity with the Illinois & Michigan Canal on the Illinois River. By this time, there was talk about closing and abandoning the Hennepin Canal, and 1914 saw only 12,222 tons moved, far less than one-tenth of one percent of the planned volumes. Even with the economic and manufacturing activity caused by World War I, the 1914 volume wasn't matched until 1921. The other business moving on the canal during the 1910s was passenger boats. This was the peak of this business, with 35,000 passengers in

1918. The numbers reduced before the business completely ended during the Depression of the 1930s.

Hennepin Canal Freight Volumes (1895-1918)

Year	Tons	Year	Tons	Year	Tons
1895	6	1903	1,333	1911	9,118
1896	1,865	1904	544	1912	9,103
1897	9,583	1905	10,555	1913	11,856
1898	20,430	1906	669	1914	12,222
1899	15,005	1907	3,472	1915	11,279
1900	18,682	1908	1,568	1916	9,282
1901	6,238	1909	2,225	1917	15,662
1902	1,478	1910	8,720	1918	11,164

The above table shows that freight volumes were highest during the late 1890s, and then increased again during World War I (1914-1918). It should be noted that the tonnages for 1895-1907 are for the Milan Section only. Another interesting note about these volumes is that until the entire canal opened in 1908, the freight volumes quoted included both commercial freight and the government materials moved for canal construction and maintenance. Beginning in 1908, the freight volumes only included commercial freight.

To keep the canal maintained and operating, the Corps of Engineers employed a large staff at a budget of almost $200,000 a year. For example, the expenses for fiscal year 1911 (July 1, 1910 - June 30, 1911) totaled $168,537.76, with more than a third of the expenses related to labor and emergencies. The report for that year showed the expenses as follows.

Fiscal Year 1911 Expenses

$65,716.18	Labor and emergencies
$28,797.82	Patrolmen
$23,102.59	Miscellaneous
$15,836.49	Lockmen
$12,456.34	Engineering, superintendence and office
$11,359.76	Boats, operating, etc.
$10,892.83	Overseers
$375.75	Telephone line
$168,537.76	Total

The 1910s seemed to be a period of keeping the workers busy and finding alternative uses for the canal property. Although originally the Corps of Engineers fenced the property and declared that it was for the use of government employees only, public uses were soon promoted. Walnut, elm, catalpa and other trees were planted along the canal banks to make the canal route more pleasant. In 1915 alone, 7925 catalpa trees, 2350 elm trees, and 2055 walnut trees were transplanted from nurseries and planted along the canal. Picnicking on the canal banks became popular, and fishing was soon a major attraction, with some fish caught setting Illinois records. The Rock Island YMCA was even given permission to hold swimming classes in the Milan Section of the canal.

A final difference between the original plans of the canal and the actual operations was the use of motorized boats instead of animal power. Like all canals to that time, the route was lined with pathways for the use of horses or mules that would pull the boats. On many canals, this was still the practice. However, steam power had become common, and internal combustion engines were also starting to be used. One of the early complaints about the size of the locks was that powered boats would not fit through the locks if they were pulling or pushing an unpowered barge.

Canal Navigation – The 1920s

The 1920s were the peak years of the canal's use, and the report *Water Terminals and Transfer Facilities, Letter from the Secretary of War*, stated that there were four grain elevators on the Hennepin Canal in 1920. Generally, the canal moved 10-15,000 tons per year during the 1920s. However, a record of 30,161 tons was moved in 1929. While this was still well less than one percent of the canal's capacity, the canal was somewhat successful in that it was credited with holding down railroad rates on parallel lines. Nevertheless, the canal never became the center link in a chain of waterways that connected the Mississippi River with the Great Lakes and on to the Atlantic Ocean.

There was some improvement in service on the Hennepin Canal during this time as Ray Mechling and Fred Wolf began a commerce barge line in 1920 to serve customers on the Hennepin Canal. The company, based in Rock Falls, concentrated on serving just the Hennepin Canal. The firm acquired a steam boat and then built several barges designed to fit through the locks. The company initially bought gravel and moved it to various locations along the canal to sell for construction projects and other uses. The primary source of gravel was from a government pit east of Sheffield, where it was bought for ten cents a yard. One of their major non-gravel customers was the International Harvester Company, which received steel from the Chicago area and coal from lower Illinois coal mines.

The firm later became the A. L. Mechling Barge Lines after Fred Wolf sold his share of the company about 1925. The barge company hauled grain from the various elevators along the canal, taking it to the grain terminals in Pekin. The firm eventually moved to Joliet and expanded their operations to all major rivers and the Gulf of Mexico. In 1961, the firm moved the first Saturn missile from Huntsville, Alabama, to Cape Canaveral, Florida. In 1973, A. L. Mechling Barge Lines was acquired by the Dravo Corporation of Pittsburgh, Pennsylvania, and merged with Union Barge to create the Union Mechling Corporation, one of the largest barge companies in the United States. The company was later reorganized as the Dravo Mechling Corporation, still the barge line subsidiary of Dravo Corporation.

Hennepin Canal Freight Volumes (1919-1929)

Year	Tons	Year	Tons
1919	10,295	1925	14,929
1920	7,428	1926	14,136
1921	12,949	1927	14,513
1922	11,166	1928	18,611
1923	10,093	1929	30,161
1924	11,627		

Despite the success of the barge company, traffic on the Hennepin Canal never grew to the expected volumes. Traffic on the canal was also slowed in 1928 by a severe break, but repairs were made quickly enough to move a higher-than-average volume, and then the record volume the next year. Much of this late 1920s volume may have been gravel, as Illinois pushed a program to improve gravel roads across the state.

Canal Navigation – The Depression and World War II

The 1930s started off with the above average volume of 18,142 tons in 1930, however, the year also marked the beginning of the Great Depression. Traffic tonnage dropped steadily until 1935, and the volumes never again exceeded the 1930 total.

Hennepin Canal Freight Volumes (1930-1945)

Year	Tons	Year	Tons	Year	Tons
1930	18,142	1936	17,164	1942	4,153
1931	12,680	1937	18,086	1943	11,712
1932	6,176	1938	13,435	1944	13,554
1933	6,275	1939	6,693	1945	14,146
1934	4,559	1940	14,542		
1935	11,578	1941	12,146		

With changes in the waterway industry, the *River and Harbors Act of July 3, 1930* called for an investigation on enlarging the Hennepin Canal. A major study took place in 1931, but it noted the small volumes that used the canal and concluded that the benefits weren't worth the cost. Things became even more difficult for the Hennepin Canal in 1933 when the project to enlarge the Illinois River and the Illinois & Michigan Canal (I&M) was completed. In that year, the locks on these other waterways opened with the new standards of 600 feet by 110 feet, the minimum size of canal lock specified for the Mississippi River and its tributaries. Historically, the I&M locks were smaller than those on the Hennepin Canal, and now they were much larger. The depth of both water systems was also increased to nine feet. Both situations prevented the Hennepin Canal from truly being a part of a Mississippi River to Great Lakes to Atlantic Ocean waterway network.

The Great Depression and the changing markets were not the only challenges to the Hennepin Canal. Weather and the aging of the canal system also created problems and plenty of work for the Corps of Engineers and its employees. There was another break in the canal in 1932, and the canal was closed for some time. However, all the news wasn't bad that year. *The Dispatch* newspaper from Moline had a story about the canal in their March 14, 1932, issue.

It read: "As cold weather continues, a crew of men is steadily harvesting ice from the surface of the Hennepin canal north of Geneseo. Trucks have been hauling the material to Geneseo, to be stored in an icehouse on East Exchange street. Men are working night and day. The harvest is being carried on by means of temporary equipment to the west of the icehouse on the canal north of Geneseo. A temporary landing platform and a skid were erected on the bank of the canal, and an automobile is used to pull the cakes of ice from the water, up the skid and upon the platform, where they are loaded into waiting trucks. Workmen have been laboring at night in order to take advantage of the cold weather before the period ends."

In 1933, Gillen Construction Company was moving barges on the canal to conduct several work projects, but a break near Lock #21 drained part of the canal in early March 1934. In February 1936, ice was a problem on the canal. The news was covered as far east as the *Altoona Mirror* newspaper in Altoona, Pennsylvania, which reported that "CCC workers were called out to dynamite ice which threaten to sweep away a highway bridge over the Hennepin canal, thirteen miles north of Kewanee."

The *Freeport Journal Standard* of February 8, 1938, reported on another break in the canal. "At the east end of the Hennepin canal, near Tiskilwa, a crew of 50 men worked 24 hours repairing a 100 foot break. A dam has been built across the canal above the break to prevent Bureau Creek from flooding the canal." There were several breaks that year, and the Corps of Engineers recommended ending maintenance spending as the canal would soon be abandoned. Spending did continue, but more breaks in 1940 and 1943 took out locks and even an aqueduct.

There was some good news that probably still helps the reputation of the Hennepin Canal. The *Alton Evening Telegraph* of October 25, 1940, stated that "Conservation director Thomas J. Lynch announced today that stocking of Hennepin Canal between Rock Island and Bureau with approximately 50,000 bass, bluegills, crappies and catfish of 'breeder' and 'fingerling' size is under way." While there wasn't much boat traffic on the canal, fishing continued to be a popular activity.

The Mechling Barge Company had towboats and barges on the canal during World War II, hauling grain to Pekin and Peoria. The company headquarters was at Joliet, and most of its fleet operated on the Illinois Waterway. However, these shipments declined from 3753 tons in 1940 to 700 tons in 1945. Because of the war effort, during 1944-1945 the main westbound freight was rolled steel and bars, with much heading to the manufacturing in the Rock Island area. Eastbound, the freight was primarily scrap iron and steel heading to the mills near Chicago.

Canal Navigation – The End of Operations

Traffic picked up some toward the end of the Great Depression and during World War II, but then plummeted in 1946. With almost no traffic moving on the Hennepin Canal, the Corps of Engineers issued a navigation notice on April 7, 1948, that placed the canal on limited service basis. The notice stated that the Hennepin Canal would be open Thursdays and Fridays with one day advance notice, with other days available with one week advance notice. The result was that in 1948, there was no recorded traffic, with only maintenance boats reportedly operating on the canal.

Supporters of the canal complained that the schedule prevented freight movements, and that the Corps of Engineers was to blame due to the poor condition of the canal. There were also calls for the locks and canal to be rebuilt to modern standards, something that was estimated to cost $12 million. Even fishing was being impacted as the water depth was unreliable due to regular breaks in the embankments. As seen below, even with some maintenance work, traffic did not recover.

Hennepin Canal Freight Volumes (1946-1951)

Year	Tons	Year	Tons
1946	866	1949	1,034
1947	394	1950	1,198
1948	0	1951	0

By 1950, much of the canal had less than four feet of water in the main canal, and only four feet in the Feeder Canal, due to embankment and lock deterioration. There were multiple locations where the embankments were failing, and many of the locks needed major repairs to their gates and spillways.

In 1951, the Corps of Engineers completed a study of canals and waterways nationwide, and suspended lock operations and eliminated nonessential maintenance on seven canals and waterways. These waterways were all determined to provide little or no benefit to general commerce and navigation nationwide. Among the studies was one on the Hennepin Canal, which included a 1951 driving inspection of the canal, detailed photographs of many of the problems, and estimates for various options. On June 20, 1951, the Corps of Engineers issued a public notice that the Hennepin Canal would be closed to commercial navigation after June 30, 1951. Recreational use would still be allowed, but no lock operations or significant maintenance would be provided, making use of the canal essentially an "at your own risk" proposition.

A final report on the Hennepin Canal showed that from 1908 until 1951, the Corps of Engineers had spent $6,900,653 to operate and maintain the canal. During this time, only 446,640 tons moved on the canal, approximately

2.5% of what the canal was built to handle in a single year. The cost to operate and maintain the canal was approximately $160,000 per year, or $15.45 for every ton moved. Few could argue that the canal still had a commercial purpose, but there were still protest meetings along the route. Nevertheless, the canal was closed and plans were made to abandon the property. However, that didn't end efforts to save and preserve the Hennepin Canal.

Recreational Use of the Hennepin Canal (1951-current)

Even before the closing of the canal for commercial navigation, there were efforts to save the canal for recreational purposes. Protest meetings were organized and several letter writing campaigns began, leading to both Washington, D.C., and Springfield, Illinois, receiving a large number of letters and petitions. Among the letters were a mix of causes from conservationists to farmers to industry leaders to those supporting recreational activities. One of the first was a letter to Illinois Governor Adlai Stevenson from the Illinois Branch of the Izaak Walton League calling for the creation of a state park along the entire canal route. Almost immediately, the 68th Illinois General Assembly petitioned the federal government to preserve the canal for recreational and conservation purposes.

Late in 1951, the Corps of Engineers reduced the water level in the Hennepin Canal to five feet and did some minor work to maintain basic canal operations. At the same time, several studies were conducted on what to do with the canal. It was estimated that it would cost at least $10 million to abandon the canal, but only $1.7 million to end commercial operations but maintain the basic system. Another study by the Illinois Department of Conservation stated that it would cost $2,521,439 to convert the canal for recreational use. All of these cost estimates scared off any decisions, and the canal remained under Corps of Engineers control, but with no commercial operations.

With the canal already in control of the federal government, the National Park Service (NPS) was asked to consider making it a national park. However, the NPS declined the offer. The Illinois-Mississippi Canal and Lake Sinnissippi Commission was created in 1953 by Illinois to study the feasibility of saving the canal and lake for recreation. An issue was that the Illinois constitution forbade the General Assembly from spending money to aid railroads and canals. However, interest in saving the canal led to a November 1954 referendum that removed that restriction. Almost immediately there were several unsuccessful attempts to lease the canal, and in July 1955, Illinois Governor William Stratton signed House Bill 1202 which authorized the Illinois Department of Conservation, and the Illinois Department of Public Works and Buildings, to have the Corps of Engineers rebuild the canal and then have the state buy it as a state park. Section 110 of the *River and Harbors Act of 1958* included the authorization for the United States to sell the canal to Illinois.

Spending on the canal did not stop as embankment breaks continued to happen. For example, on March 8, 1955, there was a thirty-foot break in the north bank west of Lock #27, where one happened again in 2019. Breaks have been a routine challenge, and even today, they are a regular part of the canal's maintenance. For example, during the 1970s, there were eighty breaks that occurred in the canal's banks, with sixty taking place from February through May during the annual spring thaw.

Throughout the late 1950s and early 1960s, efforts continued to maintain the canal and to find a solution for its future. For example, on July 3, 1958, President Eisenhower signed a bill that approved a transfer of ownership to Illinois, subject to the Corps of Engineers spending $2 million to repair and/or modify parts of the canal, to allow continued use of water from the Rock River, and to clarify the role of the various parties involved. But it wasn't until December of 1960 that an agreement was signed to begin rehabilitation of the canal. In 1961, the Corps of Engineers began rebuilding a number of locks, but soon ran out of money and asked for another $800,000 to finish the work then underway. A report from the time estimated that it would cost another $10 million to finish the work.

Looking for other sources of money, the National Park Service was again approached in 1963, but denied the request. In 1965, a campaign to rebuild and reopen the canal for freight was launched in the Rock Island area, but the $100-200 million estimated cost quickly shut down the discussion. In 1969, a final rebuild of the canal was agreed upon at an estimated cost of more than $6 million. After the final work, Illinois accepted ownership of the Hennepin Canal on August 1, 1970, creating the Hennepin Canal Parkway State Park.

Since that time, the canal has continued to change. Most of the historic bridges are now gone, replaced by causeway fills, but the waterway still flows through what is mostly a rural environment. Almost all of the canal houses have been torn down or moved, but a few can still be found along the route. A few of the lock gates have been restored, although none are currently used. Today, the Hennepin Canal is used for recreational purposes, including walking, biking, horseback riding, snowmobiling, and fishing.

Hennepin Canal Parkway State Park

After almost two decades of debate, negotiations and restorations, the Corps of Engineers transferred the Hennepin Canal to the State of Illinois on August 1, 1970. It was immediately assigned to the Illinois Department of Conservation (now the Department of Natural Resources), with the name Hennepin Canal State Trail, later established as the Hennepin Canal Parkway State Park. Since that time, the property has been listed on the National Register of Historic Places. Officially, the Hennepin Canal Historic District is 89.8 miles in total length. The main channel stretches 60.5 miles from Lock #2 at mile 1.3 to the Rock River at mile 61.8. In addition, there are the 29.3 miles of the Feeder Canal. All are followed closely by walking and biking trails.

The logo of the Illinois Department of Natural Resources can be seen all along the Hennepin Canal, including on this truck at the Visitors Center near Sheffield. Photo by Barton Jennings.

The State Park includes a Visitors Center near Sheffield, a number of parking areas, several campgrounds, and more than 170 miles of hiking, biking, equestrian, and snowmobiling trails. Along the canal, there are 33 locks and six of the original nine aqueducts. Five of the locks have been restored to working condition, although they are not used at this time. Most of the original highway bridges have been replaced, but some still remain to be explored by historians. The Hennepin Canal Parkway State Park is one of the longest parks in the United States, and spans Bureau, Henry, Lee, Rock Island, and Whiteside Counties in Illinois.

The trails use the former canal towpaths, which are generally located on both sides of the canal. The trails today are either a paved oil-and-chip, gravel, or grass surface. The paved and gravel sections are designed for hikers and cyclists, while the grass is primarily for equestrian use. In some places only one trail exists due to an aqueduct, bridge, or lock. Here, the trail is shared but equestrians have the right-of-way. The landscape along the canal varies from forest to grasslands, with marsh along the streams. There is also a great deal of farmland.

The Hennepin Canal Parkway Trail is often well-marked, warning users of hazards along the route. Photo by Barton Jennings.

Picnicking, boating and fishing are also popular activities along the canal. The summit level and the connecting Feeder Canal provide forty miles of connected boating for small craft that can pass through the twelve-foot culverts used in many of the roadway fills. Fishing on the Hennepin Canal is allowed at all times of the day and night throughout the year. The most common fish caught include large and smallmouth bass, catfish, walleye, crappie, and bluegills. Trout fishing is also a special event on the Hennepin Canal. Several times a year, the canal near the Visitor Center is netted off and trout released.

Supporting the state park is the organization Friends of the Hennepin Canal. This group regularly conducts walks to clean trash, make minor repairs, and to promote the preservation of the canal. The Friends also promote the restoration of parts of the canal and locks to enable pleasure boats to cruise the canal. More details can be found on their website.

Details on the trails, fishing and other events can be found through the park's website and at the Visitor Center. There are a number of trail maps available to assist those who wish to explore the canal. A basic description of the walking and equestrian trails follows. Note that maintenance and repair efforts can often change these conditions temporarily, or even permanently.

Main Channel Canal Trail

Location	Side of Canal	Surface Material
Lock #2 to Lock #12	south side	oil & chip
Lock #12 to Bridge #15 with horse trail	south side	gravel – joint
Bridge #15 to Lock #22	north side	oil & chip
Lock #22 to Bridge #20 with horse trail	north side	gravel – joint
Bridge #20 to Bridge #23	north side	oil & chip
Bridge #23 to Bridge #24 with horse trail	north side	gravel – joint
Bridge #24 to Bridge #32	north side	oil & chip
Bridge #32 to Bridge #33 with horse trail	north side	gravel – joint
Bridge #33 to Bridge #39	north side	oil & chip
Bridge #39 to Lock #25	south side	oil & chip
Lock #25 to Bridge #40A	south side	gravel
Bridge #40A to Bridge #40	south side	oil & chip
Bridge #40 to Lock #2	north side	oil & chip

Feeder Canal Trail

Location	Side of Canal	Surface Material
Lock #33 to Bridge #46	west side	oil & chip
Bridge #46 to Bridge #56	west side	gravel
Bridge #56 to Bridge #18A	west side	oil & chip

Hennepin Canal Parkway State Park

Main Channel Horse Trail

Location	Side of Canal	Surface Material
Lock #2 to Lock #4	north side	grass
Aqueduct #1	south side	paved bridge
Lock #4 to Lock #12	north side	grass
Lock #12 to Bridge #15	south side	grass
Bridge #15 to Lock #22	south side	grass
*Lock #22 to Bridge #20	north side	gravel
Bridge #20 to Bridge #23	south side	grass
*Bridge #23 to Bridge #24	north side	gravel
Bridge #24 to Bridge #32	south side	grass
*Bridge #32 to Bridge #33	north side	grass
Bridge #33 to Lock #24	south side	grass

*Trail is shared between pedestrian and equestrian use.

Special signs are often used to identify the equestrian routes along the Hennepin Canal. Photo by Barton Jennings.

Feeder Canal Horse Trail

Location	Side of Canal	Surface Material
Bridge #46 to Bridge #60	east side	grass
*Bridge #60 to Bridge #61	west side	oil & chip
Bridge #61 to Bridge #17A	east side	grass

*Trail is shared between pedestrian and equestrian use.

Main Channel of Hennepin Canal

The mileposts of the various locations on the Hennepin Canal are based upon those recorded in the State of Illinois Rivers and Lakes Commission October 1, 1911, report: *Bulletin 1, The Conservation of Water Power in the Des Plaines and Illinois Rivers and the improvement of these rivers for navigation.* The distances provided are from the Illinois River. Heading west, the first eighteen miles climb out of the Illinois River valley, gaining 196 feet. The next twelve miles are the summit level and the area is essentially flat between Locks #21 and #22. The Feeder Canal enters the Main Channel between these two locks, historically providing forty miles of open canal. West of Lock #21, the canal drops 93 feet over the next 46 miles as it reaches the Rock and Mississippi Rivers.

The goal of the original Main Channel of the Hennepin Canal was to connect the Illinois and Mississippi Rivers and provide a route for through boat movements. Water was allowed to enter the Main Channel on October 24, 1907, and by May 1908 the canal was fully open for commercial service. However, the route never came close to the volumes projected. In fact, in no single year did the traffic even reach one percent of the canal's designed capacity.

The Main Channel of the Hennepin Canal follows a natural low area between the Illinois and Rock Rivers. This is actually the ancient channel of the Mississippi River, which at one time flowed from the Quad Cities area to near today's Hennepin, and then south along what is today the Illinois River. The Main Channel route is 61.8 miles long and features 29 locks, the site of eight aqueducts, and the Visitor Center of the Hennepin Canal Parkway State Park.

The Illinois State Park breaks the route up into its historic East Branch (or Section) and West Branch, divided by the location of the Feeder Canal basin. The route is now a series of trails useable for hiking, biking, snowmobiling, and even horseback riding.

This route guide follows the main channel of the canal from Milepost 0.0 at the Illinois River, to Milepost 61.8 at the Rock River near Colona, Illinois. The information provided is based upon walking trips along the canal, historical records, and various other sources of information both public and private.

0.0   **ILLINOIS RIVER** – The Illinois River is created when the Des Plaines River and the Kankakee River merge approximately 10 miles southwest of Joliet. The river flows to the southwest almost 275 miles before entering the Mississippi River near Grafton, Illinois. Grafton is 25 miles northwest of downtown St. Louis, and only 20 miles upstream from where the Missouri River also flows into the Mississippi.

The Illinois River follows an old channel that was created by a flood caused by a giant lake at what is today Indiana. The lake was caused by melting glaciers approximately 10,000 years ago. The water was blocked by a glacial moraine that eventually failed, causing water to flow southwest creating a narrow channel. Below today's Hennepin, the flood reactivated the original channel of the Mississippi River. The Mississippi River once flowed east from near today's Rock Island, and then south at Hennepin. About 200,000 years ago, the channel was blocked near Rock Island, forcing the Mississippi River to flow south along today's channel. The Hennepin Canal roughly follows the ancient channel of the Mississippi River between Rock Island and Hennepin.

The Illinois River is part of the Illinois Waterway, a commercial river route from the Mississippi River, up the Illinois River and then the Des Plaines River, to the Chicago Sanitary and Ship Canal (CSSC) at Lockport Lock and Dam. The route then continues up the CSSC and the Chicago River to Lake Michigan. A second route is the Calumet Sag Channel (CSC), which splits from the CSSC near Lemont, Illinois. The CSC eventually also connects to Lake Michigan using the Little Calumet and Calumet Rivers. The Hennepin Canal was originally designed to connect to the Illinois & Michigan Canal, the upper end of the Illinois Waterway, to connect Chicago with the Mississippi River near Rock Island.

The *River and Harbors Act of 1930* established standards for the Illinois Waterway that included a nine-foot deep navigation channel that had to be 400 feet wide for multiple-barge tows. These regulations were really the end of the Hennepin Canal as it already was too small for most water vessels, and work on the Illinois Waterway resulted in changes that flooded the start of the canal near Bureau Junction.

The construction of the Hennepin Canal from the Illinois River to Lock #1 was through swamp and overflow waters, including Spring Lake. Because of this, the 1800 feet in distance was dredged using boats. The work started during the fall of 1901, and the boats were laid up in the canal for winter until April 14, 1902, when work began again. The dredging ended on May 8, 1902. Reports of the Corps of Engineers state that the boats used were tow boats *Fox* and *Pearl*, dredge *Apache* (which had also worked on the Rock River end of the canal), three dumping scows, and a coal barge.

Hennepin Canal Parkway: History Through the Miles

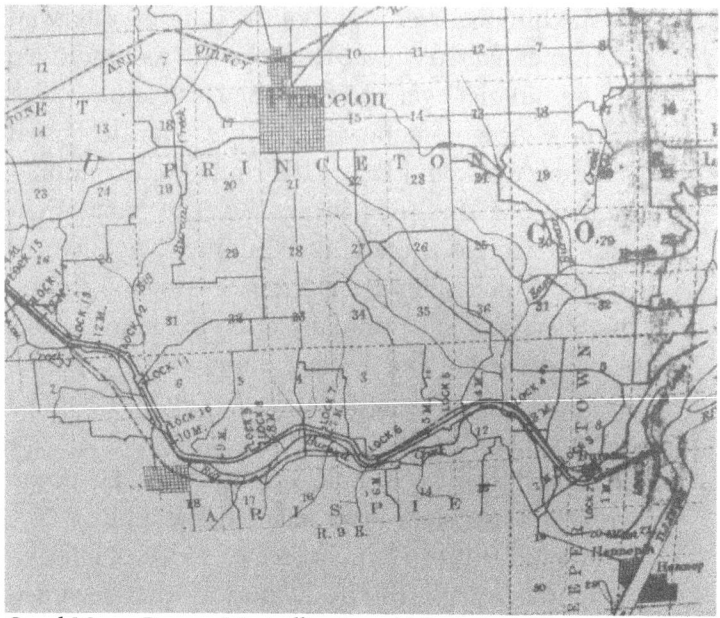

Canal Map – Bureau West. Illinois and Mississippi (Hennepin) Canal, "Canal Route Plat Files," Record Series 497.008, Illinois State Archives.

0.3 LOCK #1 – Lock #1, built starting in 1894, controlled the movement of boats between the Illinois River and the Hennepin Canal, providing a nine-foot lift. During the 1930s, in response to the *River and Harbors Act of 1930*, the U.S. Army Corps of Engineers worked on the Illinois River as a part of the 9-Foot Channel Project. This made the river reliable for barge service. However, it also flooded the original junction between the Illinois River and the Hennepin Canal. This also flooded the area around Lock #1, including the lock itself. At lower water levels, the remains of the concrete walls can still be seen, showing that the gates of the lock are gone.

Water has long been an issue in the area of Lock #1. This part of the canal was dug using boat dredges. Keeping the facilities above water was a tough challenge. For many years, the lock tender at Lock #1 used a houseboat instead of a typical lock tender's house, although a one-acre lot was planned to the north of the lock as a place for a house. When built, there was a pontoon bridge at Lock #1, as noted by an October 18, 1905, drawing.

An interesting feature of the lock is the water depth gauge at the west end of the lock, formed in the concrete wall and using Roman numerals. All locks had this marking, as the Hennepin Canal regulations stated that "A boat must not attempt to leave or enter a lock when its draft is greater than the depth of water on the miter sills, as shown by the gauges at that time."

The canal between Lock #1 and Lock #2 is only one mile long, and heads to the southwest. The locks on the Eastern Section of the Hennepin Canal are much closer than on the Western Section as the distance is less and the climb is more. The area between the locks on a canal is known as a level or pool in the United States, but is also known as a pound or reach around the world. The level often has places for boats to meet, and docks to serve local customers. The Hennepin Canal was built to handle as many as 18 million tons of freight a year, so the levels are often wide with numerous pullouts. However, there were few docks along the route due to the lack of local business.

When the water levels are low, or when the water is very frozen, it is possible to walk the route between Lock #1 and Lock #2. However, be warned that it is heavily vegetated and very buggy during the summer, and a possible death trap in the winter should you fall through the ice. However, the route can be fun to take as it passes through heavy woods, and much of the canal's old embankments still exist as an elevated walkway.

1.3 LOCK #2 – This lock, which provided a nine-foot lift, marks the east end of the Hennepin Canal Parkway Trail. Construction on this lock started in 1894, and like all on the system, it was built of concrete. Both gates and their machinery are gone, removed in 1965 by the Corps of Engineers, with the west or upper gates replaced by a concrete dam (breastwall) to maintain five-foot water levels west of here. Note that the dam is built to resemble the former miter gates that were once here, forming a point upstream.

This photo shows the concrete dam that has replaced the west miter gates at Lock #2. Note that the dam points upstream, just as the lock gates once did. Photo by Barton Jennings.

Over the east, or lower gate, is a roller bridge (called a retractile farm bridge on an April 10, 1928, drawing) that allowed road traffic to cross the ca-

Main Channel

nal. The bridge was not original to the lock and was built a number of years after the construction of the lock, June 1929, according to one Corps of Engineers document. When a boat needed to move through the lock, the 54-foot bridge was rolled to the north to clear the route. Known as the Hennepin Canal Lock #2 Roller Bridge, the pocket where the bridge once moved to has now been filled for the trail. However, some of the rollers and steel rails can still be seen. The steel stringer roller bridge is now set in place and is used by pedestrians as part of the Hennepin Canal Parkway Trail. Substantial guard rails have been added for safety. The State of Illinois Rivers and Lakes Commission reported in 1911 that there was a "Pontoon bridge at upper end of lock." This upper bridge was also called the farm bridge, and records show that it washed out several times before the canal even opened due to the spring thaw and large ice flows.

This title of the 1928 drawing of the Lock #2 "Retractile Farm Bridge" was made under the authority of Major C. L. Hall. Illinois and Mississippi (Hennepin) Canal, "Map, Drawing, and Plan Files, G-Q," Record Series 497.001, Illinois State Archives.

The Retractile Farm Bridge is now set in place and is used as a pedestrian bridge to connect the Parkway Trail with the parking lot to the north. Photo by Barton Jennings.

This photo shows the rollers that allowed the bridge to retract when boats passed through the lock. Photo by Barton Jennings.

There is a parking lot on the north side of the lock which can be reached from West Street in Bureau Junction, Illinois. Many of the canal access points are identified by signs on area highways. On the Hennepin Canal Parkway Trail, many of the locks, aqueducts, and other points are marked by small green signs. Heading west, the canal and trail are heading to the southwest, and then make a bend to turn to the northwest, passing under the Iowa Interstate Railroad bridge – Railroad Bridge #1.

Bureau Junction

Although its official name is Bureau Junction, the village is more commonly called Bureau, and Bureau is the main name used by phone companies, the Federal Board on Geographic Names, and the United States Post Office. The name came from Michel or Pierre de Beuro and their trading post on the Illinois River.

Bureau grew quickly after the Rock Island Railroad reached here on September 12, 1853. In the June 6, 1872, edition of the *Henry Republican*, it was stated that "Bureau Junction has the significance of being the midway station between Chicago and Rock Island, and nothing more nor less than being a railroad town, relating solely to the interests of the C. R. I. & P. R. R. (Chicago, Rock Island & Pacific Rail Road). Here is where railroad men live; here is where trains come and go, conductors stop, trains are dispatched, cars and locomotives repaired, passengers get their 'inner man' replenished, and where there is cessation of locomotive snorts neither day, night or Sundays. Look which way you will and you see endless tracks side by side, and a sea of cars everywhere. The houses are occupied by railroad men and their families. The school is filled with scholars thereof, and its railroad business forever and aye."

This subject was continued in the September 13, 1877, issue of the *Henry Republican*. An article stated that "the staid little 'City of Side Tracks' remains in status quo. It is always lively when trains are passing and this is about every hour in the day and night. It's a railroad town, having the advantage of other places, being a railroad town and nothing else. Here is a round house with a dozen locomotives ready for use, and where exchanges are hourly made. And it might be said to be the 'seat of government' of the C. R. I & P. R. R., so much business of the line seemingly centers at this point."

Bureau was the junction point between the line from Chicago to Rock Island, and the Peoria line of the Peoria & Bureau Valley Railroad Company, chartered on February 12, 1853, to "locate, construct and finally complete a railroad from the City of Peoria, in Peoria County, to the Valley of the Bureau in Bureau County." The line was leased in perpetuity to the Chicago & Rock Island Rail Road Company on April 14, 1854, and finally sold to the Chicago, Rock Island & Pacific (CRI&P) on November 17, 1950. The line was built from Bureau Junction to Peoria, a total of 47 miles, by November 7, 1854.

The former CRI&P wood station still stands at Bureau Junction, just inside the east wye switch. Maps from 1892 show the Bureau House Hotel just west of the station, and a railroad office, a five-stall roundhouse, and a repair shop further west, all inside the wye. South of the depot, the town had two blocks of business and houses, with three more blocks to the north. Except for the depot, none of the rail structures remain, although some of the foundations can still be found in the brush.

Former CRI&P station at Bureau, Illinois. Photo by Barton Jennings.

The two-block community to the south of the railroad fronted on the Hennepin Canal, although it was built forty years earlier when the railroad opened. There are few reports about businesses locating here specifically due to the canal. Today, there are only a few houses in this area.

Bureau County

The name Bureau is also shared with the county. **Bureau County** was organized out of Putnam County in 1837 with its county seat at Princeton. It was named for Michel or Pierre de Beuro, French Creoles, who ran a trading post from 1776 until 1790 near where Big Bureau Creek empties into the Illinois River. The southern part of Bureau County includes part of the Military Tract. In May 1812, an act of Congress was passed which set aside bounty lands as payment to volunteer soldiers who participated in the War of 1812. The bounty land in Illinois was located in the western part of the state between the Illinois and Mississippi Rivers. Of the 5.4 million acres included in the tract, approximately 3.5 million acres were deemed fit for cultivation and were set aside for military bounties. The tract was surveyed in 1815-1816 and opened to settlement. At the time, the land was a mix of forest and wild prairie. Today, major parts of the county are planted in corn or soybeans and the county's population is less than 40,000.

1.6 RAILROAD BRIDGE #1 – By the time the Hennepin Canal was built, railroads already served or passed through much of the route. This required that the Corps of Engineers build nine railroad bridges. In many cases, to provide the required clearance for boats to pass under the bridge, the railroad's grade was raised significantly, greatly complicating the work.

This bridge has historically been known as the Rock Island Bridge, and is today used by the Iowa Interstate Railroad (IAIS) and is located on their Bureau to Peoria line. This line was once the Chicago, Rock Island & Pacific's 3rd Subdivision of the Illinois Division. It was built by the Peoria & Bureau Valley (between Bureau and Peoria) by early November, 1854. When completed, it was immediately leased to the Chicago & Rock Island. When the Rock Island entered its court-ordered liquidation at the end of March 1980, several different operators managed the Bureau-Peoria line. Initially, the Elgin, Joliet & Eastern provided service, then segments were operated by Burlington Northern (Peoria to Henry) and Baltimore & Ohio/CSX from Bureau south to Henry (when Burlington Northern ended service north of Mossville).

Iowa Interstate Railroad engines on Railroad Bridge #1 (the Rock Island Bridge) of the Hennepin canal. Photo by Barton Jennings.

CSXT acquired the line from Bureau to Henry to keep the business from the Goodrich chemical plant just north of Henry. To keep competition to the plant, Goodrich created the Lincoln & Southern Railroad (L&S) and bought the line on south toward Peoria. In 1987, the L&S leased the operating rights over their line to Iowa Interstate (the Mossville-Henry portion had no revenue freight trains from October 1981 until IAIS began operating the line). In 2006, Iowa Interstate signed a lease on the northern half of the line from CSXT and took over operations on February 4th. Today, the IAIS operates the line with a local out of Bureau, plus a number of coal and grain trains as well as general freight for interchange in Peoria.

This three-span through plate girder (TPG) bridge crosses the Hennepin Canal between Locks 2 and 3, at Milepost 114.7 on the railroad. The original bridge, with a 60-foot TPG over the canal and a 30-foot TPG over each approach where a towpath was planned, was built by the Corps of Engineers, and manufactured by Lassig Bridge & Iron Works of Chicago in late 1899. The current bridge sits on solid piers at each end, and uses two assembled steel piers for the center span, part of the original construction. The bridge received major maintenance in 2016, removing the north approach span. The south approach span has also been rebuilt, now using an I-beam design. Note the concrete bumpers on each shore used to protect the bridge from barge traffic.

The railroad bridge deck is at an elevation of 472.386 feet. This number is acquired from a U. S. Corps of Engineers bench mark, located on the "southwest end of northwest plate girder of railway bridge over the Hennepin Canal, on Peoria branch, 5.1 inches from northeast edge of casting; center of cross cut in top of base of cast-iron bridge seat."

1.8   **BRIDGE #1** – The canal and Parkway Trail pass under the modern Illinois Highway 26 bridge at this location. This road is approximately 140 miles long, stretching from East Peoria to the Wisconsin border near Orangeville. The current bridge is located just east of where the original bridge once stood, marked by several concrete foundations.

The original Bridge #1 was part of a series of five bridges (Bridges #1, #2, #3, #4 and #10) built using the same design. Each bridge featured a 100-foot-long steel Warren pony truss span with a wooden deck. According to Corps of Engineers records, they were all built in September 1898. Only Bridge #10 still stands, used by the canal parkway near Wyanett. The original Bridge #1 was replaced with a new reinforced concrete and steel plate girder bridge in April 1928. It has since been rebuilt and upgraded again.

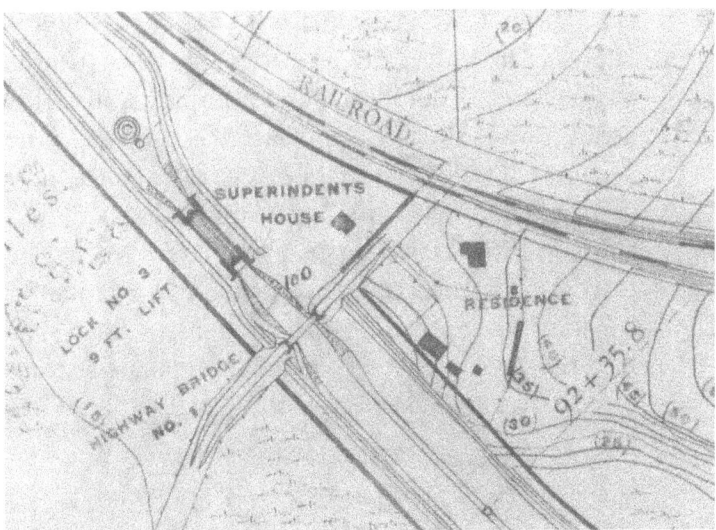

During the construction of the Hennepin Canal, the area around Lock #3 was busy due to the nearby Rock Island Railroad. Later, however, the area just included several houses and barns, as shown in this Corps of Engineers drawing. Illinois and Mississippi (Hennepin) Canal, "Map, Drawing, and Plan Files, G-Q," Record Series 497.001, Illinois State Archives.

Bridges were an unexpected issue involving the Hennepin Canal. When first planned, there were few local roads in the area, but by the time the canal was under construction, much of the modern grid of local roads was in place. As reported by the Corps of Engineers, the construction of sixty-seven highway bridges created unexpected delays.

On the north side of the canal and on the west side of the highway was once a Superintendent's House (spelled "Superindents House" on early Corps of Engineers drawings). Because of the nearby Lock #3, there was also a lock tender's house, a barn, and a few other structures here.

1.9   LOCK #3 – Lock #3, which provided the typical nine-foot lift, is located just west of the Illinois Highway 26 bridge. To the north of the lock is a large parking area with toilets, but no running water. This area is one of the most popular access points to the canal and the lot can be filled on sunny weekends. This concrete lock is missing its miter gates and machinery, with the west gate replaced in 1965 by the Corps of Engineers with a low dam to maintain a constant water level in the canal to the west. To connect the parking lot and the trail, a small pedestrian bridge has been installed over the lock.

Most locks and former bridge locations along the canal are identified with small green signs, such as this one for Lock #3 at Mile 1.9. Photo by Barton Jennings.

Main Channel

Over the concrete dam at the west end of Lock #3 is a pedestrian bridge which allows access to the large parking lot and toilets on the north side of the canal. Photo by Barton Jennings.

On the north bank of the canal is the Bureau railyard of the Iowa Interstate Railroad. This rail line was in operation more than 40 years before the canal was built, so the canal was built around this curve in the line. The canal stays just south of the railroad until west of the Interstate 180 bridge. While the railroad would be a competitor to the canal, it also aided and benefitted from its construction. The Corps of Engineers established material storage yards and built spur tracks connected to the Chicago, Rock Island & Pacific Railway at Bureau Junction, Lock No. 3, and Lock No. 6. To build the canal through this area, the Corps of Engineers used a narrow gauge railroad to move dirt and materials. During the late 1890s, there was a large warehouse here that was used to store the railroad equipment each winter.

Heading west from the Bureau area, the paved Hennepin Canal Parkway Trail is located on the south bank of the canal. On the north side, hikers can walk on a sometimes-mowed path, also used by those riding horses.

2.3   CAUSEWAY – Several small fills, or causeways, have been built across the canal in this area to protect the Bureau locks from damage from flooding. Each of the fills have a gate and culvert that allows water to pass through the fill. Flooding from an overflowing stream caused by heavy rains or quick ice and snow melt is known as a freshet, a problem recorded almost every spring by the Hennepin Canal.

Arch Culvert #1, a 10-foot concrete arched culvert, once existed here. It was built with a flushing gate to allow water from the canal to enter the culvert for cleaning, or when too much water was in the canal.

2.7   CULVERT #2 – Culvert #2 featured a flushing Tainter Gate, a type of radial arm water gate. A flushing gate allowed water from the canal to be directed into the culvert to help clean out debris.

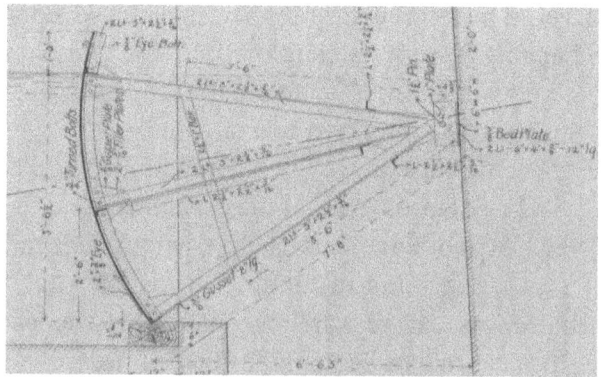

The Tainter Gates on the culverts could be opened to allow almost any volume of water to flow into the culverts. This allowed the culverts to be cleaned out or to reduce the water level in the canal. Illinois and Mississippi (Hennepin) Canal, "Map, Drawing, and Plan Files, G-Q," Record Series 497.001, Illinois State Archives.

Main Channel

To the north was once **Leepertown Mills**, the location of a flouring-mill built by John Leeper on the stream that still flows through Culvert #2. While not shown today, the name is shown on several early canal maps. John Leeper had first settled in Illinois in the early 1820s, and moved several times before moving to Putnam County during the fall of 1831. There, he claimed 2500 acres of land three miles northeast of Hennepin, and built a stockade during the Black Hawk War. He bought an unfinished saw-mill here in 1833, moved his family to the site, and claimed a great deal of land in the area. He finished construction of the sawmill and added a grist mill and a carding wool mill. John Leeper died in 1835, but his family continued to operate the mill and farm. The town slowly wilted away, but the area around Bureau Junction is now Leepertown Township, one of twenty-five townships in Bureau County.

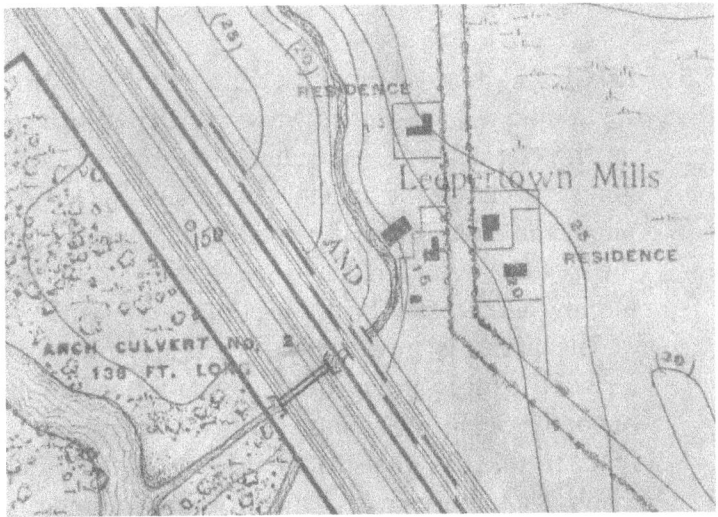

This early map of the canal clearly shows Leepertown Mills just north of the canal, where little but farmland and woods exist today. Illinois and Mississippi (Hennepin) Canal, "Map, Drawing, and Plan Files, G-Q," Record Series 497.001, Illinois State Archives.

3.0 CAUSEWAY – This fill is larger than the one at mile 2.3, but serves the same basic purpose. To the south is a marshy and heavily wooded area, and wildlife sightings are common.

This photo shows a typical paved trail section with plenty of shade from trees to the south, and views of the canal to the north. Photo by Barton Jennings.

3.5 LOCK #4 – Lock #4 provided a lift of nine feet. This was a unique arrangement where a lock was located on the east end of an aqueduct. The Corps of Engineers replaced the aqueduct with an inverted siphon, and built a full wall placed at the upper end of the lock chamber to replace the removed gates. Water now enters from the upper pool via the siphon.

The lift that is provided by a lock is also known as a rise. The lift is provided by moving water into or out of the canal. The amount of lift or rise is normally determined by the structural limits of the canal material and the terrain of the surrounding land.

The area between the lock walls where the boat is raised or lowered is known as the chamber. It is this part of the lock that limits the size of the boats that can use the canal. The lock chambers on the Hennepin Canal were 170 feet long and 35 feet wide, large when originally planned but soon out of date when the new Mississippi River standard became 600 feet long and 110 feet wide.

To the south of Lock #4, and just to the east, was once the lockkeeper's house, with a barn further to the east. This area has grown up with trees and is just east of a clearing.

The original plans for the Illinois & Mississippi Canal had the canal curving off to the south, starting just east of Lock #4. The lock and aqueduct would have been where East Bureau Creek flows into the main channel of Bureau Creek. The canal would have stayed to the south and come back to the current alignment east of Lock #6.

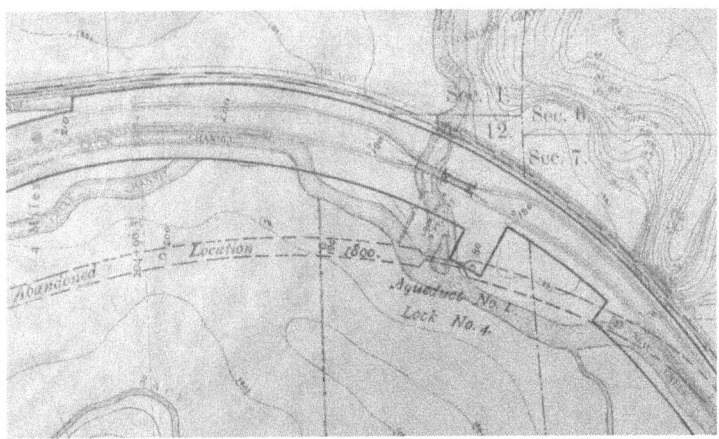

This Corps of Engineers drawing shows the planned 1890 route of the canal, and what was actually built to the north, at Lock #4. Illinois and Mississippi (Hennepin) Canal, "Map, Drawing, and Plan Files, G-Q," Record Series 497.001, Illinois State Archives.

J. C. Long, the project's assistant engineer based in Tiskilwa, reported that in 1895-1896, land was "acquired and a gravel pit opened adjacent to the right of way near Lock No. 4, for the purpose of furnishing gravel for the construction of concrete masonry, and 21,000 cubic yards of gravel uncovered for use, by stripping off the overlying sand and earth." This area, known as the Carlson Gravel Pit and located north of the canal, is now heavily vegetated and impossible to find.

3.6 AQUEDUCT #1 – This aqueduct was built as a concrete trough on concrete piers, typical for the Hennepin Canal. The original aqueduct, a bridge designed to carry a canal across another waterway, was built as a part of the original canal. The aqueduct is now gone, replaced by a 36-inch inverted siphon during the 1960s by the Corps of Engineers, as well as a pedestrian bridge. An inverted siphon is shaped like the letter "U" and water flows through the system, maintaining the water level on both sides of the former aqueduct location. At the west end of the aqueduct is a modern bridge to carry horseback riders over to the north bank of the canal.

Aqueduct #1 is gone and the trail uses this newer bridge to cross East Bureau Creek. Photo by Barton Jennings.

Main Channel

The aqueduct once crossed East Bureau Creek, giving it the nickname of East Bureau Creek Aqueduct. Bureau Creek is the stream on which Michel and Pierre de Beuro had their trading post, located not far downstream at the junction with the Illinois River. East Bureau Creek Aqueduct was located about 600 feet upstream of where this stream flows into Bureau Creek. Bureau Creek starts about ten miles north of Mendota, Illinois, and flows south for about 75 miles in total length.

The Hennepin Canal crossed Bureau Creek and two of its tributaries, all three known for flooding. Aqueduct #1 crossed over the East Branch, Aqueduct #2 crossed over Bureau Creek, and Aqueduct #3 over the West Branch.

To the north is the Iowa Interstate Railroad's mainline, once the Chicago, Rock Island & Pacific Railroad. The railroad bridge has been rebuilt and now consists of large I-beams supporting a concrete deck. The canal and railroad follow each other closely between Bureau and the Quad Cities area. The presence of the all-weather, faster railroad certainly made it difficult for the canal to survive. Further to the north was once the grade of the "Illinois Valley Electric Railroad," an interurban railroad that operated west out of the Chicago area. An interurban railroad is an electric railroad, generally designed to handle passenger service between various communities. Many of these railroads were built in the early 1900s, but most were gone by World War II.

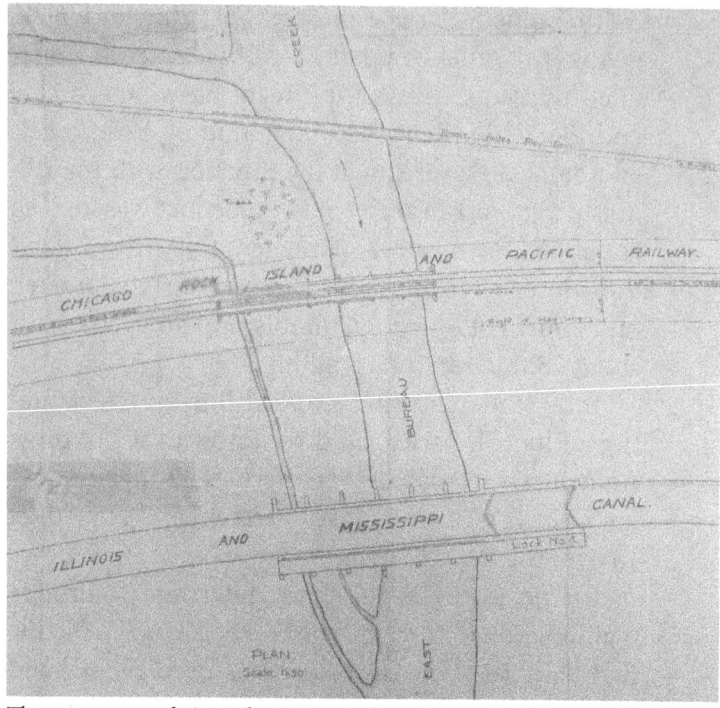

The area around Aqueduct #1 was heavily studied due to the almost yearly flooding and canal damage. This early drawing from one of those studies shows the canal, as well as the adjacent railroad and interurban railroad, located upstream and to the north. Illinois and Mississippi (Hennepin) Canal, "Map, Drawing, and Plan Files, G-Q," Record Series 497.001, Illinois State Archives.

Bureau Creek Flooding

The subject of flooding along Bureau Creek was a common problem for the entire life of the canal, and it is still an issue today. Even before the canal was completed, the canal work was damaged by high water on East Bureau Creek. Numerous reports on flood damage and how to prevent it in the future filled the files of the Corps of Engineers, and there were multiple proposals to raise the canal's aqueduct, move the canal, enlarge the bridge on the adjacent railroad, and even build a dam and large lake upstream.

A 1911 report by the Corps of Engineers commented upon plans to raise Lock #4 and Aqueduct #1. The reason for the proposed project, which was never completed, was that the Corps of Engineers had determined that the "entire valley of Bureau Creek below aqueduct 1 is 4 feet and more above its original level, due to obstruction to the discharge of the Creek caused by the solid embankment of the Peoria Branch of the Chicago, Rock Island & Pacific Railway, which in times of freshet sustains a head of 8 feet." Basically, because the area was now holding water, sediment was being deposited and the ground level was rising. There were also several studies to build a dam on the north side of the aqueduct to control the flow of the water in the stream.

3.8   INTERSTATE 180 BRIDGE – Look up to see one of the least used Interstate highways in the country – it sees only 2000 to 4000 vehicles daily. Stretching from I-80 east of Princeton, south to Hennepin, Illinois, it is just more than 13 miles long. Completed in 1969, it was built to provide access to a new Jones & Laughlin steel plant built at Hennepin in 1965. The steel plant has opened and closed over the years, reducing the need for the highway.

Heading west toward the Mississippi River, the Hennepin Canal turns sharply from heading northwest to heading southwest. In this area, the trail is well shaded by the woods to the south. With the open fields scattered throughout the area, deer and coyote sightings are common.

4.1 CAUSEWAY – This fill has a culvert to allow a limited amount of water to flow through. The fill is used by canal maintenance equipment and mowers to cross from one side of the canal to the other. Horseback riders also sometimes use the causeway. To the north are several large lake and marsh areas.

4.3 BRIDGE #2 – This bridge no longer exists, but a causeway across the canal marks its former location, as well as the former concrete abutment beside the trail on the south bank. When the canal was built, this was an important road that connected a local school, located at what today is the junction of 1120 North Avenue and County Road 2300 East, and a number of farms to the south on what is today Tiskilwa Bottom Road. Signs of the road grade can still be seen where it crosses through the marshes and Bureau Creek, but it is no longer a road or even a trail, so access to here is only via the canal trail.

The large concrete abutment for Bridge #2 still stands on the south bank of the canal, forcing the trail to curve around it. Photo by Barton Jennings.

Main Channel

This bridge was of a unique design for those on this part of the canal. While most were a single span, this one required two truss spans. The south span was a 100-foot Warren pony truss with a wooden deck, like Bridge #1. The north span, a through truss, was larger to cross the water to the north of the canal. A concrete abutment and a pier for the bridge were built 1895-1896, one of the first built. According to Corps of Engineers records, the bridge was built in September 1898.

The lake to the north of the canal and railroad, and west of the former road, is Lake Arispie. On the north side of the lake are about twenty houses and an apartment complex, although the private community was built for about sixty houses. Those that live in this small community are represented by the Lake Arispie Homeowners' Association. This area is within the Arispie Township, one of twenty-five townships in Bureau County.

Heading west from Bridge #2 to Lock #5, the canal prism (water channel) is wider than normal. This allowed canal boats to pass, and to wait their turn through the lock. There are thick woods to the south and open marshland to the north of the canal through this area.

4.6 LOCK #5 – Like most of the locks along the canal, this lock has had its gates and gate machinery removed, and a low dam installed on the upper (west) end to maintain a five-foot water depth in the canal. The changes were made in 1965 by the Corps of Engineers. Lock #5 was one of the smaller locks and only provided an eight-foot lift for boats on the canal. A map from 1911 indicates that the lock tender's house was on the south bank just east of the lock, while a later diagram showed a house and barn to the west of the lock. An ice house was built here for the lock tender in 1909-1910.

Lock #5 is overgrown and difficult to get to except by the Parkway Trail. This view is of the east gate area. Note the recess in the lock walls that housed the gates when they were open. Photo by Barton Jennings.

Note the stone along the canal's banks for several hundred feet to the east of the lock, a feature known as revetment. The shoreline was lined with stone in this area to reduce erosion from the swift changes in water flows due to the opening and closing of the lock. At one time, all of the locks included this in their construction design. The practice was also used anywhere the shoreline tended to wash away.

There is a new pedestrian bridge spanning the west end of the lock to allow hikers to explore both sides of the canal and lock. The Hennepin Canal Parkway Trail remains on the south bank of the canal, actually heading to the southwest as walking toward the Quad Cities. The trail is often far above the surrounding land, required to maintain a steady grade for the canal.

Note the timber pile mooring clusters that were once found at the ends of each lock along the canal. These timbers protected the lock from being rammed by out-of-control boats, and they provided a place to secure a boat while waiting its turn through the lock. Photo by Barton Jennings.

5.1 ARCH CULVERT #3 – It is hard to see, but this stream passes through a 10-foot culvert under the canal, and flows south into Bureau Creek. The stream drains several miles of fields to the north of the canal. Notice the old access road on the west side of the stream.

5.7 CAUSEWAY AND STREAM – The canal has had a large causeway installed across it to allow a small stream to drain the farmlands to the north. This stream once used a four-foot pipe under the canal. Today, the Hennepin Canal Parkway Trail dips down to cross the stream using a low-water bridge, one of the few places along the trail where there is a chance that you could get your feet wet. The fields to the south often attract deer, a common sight for early morning hikers.

5.9 CAUSEWAY – This is another small fill and culvert designed to provide a way across the canal, and to control the water flow in the canal.

6.2 BRIDGE #3 – This wooden deck bridge is now gone, replaced by a causeway across the canal. The main span of the bridge was a 100-foot-long steel Warren pony truss design, part of a series of five bridges (Bridges #1, #2, #3, #4 and #10) built using the same design. On the south end of the span was a concrete abutment. On the north end was a short approach span set on 40-inch "tubular" piers. Corps of Engineers records state that this bridge was built in September 1898, and removed as part of the plan to turn the canal over to the State of Illinois.

The Corps of Engineers owned these road bridges across the canal, even though local roads used them. Therefore the cost of repairs and maintenance continued despite the reduction in canal use. During the 1930s, these costs varied from $250 to $600 per mile per year, depending upon the work done. In 1936, basic deck repairs were required for this bridge. A February 1938 drawing indicated that the bridge needed to have a number of parts replaced. Apparently, this was at the same time as Bridge #10 was being replaced, because the drawings noted: "Replace all damaged members of truss with corresponding members of Bridge No. 10, provided such members can be salvaged in good condition."

Getting here by road is complicated. From Tiskilwa, take First Street east alongside the railroad tracks. Head north on County Road 2050 across Hennepin Canal Bridge #4, and then turn east on County Road 1180 North. Follow the road as it curves south and becomes 2125 East Street. The road curves around as it heads south, passing the access road to Lock #6. By the time it gets here, the road that crosses the causeway is 2160 East Street, which ends just south of the canal as a farm field road. Here, the canal, which has been heading to the southwest, curves to the north to pass under the former Rock Island Railroad line. There is very limited unofficial parking here that is popular with local fishing enthusiasts.

Parking is limited at a number of the former bridge locations, and signs such as these warn about blocking the trail. Photo by Barton Jennings.

6.4 RAILROAD BRIDGE #2 – This bridge is used by the Iowa Interstate Railroad, but was once the Chicago, Rock Island & Pacific mainline. The bridge consists of two three-span through plate girder trestles for two tracks, but only the south span is used today. The bridge, including the approach spans, was built by the Corps of Engineers by 1907, and uses the same design as the Rock Island bridge at Bureau. There are two steel frame piers, set on concrete, on each bank of the canal. These piers are used to help support the end approach spans.

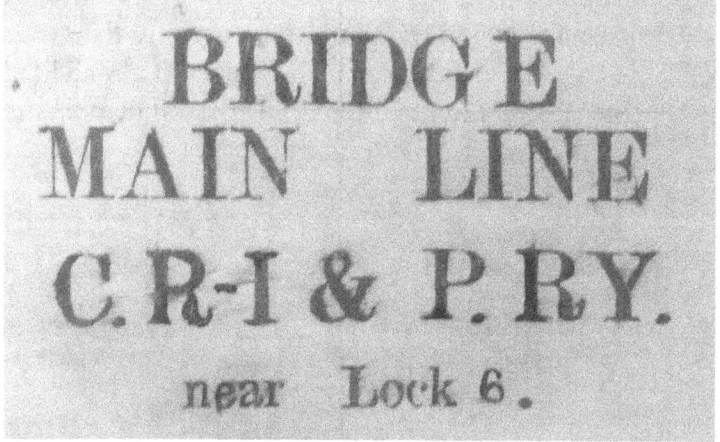

The Corps of Engineers, in their early planning, often used different names and locations as references for different structures. Instead of using Railroad Bridge #2, this drawing simply stated "near Lock 6." Illinois and Mississippi (Hennepin) Canal, "Map, Drawing, and Plan Files, G-Q," Record Series 497.001, Illinois State Archives.

Records of the Corps of Engineers state that main span of Railroad Bridge #2 was 59'-11", with spans of a few inches more than 34 feet on each end. The bridge was built by Lassig Bridge & Iron Works, a Chicago company. Since the canal was built after the railroad, the bridge was built as part of the canal and remained the property of the Corps of Engineers.

This meant that the Corps was responsible for maintaining the bridge. Several reports were made about making repairs, including one in 1932 that included a rebuilding of the bridge's deck. The railroad was responsible for the tracks above the deck.

Corps of Engineers Railroad

The construction of the Hennepin Canal required the construction or improvement of nine different railroad bridges for three different railroad companies. These were for the Chicago, Rock Island & Pacific; the Chicago, Burlington & Quincy; and the Chicago & North Western. The canal contractors also contracted with each of these railroads to move materials. However, these were not the only railroads involved with the Hennepin Canal.

The Hennepin Canal was actually built using a railroad. The railroad was built along the entire line, being extended as it moved dirt and stone for the construction of the canal embankments. Early reports indicate that the first two locomotives were named *Hennepin* and *Davenport*. Photos of the equipment indicate that at least some of the steam locomotives were built by the H. K. Porter Company. Porter started manufacturing in 1866 and became the largest producer of industrial locomotives, building almost eight thousand of them by the end of production in 1950. Looking at the construction records of H. K. Porter, the U.S. Corps of Engineers bought a number of three-foot gauge locomotives from Porter.

In the various reports produced by the Corps of Engineers, there were many references to the 3-foot narrow gauge railroad. For example, in 1896, the

Corps of Engineers built several miles of track on the east end of the canal. Their 1896 report stated: "A narrow gauge railroad track built along the canal embankment, as fast as it was completed, for a distance of 3½ miles from Station 68 (Mile 1.3) to Station 253 (Mile 4.8), and connected by 1½ miles of additional narrow gauge tracks with the gravel pit, storage yards, and lock sites. A house to shelter locomotives, a blacksmith shop, an oil house, and three warehouses in the storage yard near Lock No. 3, a warehouse at Lock No. 2, another at Lock No. 5, and another in the storage yard at Lock No. 6, built."

The equipment and track was moved around frequently. For example, in January 1903, a steam shovel, three locomotives and sixty cars were sent to Colona from the Feeder Canal to work on a cut. As the railroad was expanded, six more miles of railway materials were purchased. At the same time, an evaluation was being conducted on the existing rail line between miles 5 and 20. A report stated that along with the narrow gauge tracks in this area, there were water tanks, flat and dump cars, and one locomotive.

In July 1903, Assistant Engineer James Long wrote a report on the railroad at the eastern end of the line. "From mile 5 to mile 15, it has not been in use and is so out of repair that it is not safe for a locomotive to run over it, and can only be used by hauling cars drawn by horses over it. A question to be considered is whether it would be best to take up this part of the track before it becomes impassable, even for cars drawn by horses, and store the material or keep it in repair to be used for the delivery of material in the construction of lock gates, aqueducts and buildings. It might also be useful in repairing the canal banks

Main Channel

in case they should break at any time to convey earth to be used for repairs."

As stated, the railroad equipment was moved around as needed. In 1904, much of the eastern part of the railroad was moved to Cecil's Slough for the construction there. About the same time, trains were also active near Colona and along the Feeder Canal. The railroad's use ended with the completion of the canal. Eventually the equipment was sold off, moved to other projects, or scrapped.

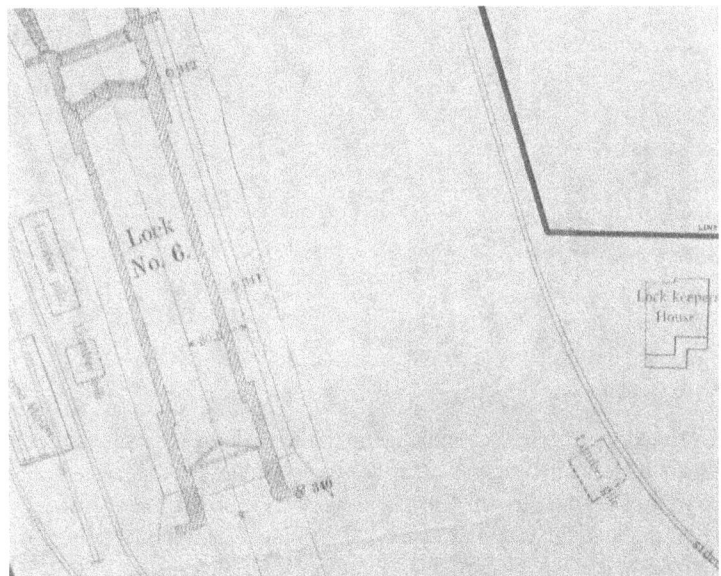

During the construction of the Hennepin Canal, the area around Lock #6 included many tracks, warehouses, piles of lumber, and even a railroad engine house for the Corps of Engineers railroad. These drawings show much of this complex facility. Illinois and Mississippi (Hennepin) Canal, "Map, Drawing, and Plan Files, G-Q," Record Series 497.001, Illinois State Archives.

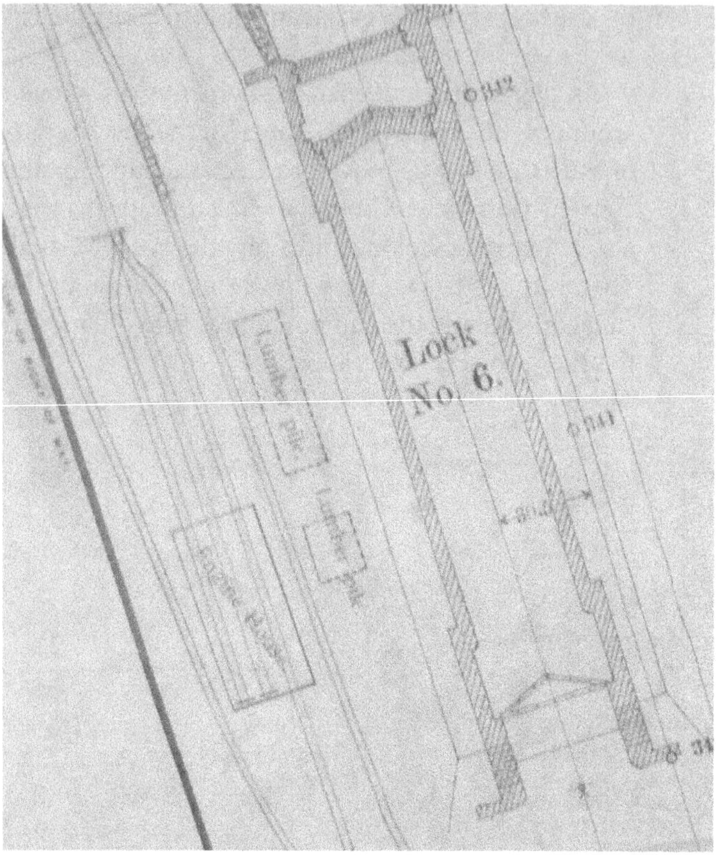

During the construction of the Hennepin Canal, the area around Lock #6 included many tracks, warehouses, piles of lumber, and even a railroad engine house for the Corps of Engineers railroad. These drawings show much of this complex facility. Illinois and Mississippi (Hennepin) Canal, "Map, Drawing, and Plan Files, G-Q," Record Series 497.001, Illinois State Archives.

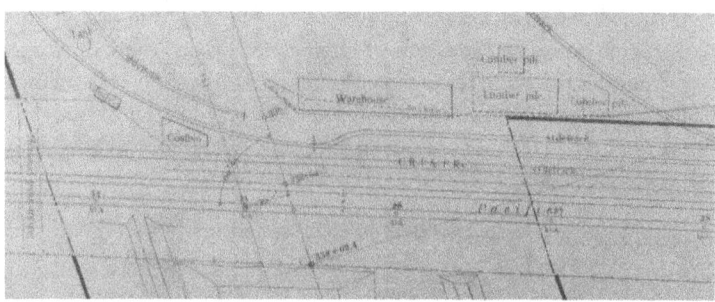

Lock #6 Railroad Yard, Warehouse and Shops

To the north of Railroad Bridge #2, and all around Lock #6, was a series of Chicago, Rock Island & Pacific tracks, and Corps of Engineers railroad tracks, plus a number of support facilities. Before the railroad bridge was built, the Rock Island consisted of two main tracks, plus a siding used to transfer supplies to the canal builders. Several side tracks were located further to the north that served a lumber yard and warehouse. There was another spur track that went east of Lock #6, passing by the lockkeeper's house and more lumber storage areas. Several tracks looped around the west side of Lock #6. These passed a coal bin, water tank, a 3-track engine house, and more lumber storage areas.

6.4 **LOCK #6** – Lock #6 is located just north of the Iowa Interstate rail line and once provided a ten-foot lift. Like most of the locks, the gates and machinery were removed in 1965 by the Corps of Engineers. Also, like many, a concrete breastwall (dam) was installed at the upper end of the lock to maintain five feet of water in the canal. There is also a pedestrian bridge over the west end of the lock to allow hikers to cross the canal.

To the east of the lock on the north bank was once a lockkeeper's house, with a barn further to the east. A diagram of the lockkeeper's house shows that the house had a kitchen, dining room, living room and bedroom on the first floor, two bedrooms on the second floor, and a basement. It was one of the smaller houses along the canal. The buildings are gone, and this property is now used as a public area, made possible because this lock is one of a number along the line that can be reached by private car. The canal is reached from the north by using Bureau County Road 2160 East. At the lock, there is also an official camping location on the north bank of the canal east of the lock, and there are public toilets, picnic tables and grills for day use. Except for when a train passes, this is one of the quietest campsites on the canal.

The entire Hennepin Canal was once lined with a fence, generally using concrete fence posts manufactured by the Corps of Engineers. This fence post can be found at Lock #6. Photo by Barton Jennings.

Just west of Lock #6, the canal turns to the west-northwest, and continues to follow Bureau Creek. The trail generally stays sheltered from the sun, but there are a number of views of area farmland.

Main Channel

6.6 CAUSEWAY – This fill is often used to connect the fields to the south of the canal with farms and roads to the north. Notice the small farm complex with the blue house across the canal.

Just west of this fill, another small local stream passes under the canal. A 10-foot concrete arch culvert, designated as Arch Culvert #4, was built for this stream in 1895-1896.

6.8 BIG BUREAU CREEK – This is where Arch Culvert #4, a 10-foot concrete structure, was built to move water under the canal. Immediately to the south is Big Bureau Creek, and only the canal's embankment separates the canal and stream. The bank in this area has a tendency to erode as Big Bureau Creek makes a tight horseshoe turn. The paved trail is sometimes impacted by this erosion, but several fills and causeways across the canal provide access to the grassy trail on the canal's north bank.

The various channels of Bureau Creek were adjacent to the canal between Miles 2 and 16, and were a common cause of breaks in the embankments. The large number of muskrat and groundhog dens in the embankment just added to the problem, and a number of breaks were blamed on water that ran through a muskrat den in the embankment. Even before the Eastern Section opened in 1907, breaks were reported "600 feet east of Lock #1", "1000 feet east of Lock #4", and in April 1905, "miles 4, 5, and 6."

Numerous other floods occurred over the years, and there were plenty of studies performed by the U.S. Corps of Engineers to solve the problem.

7.0 CAUSEWAY – This fill connects the paved Hennepin Canal Parkway Trail on the south bank with the horse trail along the north bank.

7.2 LOCK #7 – This lock has an angled dam in place of its upper (west) gate, with the east gates removed, a change made by the Corps of Engineers in 1965. The lock was originally built to provide an eight-foot lift, and a pedestrian bridge is located over the west end of the lock. Note the water level markings on the east end of the bridge, written in Roman numerals, something commonly found on all of the locks.

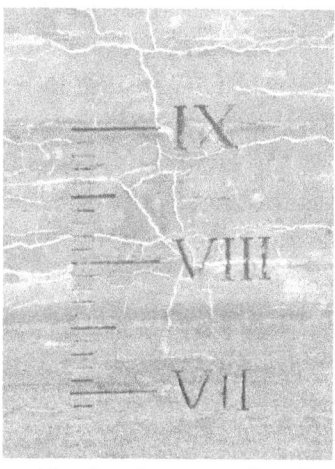

Water level gauges can be found imprinted in the walls of each lock. They were used to ensure that the water depth was adequate for the boats moving through the canal. This one is located at the east end of the lock. Photo by Barton Jennings.

There was a barn and a lockkeeper's house on the south bank, just east of the lock. The canal also included the approximately 200'x200' block of woods on the north side of the canal. It was common for blocks of land around canals and bridges to be acquired so that there would be room for construction, and to build support structures.

Main Channel

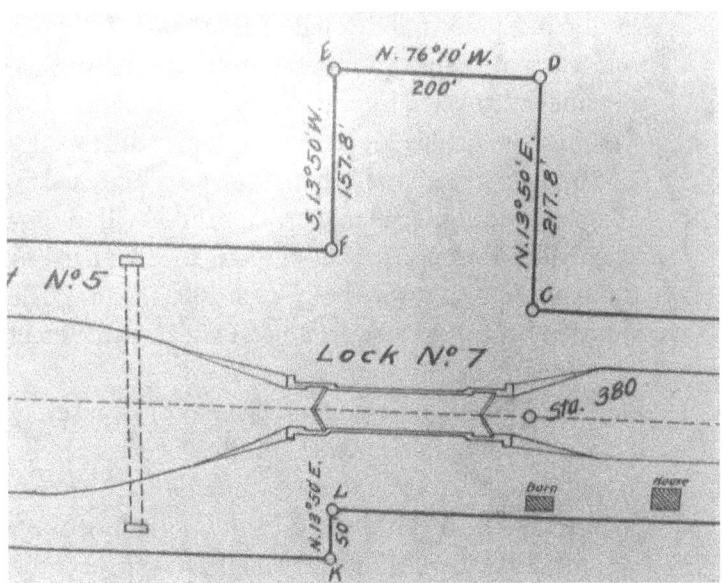

This drawing by the Corps of Engineers shows the location of the canal house and barn, as well as the canal lot to the north of Lock #7. Illinois and Mississippi (Hennepin) Canal, "Map, Drawing, and Plan Files, G-Q," Record Series 497.001, Illinois State Archives.

During February 2019, the Hennepin Canal suffered a breach during high waters just west of Lock #7. Water typically flows through a concrete box culvert under the canal, known as Culvert #3 in the original construction plans, moving water from two small streams southward to Bureau Creek. During the flooding caused by rain and melting snow, some of the water washed around the culvert, taking out the canal's south embankment. The parkway trail was closed for some time and the canal was dry between Locks #7 and #8 until repairs were made.

7.5   **BRIDGE #4** – When the canal was under construction, this was one of the first bridges built, being installed in September 1898. It used a 100-foot-long steel Warren pony truss design – a Warren truss with no top like a normal through truss bridge. The Warren truss consists of a top and bottom longitudinal member connected by angled cross-members. From the side, the bridge looks like a number of triangles all connected together. The design was patented in 1848 by its designers: James Warren and Willoughby Theobald Monzani. This design was the first used by the canal, and five were built, each 100 feet long. The wooden bridge decks were 14 feet wide, with 12 feet clear for the roadway.

This bridge is now gone, replaced by a causeway across the canal for Bureau County 2050 East Street. To get here, take First Street east alongside the railroad tracks from Tiskilwa, and then turn north on County Road 2050. There is a small parking lot at the northwest corner of the causeway. Heading west, the canal and trail curve so that they are heading to the southwest. The land around the canal also changes from mostly marsh to more open farmland, providing more views but less shade on a summer day.

Street signs often help hikers to keep track of where they are, such as this 2050 East Street sign at Bridge #4. Photo by Barton Jennings.

Main Channel

8.2 **LOCK #8** – Like most locks, this one is missing its gates, but with a concrete dam where the west gates once were. The upper gate on Lock #8 was originally a Marshall Gate, explaining the straight dam built in its place. Also note the different shape of the gate cutouts in the lock walls. A small pedestrian bridge in this area allows a close look at these differences. The spray from the water pouring over the dam can also create cool drafts, much appreciated on warm days.

A large pool was located just upstream to hold barge traffic as it passed through this lock and the nearby Lock #9. Both Locks #8 and #9 lifted boats eight feet.

8.4 **LOCK #9** – This lock also is used to hold water for the canal. Locks #8-#21 had Marshall Gates on their upper ends, and Miter Gates on the lower end. They were removed by the Corps of Engineers about 1965. There are still a number of related engineering structures at Lock #9. First, clusters of timber piles stand at the end of the lock, used to protect the end of the lock and as mooring posts. On the north side of the lock, the sluiceway or bypass can be seen. Because of the flow of water into the canal, there were times that there was more water than needed. Therefore, there was a spillway around all locks except #1 through #7, that allowed water to bypass the lock. The Marshall Gates required water from the spillways to operate, and the spillways ensured that there was water for locks lower on the canal when a lock was closed and being used. Some of these spillways still exist. The pedestrian bridge at the west end of the lock allows trail users to explore the area.

Just west of the lock is a large cedar tree. There are not a lot of these trees along the canal, and this one marks a former home and office location. This building was clearly shown on the April 1911 Hennepin topographical map.

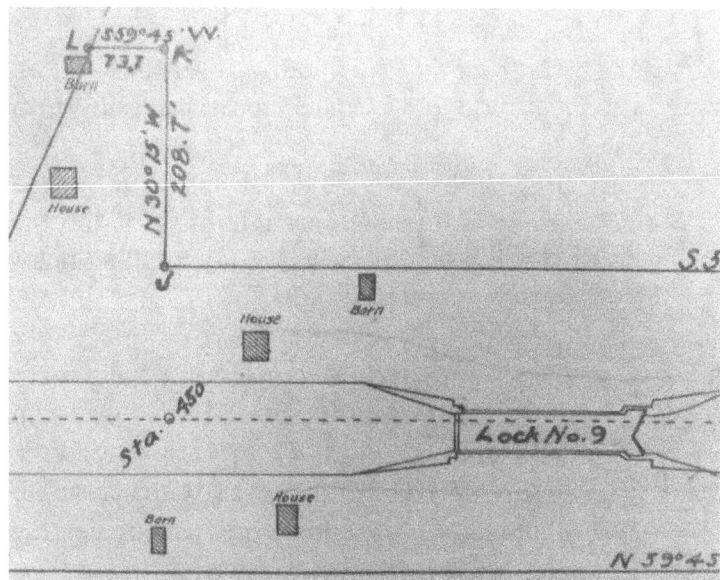

The lockkeeper's house and barn are shown in this early drawing of the Lock #9 area, as well as several other houses that once stood here. Illinois and Mississippi (Hennepin) Canal, "Map, Drawing, and Plan Files, G-Q," Record Series 497.001, Illinois State Archives.

This lock is in a scenic wooded setting, with a low hill to the south known as Owls Head, with an elevation of 597 feet. This was one location where a significant amount of dirt had to be moved to build the canal. Not far west of Lock #9, the canal widens and turns to the west.

Main Channel

Notice that the notches for the west gate are different from the east gate. This is because the west gate used a Marshall Gate, a one-piece gate that stretched between both sides of the lock. Photo by Barton Jennings.

9.2 BRIDGE #5 – The causeway for Bureau County 1890 East Avenue marks where Bridge #5 once stood. There are several small parking areas at the north end of the causeway. A benchmark in the area shows the elevation to be 533 feet. The area around this bridge featured another wide pool for the canal to hold boats waiting to move through the series of locks to the east. Just to the west, the canal turns sharply to the northwest to closely follow Bureau Creek, with only a scattered tree line to the south providing shade from the afternoon sun.

The original Bridge #5 was built by the Toledo Bridge Company and installed in December 1900, as part of a contract that covered Bridges #5-#9. It was a 98-foot steel Pratt through truss bridge, which was designed to provide 17 feet of clearance for canal traffic. For vehicular traffic, the bridge's roadway was twelve feet wide.

This was one of at least three locations that the Sterling, Dixon & Rock Falls Packet Company had leased. A lease agreement dated July 1, 1909, stated that the property was just east of Bridge #5 on the south bank. The property measured 40 feet by 100 feet. The packet company shut down in late 1910 and the property became unused.

Tiskilwa

Not far to the southwest is the town of Tiskilwa. Tiskilwa was established in 1834 and is today a small town of about 800. The town grew quickly after the construction of the Chicago & Rock Island Railroad, later the Chicago, Rock Island & Pacific, today's Iowa Interstate. At its peak, the railroad had two main tracks through town, plus a short siding to the north and a long spur track to the south. On the south side of the tracks were stockyards, the W. H. Mettler grain elevator, and the lumberyard of H. E. Curtis and Company. Today, only a single mainline plus a short spur to the north remain, plus the former CRI&P brick depot.

Because the railroad arrived first and already served downtown Tiskilwa, the canal didn't have a big impact on the community except during its construction. The Sterling, Dixon & Rock Falls Packet Company tried to provide service to the community from their dock at Bridge #5, but the firm failed by 1910. An ice house once stood near the canal, but that was about the only industry that benefitted from the waterway.

Main Channel

Tiskilwa is just a short distance south of Bridge #5, as shown by this sign which points the way. Photo by Barton Jennings.

Downtown on Main Street, the former United Methodist Church is now the home of the Tiskilwa Historical Society. They publish a newsletter regularly on their website about the history of the community. It carriers the name *The Wapsipinicon*, "from the Potawatomi name for the creek that flows into Tiskilwa from numerous springs in the hills to the west, eventually joining Big Bureau Creek east of town."

Tiskilwa is known for two festivals. The first is their Strawberry and Artisan Festival, generally held on the second Saturday in June. The festival also includes a town-wide garage sale. The second is Pow Wow Days, held the first weekend in August. Pow Wow Days is a three-day event that includes a Native American pow wow, a parade, and a number of other events.

For baseball fans, Tiskilwa is the birthplace of Warren Giles, onetime general manager of the Cincinnati Reds and then president of the National League (1957-69).

10.2 LOCK #10 – Lock #10 is an isolated lock with limited access except for the Hennepin Canal Parkway

Trail. Like most other locks, its gates – a Marshall Gate on the upper end and Miter Gates at the lower end – are gone and a concrete dam is now located at the upper gate location, where a small bridge allows hikers to cross the canal. The lock was designed to provide a lift of nine feet when in operation.

The dam at Lock #10 is straight, just like the Marshall Gate that it replaced. The pedestrian bridge crosses the lock near the dam, which provides a needed cooling spray during hot weather. Photo by Barton Jennings.

Just west of the lock is Arch Culvert #6, a 12-foot concrete arch span. The culvert allows a stream from the northeast to pass under the Hennepin Canal and flow into Bureau Creek, just southwest of the canal. Further to the west and on the north bank was a

Main Channel

lockkeeper's house and barn. These buildings sat on a 200'x200' block of land, now covered by trees. Today, on its northwest side is a farm road, marking the property limits.

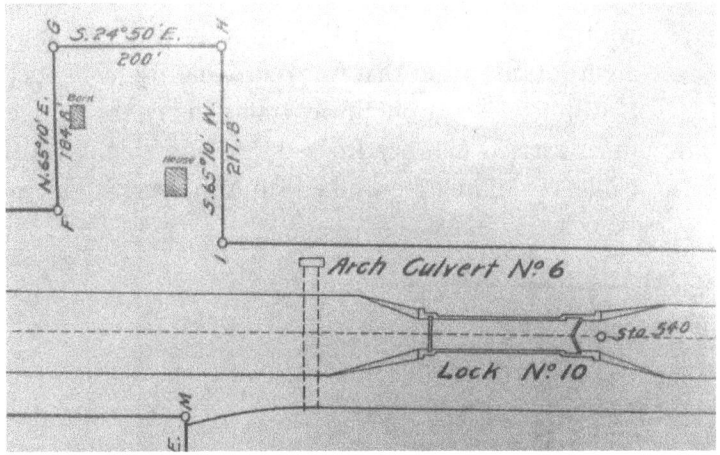

At Lock #10, the typical 200'x200' block of land was located north of the lock, and was used for the lockkeeper's house and barn. Illinois and Mississippi (Hennepin) Canal, "Map, Drawing, and Plan Files, G-Q," Record Series 497.001, Illinois State Archives.

10.4 CAUSEWAY – Just to the west of Lock #10 is a causeway that provides access for a local farm. Across the south canal embankment is still Big Bureau Creek.

This area of the Hennepin Canal Parkway Trail passes through open farmland. Between the canal and the fields to the west is one of the largest collections of concrete fence posts that still exist along the trail that can easily be photographed. Some with "U S" markings, these posts were manufactured for the Corps of Engineers and the Hennepin Canal at the Post House, near Bridge #9.

11.0 BRIDGE #6 – This is one of the few original highway bridges that still stands over the canal, and marks the east end of the Lock #11 complex. Known by many as Hennepin Canal Bridge #6, this structure is a Pratt through truss bridge built by the Toledo Bridge Company and installed in May 1900. The bridge is 98 feet long, with a reported wooden deck width of just more than 19 feet, the only one built as a part of this order that was more than 12 feet wide.

While closed to highway traffic today, the bridge once carried County Road 1150 North across the canal. It can now be walked from the parking lot at Lock #11.

This through truss bridge still stands as Bridge #6. Photo by Barton Jennings.

11.0   LOCK #11 – This lock, which provided nine feet of lift, has also had its gates removed and a dam installed at the upper end. This was another lock that had a Marshall Gate on its upper end. There is also a pedestrian bridge across the lock near the west end, allowing for a great view of the lock. Note the old canal barn that still sits on the south side of the lock. It was not the only support building here, as a superintendent's house stood here during the canal's construction, and an ice house was built in 1909-1910. The Lock #11 lock tender's house, which was once at the south end of the parking lot, was sold and moved off canal property. It is reportedly now a private residence. Some drawings show that there was a second house and barn to the north of the lock from when the canal opened. Photos from 1952 show a gambrel-roofed house standing at the north end of the east gate of the lock.

This Corps of Engineers' drawing dates from the construction of the canal and shows the superintendent's house that once stood at Lock #11. Illinois and Mississippi (Hennepin) Canal, "Map, Drawing, and Plan Files, G-Q," Record Series 497.001, Illinois State Archives.

This Corps of Engineers' photo from September 1952, shows the east gate of Lock #11 and the gambrel-roofed canal lockkeeper's house. Illinois and Mississippi (Hennepin) Canal, "Photographic Files," Record Series 497.037, Illinois State Archives.

This closeup of the house in the earlier photo shows how many of the windows face the lock, as well as how close the house was to the job site of the lockkeeper. Illinois and Mississippi (Hennepin) Canal, "Photographic Files," Record Series 497.037, Illinois State Archives.

Main Channel

This photo from 1953 shows the Marshall Gate at Lock #11. Here it is in the raised position while the canal has been drained for an inspection. Illinois and Mississippi (Hennepin) Canal, "Photographic Files," Record Series 497.037, Illinois State Archives.

Between Bridge #6 and Lock #11 is a parking lot, picnic tables, campground, and toilets, an area known as the Lock 11 Access Area. There are no showers or electricity at the campground, but there are several information and educational signs about the canal, its engineering, and the Hennepin Canal Parkway. The park can easily be reached from Tiskilwa by heading north on Galena Street. Note that there is a charge for overnight stays.

11.2 **BUREAU COUNTY ROAD 1790 EAST** – The new embankment of this road curves across the canal, and is known as **Bridge #6A**. Both the paved Hennepin Canal Parkway Trail on the south bank, and the grassy trail on the north side, have concrete underpasses. There is also a large concrete culvert for the canal's water. There is parking available along access roads at both ends of the causeway, often used by people fishing in the area.

The new "Bridge #6A" features large concrete underpasses for the Hennepin Parkway Trail. Note the Hennepin Canal sign on top next to the highway. Photo by Barton Jennings.

This fill was also once a traditional bridge, built in December 1934. Records from the Corps of Engineers, found in the Illinois State Archives, state that the bridge was 158 feet long, with a 102-foot steel Pratt truss span over the canal, and deck plate girder approach spans off each end. The records also show that the bridge was built for Illinois Highway 89 and was owned by the State of Illinois, and thus was not a part of the canal's property.

Older maps show the name of this road to be Indian Head Trail. In the January 1917 issue of *Illinois Highways*, it was reported that Indian Head Trail

Main Channel

went from Peoria to Galena, with plans to expand it north to Minneapolis, Minnesota.

11.7 LOCK #12 – Just east of this lock, the canal curves to the west. Like Lock #4, this lock was located at the east end of an aqueduct. Also like Lock #4, the aqueduct is now gone and the lock is part of an inverted siphon to move canal water under the stream where the canal once crossed using a bridge.

Lock #12 once provided a lift of eight feet as part of the climb out of the Illinois River valley. The upper gate on this lock was one of the unique Marshall Gates, an attempt to have automatic gates on the canal. About 100 yards east of the lock and on the north bank is a 220'x200' square of woods, once the location of the lock tender's house and barn. The property was acquired through condemnation from John Kitterman, who owned quite a bit of property in the area at the time.

This lock and the adjacent aqueduct received damage on a regular basis from the waters of nearby Bureau Creek. Because of this, the foundations and surrounding embankments were repaired on a regular basis. For example, in 1942, the lock received a new concrete floor and piling on the Marshall gate end. To try to reduce the flooding, a dam was proposed on Bureau Creek just north of Aqueduct #2 and Lock #12 in March 1904. This dam, although not built, would have covered 15.75 acres of land owned by John and George Kitterman. John Kitterman had a farm of about 800 acres at the time; his brother George also had a farm in the area.

At the west end of the lock is a bridge that can be used by horseback riders to move from the north side of the canal to the south side for the bridge that has replaced the aqueduct.

At the west end of Lock #12 are two bridges – one where Aqueduct #2 once stood, and a second to allow horse riders and pedestrians to cross the lock. Photo by Barton Jennings.

11.7 **AQUEDUCT #2** – This aqueduct was used to cross over Big Bureau Creek. Bureau Creek is the stream where Michel and Pierre de Beuro had their trading post, located not far downstream from the junction with the Illinois River. Bureau Creek starts about ten miles north of Mendota, Illinois, and flows south for about 75 miles in total length.

Like several others, this aqueduct was taken out of service during the 1960s by the Corps of Engineers and replaced by a 36-inch inverted siphon. It was also replaced by a pedestrian bridge on the south bank for the Hennepin Canal Parkway Trail. The remains of the aqueduct and the pedestrian bridge were damaged in a 1998 flood, but some of the aqueduct's footings remain in the creek bed on the north side of the pedestrian bridge.

Main Channel

While Aqueduct #2 is gone, the footings for some of the piers can still be seen in Bureau Creek. Photo by Barton Jennings.

Heading west, the Hennepin Canal curves to the west-northwest for a short distance. This area features a wide pool once used to hold boats waiting to go through Lock #12 to the east and Lock #13 to the west. Just south of the canal can be seen West Bureau Creek as it meanders through a marshy area.

12.4 **LOCK #13** – This is another concrete lock that originally had a Marshall Gate on its upper end. It was built with a ten-foot lift. Its gates were removed about 1965 by the Corps of Engineers and a dam for water control built in place of its upper gate. A pedestrian bridge was also built over the lock in this area.

Lock #13 also has a straight dam and a pedestrian bridge on its west end. Photo by Barton Jennings.

About 100 yards west of the lock and on the north bank was once the location of the lockkeeper's house and barn. The house was relatively large when built, with a kitchen, parlor, dining room and two bedrooms on the first floor, plus three bedrooms on the second floor. There were also three storerooms and a large attic, as well as a basement, but no bathrooms. In 1926, the house received central heating thanks to a basement furnace installed by the Rock Island Stove Company. Most of the houses also received electricity by the late 1930s.

Main Channel

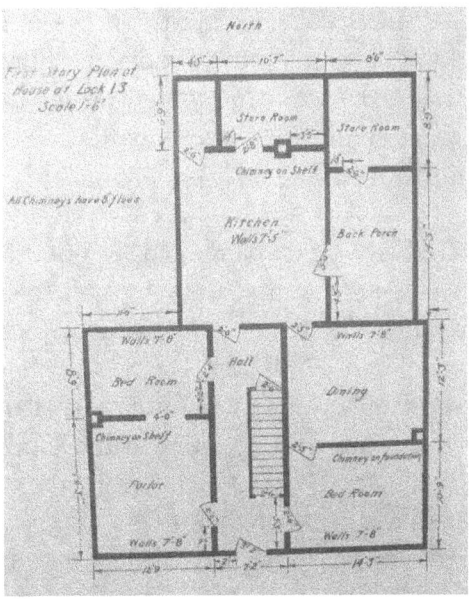

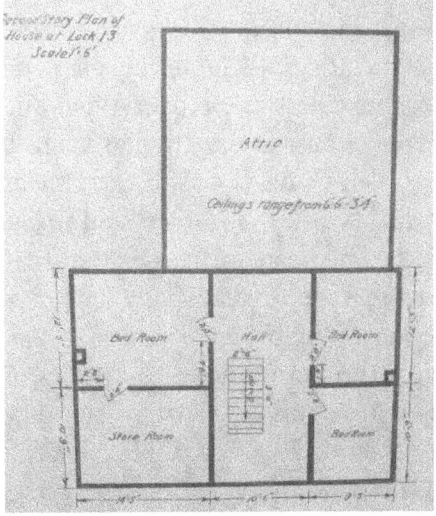

These Corps of Engineers' drawings show the floor plan of the canal house at Lock #13. These houses were pretty basic with a kitchen, dining room, parlor, and several bedrooms. Note that there were no bathrooms in the original plans; outhouses were located nearby. Central heat was installed in most of these houses during the 1920s. Illinois and Mississippi (Hennepin) Canal, "Map, Drawing, and Plan Files, G-Q," Record Series 497.001, Illinois State Archives.

Like many of these locations, the buildings are gone and the area is now wooded. Heading west, the canal and the Iowa Interstate, former Rock Island Railroad, come side-by-side as the canal curves to the northwest.

12.6 BRIDGE #7 – This abandoned 98-foot Pratt through truss bridge, manufactured by the Toledo Bridge Company, still stands on the original alignment of County Road 1700 East. However, it has been replaced by a causeway just to the east (**Bridge #7A**), with some unofficial parking at the south end. The causeway closely follows the original alignment of the road that was here before the canal was built.

This Pratt through truss bridge was the second design used on the canal, and there were at least four built, including Bridges #5, #7, #8 and #9. The bridges includes a 14-foot-wide plank deck, and this one was installed in October 1900. The Pratt truss was invented in 1844 by Thomas Willis Pratt and his father Caleb Pratt. It was known for being able to cover distances up to 250 feet and was popular with railroads. The basic form of a Pratt truss has triangular trusses whose diagonal members slope toward the center of the bridge. Because of this, the bridge design is also known as an N-truss.

The bridge was built with a curved ramp up on the south end. The road approached from the area of the current causeway and made a sharp right turn to cross the bridge, which was raised to clear boats on the canal. The tall concrete abutment has "JUNE 1900 EMPIRE" cast into it, clearly visible from the trail. Empire was one of the concrete types being tested and used during the canal's construction. Others were Atlas, Utica, Alpha, Alsen's White Label, and Star Stettin. The various brands and types were heavily tested during the first few years of construction, and many reports about their strengths and resistance to deterioration were made.

This is another example of an original bridge built for the Corps of Engineers. The diagonal braces provide strength to the Pratt through truss bridge and give it its nickname of an N-truss Bridge. Photo by Barton Jennings.

On the north bank of the canal and to the east of the bridge, Justus Blythe once had a lease on canal property. There, he built an ice house to take advantage of the winter freeze on the canal. By 1940, Justus Blythe was out of the natural ice business and wanting to end the lease. However, the lease agreement had to be extended because the First National Bank of Wyanet still had a mortgage on the ice house structure.

Heading west toward Lock #14, the canal and trail head northwest, and are shaded by a tree line on the north side of the railroad tracks to the south.

13.0 ARCH CULVERT #7 – On the north side of the canal can be seen a concrete culvert, the flushing arrangement for this double 10-foot concrete arch culvert. The culvert allows a small stream to pass under the canal. The additional concrete structure on the north bank allows canal water to also flow into the culvert to get rid of excess water, or to flush sediment out of the culvert.

On the north bank is this flush duct, a good landmark to find Arch Culvert #7. Photo by Barton Jennings.

13.1 BRIDGE #8 – This is another Toledo Bridge Company, 98-foot Pratt through truss bridge that has been retired and replaced by a causeway across the canal, located just to the east. The canal trail passes through the causeway using a large culvert. A trail sign calls the causeway **Bridge #8A**.

Main Channel

Bridge #8 is another 98-foot Pratt through truss that still stands from when the canal was built. In this photo, which looks west, Lock #14 can be seen in the distance. Photo by Barton Jennings.

The original steel bridge, which still stands on its concrete abutments, was once used by Bureau County Road 1280 North Avenue, now located on the adjacent causeway. The south approach to the bridge came in from the west on the road's current alignment, with a "T" on the north end that connected to the highway alignment to the north, and a farm road to the west. Like Bridges #7 and #9, this bridge also features a 14-foot-wide plank deck. The concrete abutment next to the paved trail is stamped with "JULY 1899 ATLAS".

Hennepin Canal Parkway: History Through the Miles

The concrete abutment of Bridge #8, located on the south bank of the canal, is clearly marked with Atlas for the concrete used in its construction. Photo by Barton Jennings.

13.2 LOCK #14 – There is a parking lot alongside the lock to the south, accessed from Bureau County Road 1280 North Avenue. Just to the south of the parking lot is the Iowa Interstate Railroad. The railroad and the canal stay close to each other through this area. Heading west, there are three more locks over the next mile as the canal climbs out of the Big Bureau Creek valley.

Lock #14 is another lock area that is now a recognized canal access area, as indicated by this sign. Photo by Barton Jennings.

This lock once provided a ten-foot lift and featured a Marshall Gate at the upper end, where there is now a pedestrian bridge. Like others, its gates are gone and the west end has a dam installed, the work done in 1961 by the Corps of Engineers. There was once a lock house south of the canal near the west gate, and a barn on the north bank about the middle of the lock. The buildings are gone and both areas are wooded.

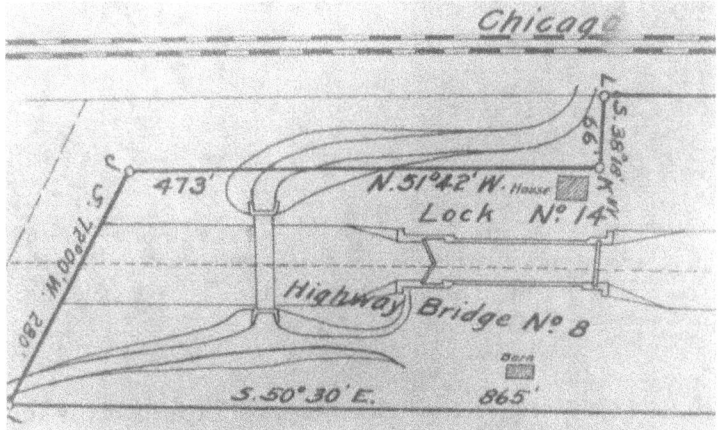

This drawing of the Lock #14 area shows how the lock house and barn were on opposite sides of the canal, and how the road using Bridge #8 curved around the site. For some reason, many of the drawings of the canal through this area have south to the top of the page. Illinois and Mississippi (Hennepin) Canal, "Map, Drawing, and Plan Files, G-Q," Record Series 497.001, Illinois State Archives.

Heading to the northwest, the canal soon widens significantly. This area was wider than usual due to the three locks to the west. The planned volume of boats required that an area be provided here to hold the many boats waiting to move through this series of locks. West Bureau Creek is to the south, providing woods in that direction. The Hennepin Canal follows West Bureau Creek, passing through a mix of woods and farms, until near Wyanet, about three miles further west.

Looking east, this 1971 photo from the Corps of Engineers shows Bridge #8 and Lock #14 after the east gates had been removed from the lock. Illinois and Mississippi (Hennepin) Canal, "Photographic Files," Record Series 497.037, Illinois State Archives.

13.8 LOCK #15 – Built with a ten-foot lift, this is the easternmost of three closely spaced locks. This lock has had its gates removed and a dam placed at its west end, where there was once a Marshall Gate. A pedestrian bridge is here now.

The lock had its own gambrel-roofed lock tender's house, with a barn, located north of the east end of the lock in a typical 200'x200' plot of land outside the regular limits of the canal property. There were thirty of these two-story homes with gambrel roofs (symmetrical two-sided roof with two slopes on each side, like many barns) and seven rooms on a foundation measuring 22 feet wide and 28 feet long.

Main Channel

This drawing shows the front plan of a typical gambrel-roofed house. The first floor featured a kitchen, dining room, parlor and bedroom. The second floor contained two bedrooms and a storeroom. The basement was open, and later had a coal stove installed to provide central heating. Illinois and Mississippi (Hennepin) Canal, "Map, Drawing, and Plan Files, G-Q," Record Series 497.001, Illinois State Archives.

14.0 LOCK #16 – This lock produced an eleven-foot lift, one of the largest on the canal. Lock #16 is one of five locks that have been restored along the canal, although it is not used. Even more unusual is that the gates on the two ends are different. The gates on the east end are traditional wooden miter gates that swing in and out, with their gate winches still in place. The Corps of Engineers was very clear on the construction of the wooden miter gates. The specifications called for Longleaf yellow pine for the timbers, Oregon fir for the sheathing, and white oak for the miter sills. Contracts show that Boeckeler Lumber Company of St. Louis provided the yellow pine, W. L. Serrell of Chicago provided the Oregon fir, and Marsh & Bingham Company of Chicago the white oak.

Lock #16 is unique in that it is functional. This is the east gate mechanism, which was used to open and close the miter gates. A crank was used to push or pull the gates to their appropriate positions. Photo by Barton Jennings.

On the west end of the lock, the Marshall gate and its operating mechanism are still in place. This is the only Marshall gate that was restored and is still functional. The lock was rebuilt and restored in 1965 by the Corps of Engineers with the goal of having limited recreational service on the canal. A Marshall gate rolls up from the floor of the lock, requiring a different design of lock wall.

Main Channel

The west gate at Lock #16 is the only restored Marshall Gate on the canal. Here it is shown in its closed position, although it now leaks due to a lack of maintenance. Photo by Barton Jennings.

The Hennepin Canal had fourteen locks that used Marshall gates. This gate design was unique to this canal, and was designed by Lieutenant William L. Marshall of the Army Corps of Engineers in 1877. The gate sits on a hinge that allows the gate to open and close like a traditional mailbox. Identified as a hinged-leaf canal gate by the U.S. Patent Office, it was classified as an improvement in automatic canal-locks.

This lock is at the east end of the Hennepin Canal Lock #17 park, and it features the three typical historical markers on the anatomy of a canal, the engineering of a canal, and information about the Hennepin Canal Trail. There is parking and picnic tables on the north side of the lock, reached from the trail using a pedestrian bridge at the west end of the lock.

While exploring the canal and its locks, bollards such as this one at Lock #16 can be found. Also known as snubbing posts by the Corps of Engineers, they were used to tie boats to the banks, or for boats to hold their position in locks as the water level changed. Photo by Barton Jennings.

Lock #16 also had its own lockkeeper, and thus its own house and barn. They were located on the north side of the canal and west of the lock about 200 feet. This area is now used for parking and as a picnic area.

14.2 **LOCK #17** – Lock #17 is a busy and popular location on the Hennepin Canal Parkway Trail. Bureau County Road 1550 East reaches the canal, and there is a parking lot to the north. Adjacent to the parking lot are toilets, picnic tables, and a campground. It is signed as the "Hennepin Canal Parkway Lock 17 Day Use Area" on several area highways.

This lock was one of the first rebuilt in 1961 by the Corps of Engineers. Like most of the locks on the Hennepin Canal, the gates are gone on the lock, replaced by a dam that maintains five feet of water in the canal as opposed to the original canal design of seven feet. Lock #17 is near the top of the grade from the Illinois River valley. The lock, with a Marshall Gate on its upper end, originally provided a lift of ten feet.

The lock also featured a roller bridge, a unique structure. The bridge was built with steel stringers on rollers and tracks which allowed the bridge to be extended across the canal, and then rolled out of way to the north to clear the canal for boats. This bridge is now in place across the canal and is open to traffic. The rails and rollers are clearly visible on the north end. There is also a pedestrian bridge over the west end of the lock.

At Lock #17, the rails for the roller bridge are clearly visible on the north bank. This bridge has been restored and the rolling system is still in place. Photo by Barton Jennings.

Reports about the canal state that the Lock #17 lock tender's house was moved to canal property on

Canal Street on the south side of Wyanet, and was leased to a private party.

14.3 BRIDGE #9 – This 98-foot Pratt through truss once carried Bureau County Road 1550 East across the canal, but it is now closed to traffic and open to pedestrians only. The concrete abutment of the bridge is stamped with "JULY 1899 ATLAS". There are concrete steps on the west side of the south abutment that go up to the bridge deck. The vegetation has not been cut in several years, but a narrow trail is still used.

Looking east from Bridge #9, Locks #17, #16 and #15 can be clearly seen as they are less than one-half mile apart. Photo by Barton Jennings.

This is one of at least four bridges built to this design, all with 14-foot-wide plank decks. On the southeast end of the steel bridge is a builders plate. It reads "Toledo Bridge Co., 1900, Toledo, Ohio" and indicates that it was built by the same firm that built Bridge #6. The Toledo Bridge Company started as the Smith Bridge Company, founded in Toledo in 1867 by Robert W. Smith. The company originally built wooden bridges, many of them covered wooden bridges, and it controlled several bridge design patents created by Smith. The firm became the Toledo Bridge Company by the late 1890s, and then was consolidated into the new American Bridge Company, which was founded in April 1900. As the firm's history states: "American Bridge Company was formed as a JP Morgan & Company engineered merger of 28 steel companies in 1900."

Bridge #9 is still original and is one of the few that still displays its builders plate – Toledo Bridge Company. Photo by Barton Jennings.

There was once an overseer's house on the north side of the canal at Mile 14.4, but it was moved away during the 1950s.

Post House

Just west of Bridge #9 is the concrete shell of a warehouse and factory, as well as the remains of a loading dock on the south side of the canal. This building, known as the Post House or Post Factory, was shown on a 1923 topographical map of the Buda, Illinois, area, but records show that it dates from not long after the initial construction of the canal. For example, one sketch of the proposed post house is dated July 30, 1910.

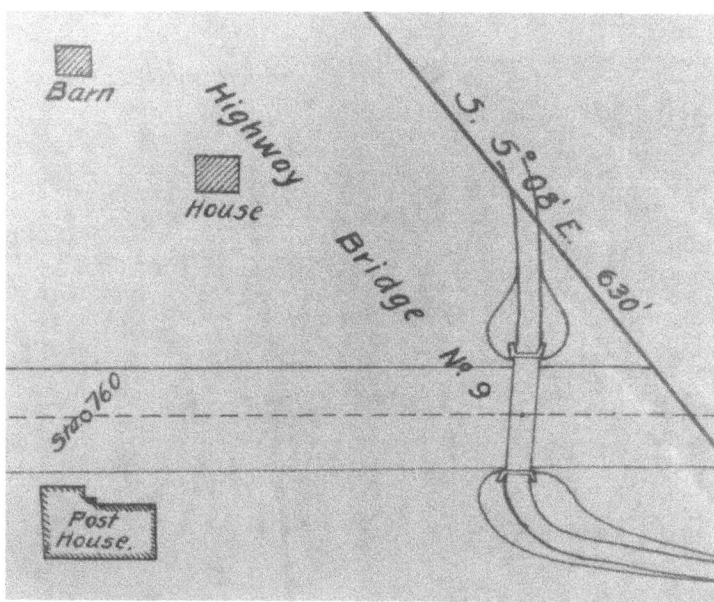

This early plat of the area around Bridge #9 clearly shows the Post House, as well as the overseer's house on the north side of the canal. Note that it also shows the curved approach to Bridge #9 along the south bank. Illinois and Mississippi (Hennepin) Canal, "Map, Drawing, and Plan Files, G-Q," Record Series 497.001, Illinois State Archives.

This facility, whose main body measured 50'x25', was built to manufacture concrete fence posts, telephone poles and bridge flooring. When the canal was being built, the fence posts and telephone poles were untreated wood, and many required replacement before the canal even opened. With so much of the canal being built with concrete, a decision was made to manufacture concrete fence posts, telephone poles, and other canal parts. Many of these can still be seen along the canal.

The remains of the Post House can still be found just west of Bridge #9. Naturally, the building was constructed of concrete, like the products it manufactured. Photo by Barton Jennings.

Reports indicate that by July 1, 1911, labor working for the Corps of Engineers had manufactured 3836 fence posts and more than 200 gate posts and braces. By mid-1912, more than 18,000 fence posts had been manufactured and installed. The telephone poles manufactured used a concrete pole with a wood cross-piece. The wood decks of some of the bridges were also wearing out, so replacement concrete flooring sections were manufactured.

The posts, poles, and decks were distributed up and down the canal by boat, thus the dock on the canal.

By 1915, the building itself needed some improvements, and the floor was leveled. Additionally, 24 new forms for telephone poles, and 6 nests of line fence post forms were made. Production apparently increased that year as 12,370 concrete fence posts, 824 braces, 710 corner fence posts, and 708 telephone poles were manufactured. Records show that several major fencing projects were underway that year, most replacing old wooden posts. Concrete blocks for three highway bridges were also made. Repair and maintenance work continued as long as the canal was in operation, and the post factory reportedly remained in service until the early 1950s. The building burned on June 20, 1957, leaving only part of the concrete shell and supports.

This photo, looking to the east, shows the Post House after it burned in 1957. Illinois and Mississippi (Hennepin) Canal, "Photographic Files," Record Series 497.037, Illinois State Archives.

Main Channel

Appropriately, heading west from the post house are a number of concrete telephone poles that were manufactured here. Check out the trail carefully for deer tracks as a number of the animals call this area home.

15.0 AQUEDUCT #3 – This four-span concrete aqueduct is set on concrete piers and crosses West Bureau Creek. West Bureau Creek flows to the southeast and eventually merges with the east branch, and then flows south to the Illinois River. This is one of six remaining aqueducts out of the nine that were originally built. Most of the metal parts for the aqueducts on the Hennepin Canal were manufactured and provided by the Springfield Bridge and Iron Company of Springfield, Illinois. The Springfield Bridge and Iron Company was founded by Joseph E. Burtle, Jerome Burtle, Thomas J. Fullenwider, and S. J. Willet in 1895. Their plant opened in 1899, but the company closed in 1913. The firm became the Jerome Burtle and Company that year and continued to manufacture and erect steel structures until at least 1924.

The Hennepin Canal Parkway Trail crosses the aqueduct on the south side. In this area, there is no trail on the north side of the canal. To the south is the Iowa Interstate Railroad bridge, consisting of two deck plate girder spans, which once supported two tracks, but only one today. Heading west, the canal turns almost directly west to pass south of Wyanet.

From the east, Aqueduct #3 is the first one that has been restored and is still standing. As at many places, the location is clearly identified by small green signs. Photo by Barton Jennings.

An aqueduct is basically a bridge that carries a stream or canal over a low area. Aqueduct #3 is made of concrete and steel, like many of the structures along the Hennepin Canal. Photo by Barton Jennings.

Main Channel

15.3 LOCK #18 – This lock provided a lift of nine feet, and is today accessible from Bureau County Highway 1400 North. There is a pedestrian bridge across the west end of the lock that allows access to both sides of the lock. For those wanting information about the canal trail, there is an information sign on the north side of the lock about the Hennepin Canal Parkway.

This sign clearly identifies Lock #18 at Mile 15.3. Photo by Barton Jennings.

Locks #15 through #18 were all built starting in 1898 and were ready when the canal was inspected in 1906. This was one of fourteen locks on the canal that once had a Marshall Gate on its upper end. It was modified by the Corps of Engineers in 1961. At the east end of the lock, and on the north side, is benchmark 15.3A, one of many along the canal used to identify locations and elevations.

15.9 BRIDGE #10 – This 100-foot Warren pony truss bridge was built with riveted connections. It is now used by pedestrians as a part of the Hennepin Canal Parkway Trail, but was once a road with a curved approach on the south end. Look for the stone wall support. The original Bridge #10 was part of a series of five bridges (Bridges #1, #2, #3, #4 and #10) built using the same design and installed in September 1898. This bridge has always been somewhat unique in that it crosses the canal at an angle instead of straight across.

While Bridge #10 is closed to highway traffic, hikers and bikers on the Canal Trail use the bridge as an access route from near Wyanet, Illinois. Notice the lack of a top, a defining characteristic of a pony-type bridge. Photo by Barton Jennings.

Just south of the trail was once a grain elevator, served by the railroad. The railroad had several tracks on each side of the elevator, including where the parkway trail now exists, as the towpath once went under Bridge #10 instead of around it.

The canal turns to the northwest on the west side of this bridge to pass under Bridge #10A and then through the Lock #19 area.

Main Channel

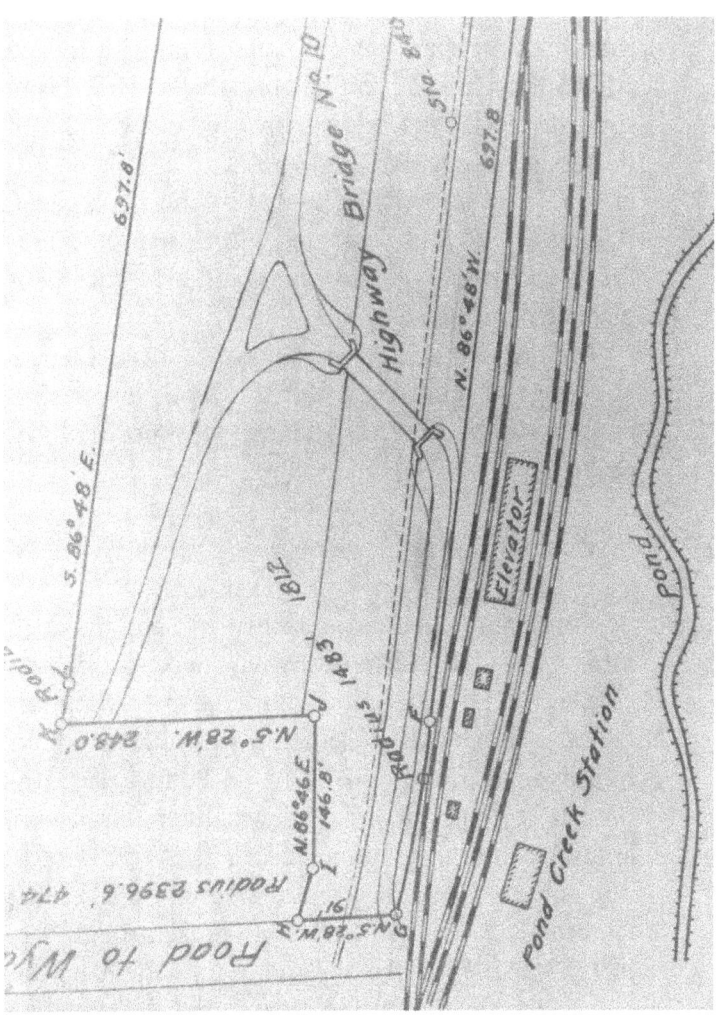

This early plat of the Bridge #10 area shows how busy it was with the railroad's Pond Creek depot and tracks, as well as the grain elevator, not far from the canal. All of this explains the tight curved approach to the bridge that is still used by the Parkway Trail. Illinois and Mississippi (Hennepin) Canal, "Map, Drawing, and Plan Files, G-Q," Record Series 497.001, Illinois State Archives.

16.0 BRIDGE #10A – This new concrete bridge, opened in 2011, replaced the earlier bridge built in 1931. The original bridge consisted of a main 115-foot Pratt through truss span over the canal, built with riveted connections in 1931 and rehabilitated in 1982. From south to north, the bridge consisted of two 40-foot deck plate girder spans, a 67'-8" through plate girder span over four tracks owned by the Rock Island Railroad, a 53-foot deck plate girder span, the 115-foot steel truss over the canal, and a 50-foot deck plate girder span.

The original bridge was relocated, strengthened, and used to cross West Bureau Creek just east of here on County Road 1400 North, just north of Aqueduct #3.

Wyanet

County Road 8 crosses the bridge, heading north into Wyanet. The first settlement here was reportedly in 1821 by an Indian trader named Bulbona. He called the location Center. A sawmill and a flour mill opened in the mid-1830s on Pond Creek, immediately south of today's Iowa Interstate tracks, and the community began calling itself Pond Creek. The name was changed again to Kingston when the Chicago & Rock Island (CRI&P) built through here in 1853, named for Henry and Mary King, who donated land for the station. It became Wyanet when the Chicago, Burlington & Quincy built through the town in 1855.

Reportedly, Wyanet for many years was one of the best grain markets in this part of the state with the first carload of grain being shipped in 1854 by William Moffatt. A warehouse was erected in 1855 and the Chicago, Burlington & Quincy (CB&Q), which passed through the center of Wyanet, added a rail car to be used as a depot. The Village of Wyanet was laid out in 1856 by the CB&Q, and in 1857 a permanent depot was built by the CB&Q, the same year that the town was incorporated.

The canal and the Rock Island Railroad never went through Wyanet, but instead passed south of the community. Nevertheless, the Rock Island once had a depot here, located on the south side of the tracks and the east side of the road. Maps show that there was also a grain elevator here. Just to the north was Lock #19. Today, Wyanet has a population of about 1000 residents. There is a gas station and convenience store downtown, about a mile from the canal.

The battle of Cecil's Slough, the fight to build the Hennepin Canal through the peat bogs west of here, actually started at Wyanet. In 1903, the materials for the overhead cableway conveyors were delivered to Wyanet. This included 600 tons of coal. Everything was moved to the Corps' narrow gauge railroad and hauled west of Lock #21.

16.1 LOCK #19 – This lock provided a 10-foot lift for barges heading west. Its gates have been removed and there is now a dam on the upper end to hold water in the canal to the west. There is also a pedestrian bridge on the west end of the lock. The work, including removing the original Marshall Gate, was done about 1965 by the Corps of Engineers.

There is a small shaded park to the north of the lock, located on the south side of Wyanet off of County Highway 8. Note the old foundations that once supported several canal buildings, and there used to be a number of Hennepin Canal facilities at Lock #19. Besides the lock tender's house, there was an overseer's house, office building, warehouse, barn, oil house, and ice house here. The large overseer's house still stands at the top of the hill to the north of the lock. Note the concrete fence posts around the area.

The Lock #19 area is another recognized access area for the Hennepin Canal Parkway State Park. Photo by Barton Jennings.

An early plat of the area showed an office and then a house to the north of the lock. There was a barn west of the house. A warehouse stood just south of the lock with a blacksmith shop to its west. The tracks of the Chicago, Rock Island & Pacific Railroad were to the south, with its Pond Creek Station further south.

Main Channel

Just north of Lock #19 is this former overseer's house. The house is unique in that there is an additional extension on the left side, while most of these houses just had an extension on the right side. Photo by Barton Jennings.

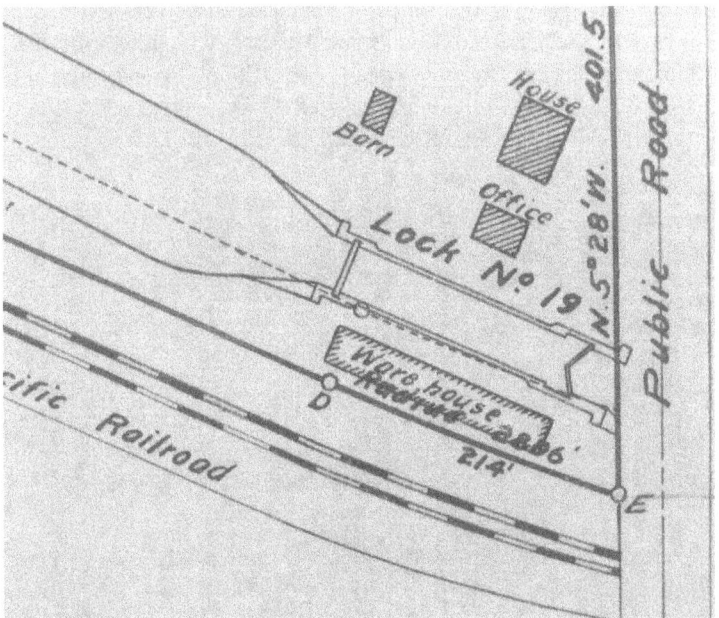

This early plat of the Lock #19 area shows some of the warehouses that were built to support the construction of the canal. None of these remain today. Illinois and Mississippi (Hennepin) Canal, "Map, Drawing, and Plan Files, G-Q," Record Series 497.001, Illinois State Archives.

This view from 1952 shows the well-maintained area around Lock #19. By this time, many of the Corps of Engineers' structures were gone, but two houses remained. Illinois and Mississippi (Hennepin) Canal, "Photographic Files," Record Series 497.037, Illinois State Archives.

This view, also from 1952, focuses on the employee houses at Lock #19. This area is now a park, but one house still stands. Illinois and Mississippi (Hennepin) Canal, "Photographic Files," Record Series 497.037, Illinois State Archives.

Main Channel

The Lock #19 area was important during the canal's construction, and it was used to handle shipments from the two railroads. Because it was an early construction station on the canal, a number of reports were written about the location that provide a great amount of detail. Some of these included information about the buildings. For example, designs for early ice houses showed them to be 18'x16', and 16' tall to the eaves; that barns measured 16'x24', and 13' tall; and an oil house measured 17'-6"x12'.

Lock #19 was also flooded several times, and the flood of October 10, 1931, heavily damaged the area. According to the Corps of Engineers report, there was "heavy erosion of canal to the west" due to the water flowing down Pond Creek and the canal. Some of the buildings were also impacted, including the blacksmith shop – "demolished by flood" – and the west end of the warehouse – "removed by flood".

Heading west, the canal turns to the northwest to pass under the BNSF Railway, and then winds along a series of low ridges to near Mile 20. The paved Hennepin Canal Parkway Trail stays on the south bank of the canal, used for a short distance as a driveway for a large home. There is no trail on the north side of the canal until the Visitor Center near Sheffield, Illinois.

This area is very scenic, with water lilies covering much of the large pool west of Lock #19. There are also a number of wood duck houses that support the local bird population. Deer, squirrel, fox and other types of wildlife are also commonly seen here.

16.7   **RAILROAD BRIDGE #3** – Today, this is the BNSF Mendota Subdivision, a busy line that connects Chicago with places like Omaha, Nebraska, and Denver, Colorado. A number of Amtrak trains also daily pass over this bridge. Originally, this was the Chicago, Burlington & Quincy Railroad (CB&Q), created in 1856. When the canal was being dug, a railroad was already built through Wyanet which became part of the CB&Q. The railroad later became part of Burlington Northern, and then today's BNSF.

Railroad Bridge #3 is in a quiet, wooded location, except for when a train rumbles overhead. Photo by Barton Jennings.

Documents show that the bridge was designed in June 1890, and that it consists of two 88' 9½" deck plate girder spans, one for each track. The bridge was built for the Corps of Engineers as a part of the canal's construction. Today, each span has an extra bent (bridge pier) to strengthen the bridge. The railroad-north span has a steel pile bent on its east end. The railroad-south span has a large wooden bent near the west end.

Because the bridge was built as part of the canal's construction, it was owned by the United States government. This required that the Corps of Engineers fund any repairs of the bridge structure. In late 1931, this led to a contract with the Kelly-Atkinson Company of Chicago for the firm to conduct a renewal of the bridge deck under the eastbound track. The

Main Channel

Kelly-Atkinson Company was a nationally known bridge building company that built bridges all across the country. They also built ships in Mobile, Alabama.

The Hennepin Canal Parkway Trail passes under the bridge on the south bank. There is no trail or walkway on the north bank. From here, the canal heads northwest to Lock #21. Heading west, the canal and trail pass through farmland, often with few trees or shade, until the Visitor Center near Sheffield.

17.1 LOCK #20 – Construction on this lock began in 1898, and it once provided an eleven-foot lift. In 1961, its gates were removed and the typical dam installed on the upper end of the lock to hold water in the canal. This was one of the locks that had Marshall Gates on its upper end, so the dam is straight. A pedestrian bridge crosses the lock above where the Marshall gate once was.

Lock #20 seems to be one of the least visited locations on the canal, or at least it seems so by the heavy vegetation which surrounds it. This view of the east gate area shows some of the large trees and heavy brush that has grown up over the years. Photo by Barton Jennings.

Today, the lock sits between several large fields. It can be reached by using a dirt farm road from the north, but the road's gate is normally closed and locked. Along this road and northwest of the lock is one of the remaining overseer houses from the canal era. At one time, there was also a barn to the north of the house.

A small stream that drains fields to the north flows into the canal just east of the lock. Through this area, the canal's embankments are often above the adjacent land, providing great views of the surrounding farmland. However, there was a break in the canal here during the 1931 flooding.

Hikers of the canal trail experience short climbs as they pass most of the locks. These climbs bring the tow path to the level of the canal on each side of the lock. Therefore, if a lock raised the water level ten feet, the trail on the towpath also needs to raise ten feet.

17.4 LOCK #21 AND LIFT BRIDGE – In this area, the canal has turned east-west for a short distance, and it enters a wooded park. Lock #21 is one of the most visited locks on the canal, being located on U.S. Highway 6/34. From the highway, the west entrance to the campground is marked by signs reading "Hennepin Canal Parkway Lock 21 Day Use Area" while the east entrance directly to the lock has no signs.

There is a small parking lot on the south side of the lock, reached by driving across the historic lift bridge (weight limit of 4 tons). Just west of the lock is also a large day use area, campground, and boat ramp. Toilets are also available there. In addition, this is the only official equestrian camping location along the canal.

A bench and the sound of falling water is a big attraction at the west gate of Lock #21. Photo by Barton Jennings.

There are also a number of signs that explain the historic nature of the canal, erected in 1976 by the State of Illinois and the Wyanet Bicentennial Committee. Sign #1 is titled *Anatomy of a Canal*. It reads:

> Canals like the Hennepin are manmade waterways for boats to travel on. Many canals are built to make shortcuts between two existing bodies of water. The Hennepin Canal was built to carry cargo barges between the Illinois and Mississippi Rivers. It cut out over 400 miles off the river route from Chicago to Rock Island. The Hennepin Canal links up with the Rock River for eight miles between Green Rock and Milan.

Sign #2, titled *The Hennepin Canal Parkway: Engineering Marvel*, provides more detail about the canal and its construction.

> *The Hennepin Canal was an engineering marvel. Many techniques and materials used in the construction industry today got their start right here. But commercially the canal never paid off. First, it got a late start. Although planning began in 1854, the Hennepin didn't open until 1908. By then, railroads were carrying most of the cargo between Chicago and Rock Island. Then, in the 1920s, the Illinois River was enlarged so it could carry bigger cargo barges and compete with the railroads. But these barges were too big to fit in the Hennepin. In 1951, the Hennepin Canal was closed to all traffic.*
>
> *A Major Milestone: The Hennepin was the first American canal to be built using concrete instead of cut stone. It was a revolutionary idea, but soon engineers around the world were copying it. The Panama Canal between the Atlantic and Pacific Oceans is patterned after the Hennepin.*
>
> *Construction Methods, 1900: It took 17 years and thousands of men to build the canal. Some of the work was done using horse driven earth scrapers. Other excavation was done by barge machines.*
>
> *In its Prime, 1929: In its peak year the canal carried 30,161 tons of cargo.*

> *This might seem a lot, but it was only 1/600th of its estimated capacity.*
>
> *The Golden Years: Although it never really enjoyed commercial success, the Hennepin Canal has always been a popular recreational destination. To this day, it's an ideal place to boat, canoe, fish, bike, hike and picnic.*

This lock provided an eleven-foot lift for barges. It was the westernmost lock that used a Marshall Gate on its upper end. Lock #21 also marked the east end of the summit basin of the canal, located 196 feet above the Illinois River. From the summit basin, it is downhill both to the east and the west. Like most locks, this one has had its gates removed by the Corps of Engineers and a dam built on its upper end to hold water in the canal. At the east end of the lock is a vertical lift bridge that can still be driven. It is located on the east park access road. Sign #4 at the lock provides information about this bridge.

> *This lift bridge, on the Illinois and Mississippi 'Hennepin' Canal, was erected in 1904. It provided farmers access to their land. A wheel 'windlass' in the center was turned to bring the large weights down, which caused the chains to lift the bridge, thus allowing ample room for canal boats to pass. The Canal was closed to barge traffic in 1951.*

The Lift Bridge at Lock #21 is a classic example of the architectural grace that such structures once featured. This bridge is essentially a piece of art. Photo by Barton Jennings.

The lift bridge, which was never assigned a number, was built in 1904 (other Corps of Engineers documents state May 1905) and rehabilitated in 1976. The bridge is 39 feet long and 14 feet wide, and is the only such bridge that can still be accessed with a public motor vehicle. It also still has its wooden plank deck, but it has metal sheets across it to protect the deck from road traffic. Builders plates on the bridge state that it was built by the Pittsburg Steel Construction Company under the direction of Major C. S. Riche, of the U.S. Army Corps of Engineers. Riche worked on a number of projects, including the Colorado River in Texas; the harbor at Ludington, Michigan; and various projects along the Mississippi River.

> THIS LIFT BRIDGE, ON THE ILLINOIS AND MISSISSIPPI 'HENNEPIN' CANAL WAS ERECTED IN 1904. IT PROVIDED FARMERS ACCESS TO THEIR LAND.
>
> A wheel 'windlass' in the center was turned to bring the large weights down, which caused the chains to lift the bridge, thus allowing ample room for canal boats to pass. The Canal was closed to barge traffic in 1951.
>
> THIS MARKER PRESENTED TO THE WYANET BICENTENNIAL COM. JULY 1976 AND DEDICATED BY THE WYANET SPORTSMAN'S CLUB

This historical marker at Lock #21 provides basic information about the lift bridge over the lock. Photo by Barton Jennings.

These bridges were known by Assistant Engineer L. L. Wheeler as drawbridges, but they were actually lift bridges. While heavy, a single worker could raise and lower the bridge. Each of the four corners of the bridge included a steel frame filled with steel leaves. These leaves weighed close to the weight of the entire bridge, balancing the weight. These corner frames were called counterpoising towers and were the key to these bridges.

This lift bridge is essentially complete, and still has the rolling mechanism used to raise and lower the structure's roadway deck. Photo by Barton Jennings.

As at all of the locks, there was a lock tender's house here, located on the north bank and just west of the canal, according to early maps. It was one of the first built and was used initially as an office for the junior engineer in charge of the overhead cableway used to dredge Cecil's Slough. Cecil's Slough was an unexpected challenge for the Corps of Engineers, as soil samples and sample drillings failed to identify the large peat deposits in the area. This peat was described as being quicksand or a peat swamp by some at the time, and failed to provide a solid footing for the canal. A drainage canal had to first be built to remove much of the water, and then a series of towers and cables were used to operate the dredging equipment. One of the conveyor towers was built near here and Lock #21 became the operational headquarters for the attack upon the peat.

During the early years of canal construction, the Corps of Engineers needed a number of offices. Some were temporary, lasting only until the work in the area was completed. To handle this need, the Corps of Engineers designed two temporary inspector's offices in 1899. The large one measured 20'x30' and included a 20'x16' bedroom for four double bunk beds, and a 20'x14' office. There was a note on the design that there was to be building paper on the roof but not on the building's sides. The smaller office measured 17'x27' and was split in half and included a bedroom for three double bunk beds, as well as an office.

This Corps of Engineers' photo from 1971 looks east from Lock #21. It shows the Lift Bridge, and in the distance, an overseer's house. Illinois and Mississippi (Hennepin) Canal, "Photographic Files," Record Series 497.037, Illinois State Archives.

17.6 WYANET BOATWAYS – In this area, there was once a boat repair facility, also known as a boatways or boat yard. Soon after the Hennepin Canal opened, the Corps of Engineers had a large number of boats and barges being used to maintain the canal. However, the only boatyard was at Milan at the very west end of the canal. In 1911, the Corps of Engineers built a boatways on the north shore here, and repaired and caulked fourteen barges. To support the activity, a warehouse and several sheds were built east of the boatways.

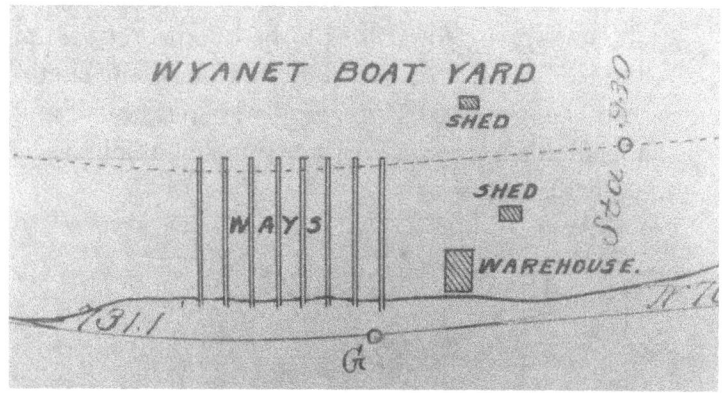

This drawing shows the general layout of the Wyanet Boat Yard during the early 1900s. The concrete boatways still exist. Illinois and Mississippi (Hennepin) Canal, "Map, Drawing, and Plan Files, G-Q," Record Series 497.001, Illinois State Archives.

The boatways, like many of the canal facilities, were made of concrete. The ways, a series of concrete ramps, began below the water level in the canal and led up onto the north shore. At first, horses were used to pull the boats and barges out of the water, later powered winches were installed to do the work. The remains of seven concrete ramps can still be seen on the north bank. There are also several picnic sites in this area.

Main Channel

What appear to be rows of concrete benches or foundations are actually the remains of the ways of the Wyanet Boat Yard. Boats would be brought up onto these ways to be worked on or stored. Photo by Barton Jennings.

17.6 **WYANET FISH HATCHERY** – Fishing had become a popular attraction on the canal by the 1920s, and Illinois wanted to support the practice. On June 2, 1925, the Illinois General Assembly created the Department of Conservation. On June 26th, further legislation was enacted which authorized the department to acquire "suitable submerged lands for breeding, hatching, propagation and conservation of fish." Two ponds to the south of the canal were acquired and converted into the hatchery, sometimes shown as the Illinois State Fish Reservation. Fresh water was taken into the hatchery here through several control gates. Water was returned to the canal through drains at Mile 17.3, just below Lock #21. Nothing but the ponds remain of the facility.

17.7 **BRIDGE #11A** – This causeway is part of the Lock 21 Day Use Area. While "day use" is used, camping is also allowed here. There is a large parking lot and several toilets to the west of the north end of the causeway. This causeway provides the primary way into the park, avoiding the weight restricted route across the historic lift bridge at Lock #21.

Heading toward the Mississippi River, the canal turns sharply to the northwest, passes under several roads, makes an S-curve, and eventually turns to the west again.

17.9 BRIDGE #11 – A large culvert with a concrete floor allows the Hennepin Canal Parkway Trail to pass under U.S. Highway 6/34. Highway 6 is the Grand Army of the Republic Highway, honoring the Civil War veterans association of the same name. The highway is 3199 miles long and connects Bishop, California, with Provincetown, Massachusetts. Highway 34 is 1122 miles long and connects Granby, Colorado, with Berwyn, Illinois. It is the highest paved through highway in the United States, passing through Rocky Mountain National Park at 12,183 feet of elevation. In this area, the two highways share the same route, which also carries the title of Walter Payton Memorial Highway. A map from 1923 showed the road as being the Cannonball Trail.

The bridge that was once here is long gone and has been replaced by a large causeway across the canal. The original bridge was one of a number over the canal whose superstructure was erected under contract with Wallace Marshall and his Lafayette Bridge Company. The Lafayette Bridge Company had contracts for at least six bridges as part of the canal's construction. The original bridge was finished in 1903, and was a design unique from the rest on the canal. It was described as being a 128'-7" through truss span manufactured by the American Bridge Company's Detroit Plant. The bridge was at an angle of 52 degrees 30 minutes, while most bridges cut

Main Channel

across the canal at 90 degrees, allowing them to be shorter. The original bridge was replaced by December 1938, using a steel Pratt truss design. The bridge was shown to be owned by the State of Illinois, so it was not a maintenance issue for the Corps of Engineers. To reduce maintenance costs, the bridge was eventually replaced by today's fill.

Heading west, the Hennepin Canal banks were often above the adjacent land as far as Lock #29 at Colona, providing some nice views of the surrounding farms. Most of the Feeder Canal was also higher than the surrounding farms. This required that bridges have approach ramps or spans, increasing their cost. It also raised the water table in the area, forcing the construction of more drainage canals to keep area farms above water.

18.5 **BRIDGE #12** – The canal is now heading north on its way to the Mississippi River. This bridge has also been replaced with a large causeway and a culvert for the water, and a concrete box tunnel for the Hennepin Canal Parkway Trail. Bureau County Road 1550 North crosses the fill. There is no official parking here, but some highway shoulder parking is available.

The original Bridge #12 was a 110-foot Pratt through truss span manufactured by Chicago Bridge & Iron, installed in December 1903. This was the most common bridge design and manufacturer on the main channel of the Hennepin Canal.

Through this area, the canal passes a number of large farms with traditional farmhouses and barns. There are also several large cuts and fills as the canal crosses this rolling landscape. Halfway between Bridges #12 and #13, there is a large stone and concrete block wall hidden in the brush on the north side of the canal. The location can often be found thanks to the sound of water flowing into the canal. All along the canal, there were a number of streams that passed under the canal using culverts. Some had flushing gates like this one where water from the canal could be used to flush debris out of the culverts. Many of these culverts are still used, but in some places the water is allowed to enter the canal.

19.0 BRIDGE #13 – This bridge is in the middle of an S-curve, and has also been replaced by a causeway fill and several culverts. Located about two miles north of U.S. Highway 3, the causeway is used by Bureau County Road 1200 East to cross the canal. The bridge that was originally here was a 110-foot Pratt through truss, the most common built on the canal. This bridge had an eighteen-foot wide plank deck when built. Located off all sides of the bridge were waste banks from the construction of the canal, some of which were used to create the fill across the canal.

At many of the highway fills, the trail uses a large culvert to pass under the roadway. The location name is often posted above the culvert. Photo by Barton Jennings.

Heading west from Bridge #13, the trail is often hard-packed gravel with a bit of grass. The canal can be very scenic with a number of blooming trees, singing birds, and great views as it curves back and forth. Photo by Barton Jennings.

Peat and Cecil's Slough

Not far west of here, the canal turns and heads directly west through what was known as Cecil's Slough. This created a problem during construction as contractors found a heaved peat bog between miles 19 and 23, forcing much of the canal in this area to be in a cut. Because of the soft peat, much of the dredge work was accomplished using an overhead cable system. Later reports stated that the Cecil's Slough area "continued to be a problem in later years and constant maintenance was needed to keep a seven-foot channel."

During the canal's planning process, there were two proposed routes through this area. The route used was actually the first route examined, and a second route was considered that was to the south. However, the initial surveys found that the second route was longer, so the Corps of Engineers went with the shorter straight route, which unfortunately encountered the peat during the construction.

Peat is a large mass of partially decayed vegetation or organic matter. It generally builds up over thousands of years, forming when vegetation doesn't fully decay because of the environment. Peat bogs are often wet areas, as the water protects the vegetation from the air needed to fully rot, and peat then works like a sponge to attract and hold more water. In many parts of the world, such as England, Finland, and Russia, peat is harvested as an important source of fuel.

Note the "No Smoking Peat Area" signs in this area. When peat catches fire, it is almost impossible to extinguish. Underground peat fires have burned for years in many places around the world, including Illinois. Photo by Barton Jennings.

The "Battle" of Cecil's Slough

In 1903, the Corps of Engineers began a major campaign to build the canal through the peat bogs in Cecil's Slough. After several attempts using traditional digging methods, it was determined that a different method was going to be required to build through the soft and wet peat. The battle began in 1903 with the arrival of a system of duplex overhead cableway conveyors, provided by the Lidgerwood Manufacturing Company of New York.

> PROPOSED PLAN
> for
> Duplex Cableway Towers
> for
> Excavating the CANAL PRISM through
> Cecils Slough Miles 21 & 22
> Ill. & Miss Canal.
> Aug. 1903.

Cecil's Slough was a major challenge for the Corps of Engineers, and an entire battle plan was drawn up just to deal with it. Illinois and Mississippi (Hennepin) Canal, "Map, Drawing, and Plan Files, G-Q," Record Series 497.001, Illinois State Archives.

Founded in 1873, Lidgerwood Manufacturing Company was promoted at the time as a manufacturer of hoisting engines, superior boilers, and conveying machines. The company actually dates further back, coming from the Speedwell Iron Works, which built the machinery for the *SS Savannah*, the first steamship to cross the Atlantic. The company later built machinery for the Corps of Engineers that was used to build the Panama Canal.

The conveyors operated between towers built by labor hired by the Corps of Engineers. Construction began in October 1903, and the towers were ready to begin operations in February 1904. The two moveable towers were described by the Corps of Engineers as being "57 feet above the car tracks, with a base about 45 feet square, resting on 24 pairs of standard-gauge wheels and trucks, which move on five 60-pound steel rails." The towers were spaced 525 feet apart and had two 2½ inch cables between them, carrying a 1½ cubic yard Haywood orange-peel bucket. The bucket was dropped into the peat, and then raised and moved to another location to dump the material. The system required support, and the necessary buildings for warehouses and shops were moved from Locks #6 and #19.

Digging with the elevated system began on April 1, 1904. To move good material in and the peat away, the narrow gauge railroad was used. In 1904, the narrow gauge railroad track between Locks #5 and #6 was taken up and moved to Lock #19 at Wyanet. From there, the Corps of Engineers railroad was active supporting the work in the peat bog. Work continued for the next several years, with more than 210,000 cubic yards of material excavated by the end of June 1905.

The following drawings show the two towers and the Haywood orange-peel bucket used to attack the peat in Cecil's Slough. Illinois and Mississippi (Hennepin) Canal, "Map, Drawing, and Plan Files, G-Q," Record Series 497.001, Illinois State Archives.

Main Channel

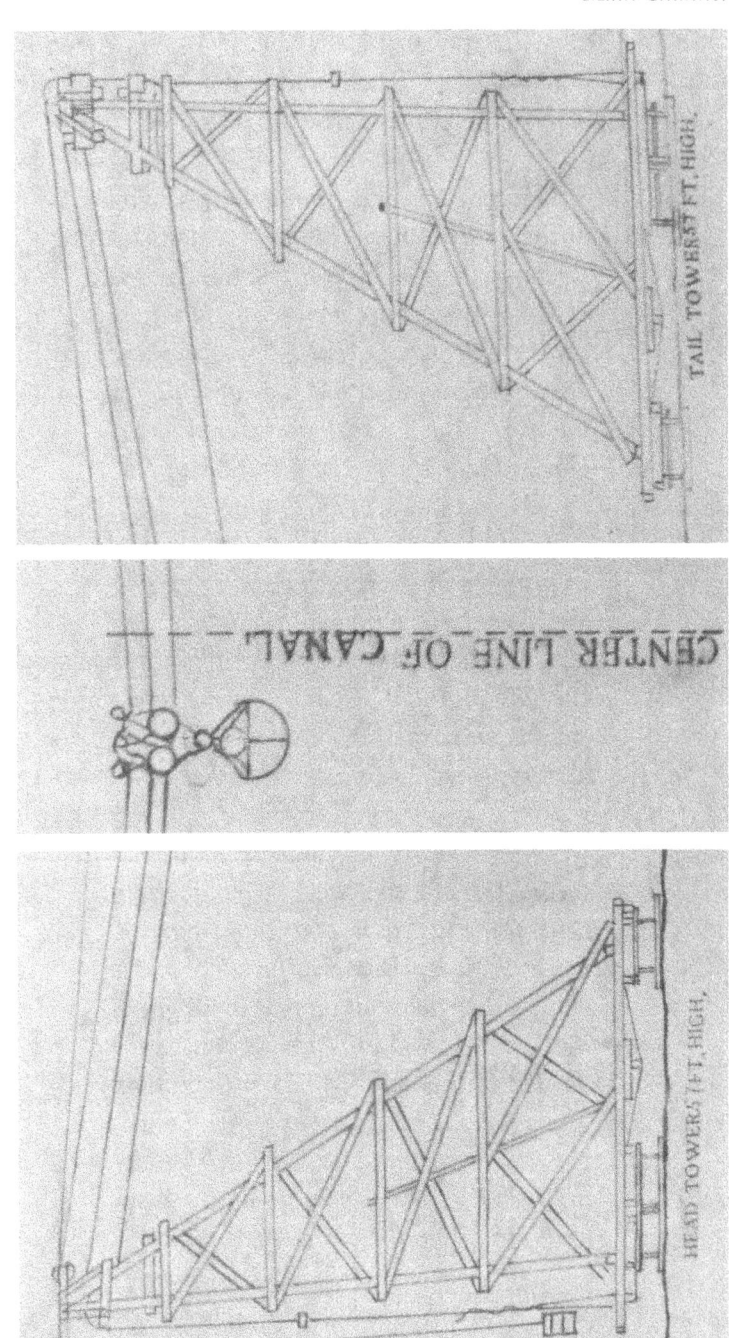

The February 10, 1906, issue of *The Engineering News* had a large article about the work and the Lidgerwood machinery. The article stated:

> *Excavation of a troublesome section of the Hennepin or Illinois & Mississippi ship canal under construction by the U.S. Government, was commenced by contractors who eventually found the difficulties so great that they abandoned the work. It is now being executed by the Government under the direction of Col. W. H. Bixby, Corps of Engineers, U. S. A. Near Wyanet, Ill., where work is now in progress, the soil is very bad, consisting mostly of peat containing quicksand and generally full of water, making the excavation difficult and causing great trouble and expense for the maintenance of surface tracks and the installation of machinery.*
>
> *The soil is so soft and unstable that the banks are constantly caving in. In spite of the fact that a berm of from 100 to 125 ft. is left between the edges of the cutting and the spoil bank, the weight of the latter on the soft ground causes the bottom of the canal to rise in the center. This makes it necessary to return the cableway for cleaning up. This extra moving increases the cost of doing the work and diminishes the output.*

Main Channel

As shown, even after the canal was built, Cecil's Slough was still an issue, reportedly a high maintenance area until the end of canal operations. The name Cecil came from James Cecil, whose father arrived here in 1857 from Monmouthshire, England. James Cecil was born on November 3, 1860, and worked on his parent's farm. James began buying land, and owned 730 acres by 1900. He served as a school director and a member of several fraternal organizations like the Modern Woodmen of America and the Independent Order of Odd Fellows. James Cecil was one of a number of local residents who were featured in the book *Past and Present of Bureau County, Illinois*, published in 1906 by The Pioneer Publishing Company of Chicago.

19.7 **OLSON'S HILL** – Olson's Hill was a unique challenge to construction in the peat bogs of this area. The hill is composed of hard clay, and it was too hard to dig and move by the Hayward buckets on the cableway. Instead, the clay was taken out with horse-drawn wheeled scrapers, typical for much of the canal's construction. Because of the challenge, the towpath was cut higher into the hillside on the south bank and was not down at water level. Reports from the time state that while the cable towers were being built, "roadbeds for the cableway tracks were graded on each side to the top of Olson's Hill, and have since been extended entirely over the hill. These are about 45 feet top width, and on passing over the hill, a 2 per cent grade was used."

At about Mile 20.2, the canal trail drops back down to the water level. To the north, a small stream flows in from the fields in that direction. Heading west, the trail for the next mile passes through fields with no tree coverage to the south. There are some nice views of farms in that direction, plus glimpses of Interstate 80 to the north. In 1916, James Cecil was shown as the owner of the land to the south of the canal, and F. R. Olson as the owner of the land to the north. The Olson family had several farms spread across Bureau County.

Because of the concerns about the canal's stability in this area, there was a patrolman's house not far west of Olson's Hill at Mile 20.0.

This view of the trail at Mile 20 shows that it passes through fields with no tree coverage in this area, but the views are great. Photo by Barton Jennings.

21.4 BRIDGE #14 – This bridge carries Bureau County Road 975 East across the Hennepin Canal. The Hennepin Canal Parkway Trail loops away from the canal to cross the gravel road, which mainly serves to provide access to several farms and fields to the north of the canal. On the north side of the canal is a small campground with picnic tables and toilets.

On the north side of the canal at Bridge #14 is a small campground, shown in this photo from the trail on the south bank. Photo by Barton Jennings.

The current bridge replaced the original 110-foot long Pratt through truss span, built for the Corps of Engineers as a part of the canal's construction. The original bridge was somewhat unique as the other similar Pratt through truss bridges had decks eighteen feet wide, while this one was only seventeen feet wide.

A 1903 report by Assistant Engineer James Long went into great detail about the complications in building this bridge. He stated that due to the soft ground, the piles for the south abutment were 36 feet long instead of the planned 25 feet. Additionally, sheet piling had to be used to stabilize the foundation pits. The foundation pit for the north abutment hit "springs spouting quicksand" that were only overcome by using bags of sand and dry cement to block the flow. The report also stated that because of the large foundations, 54 cubic feet of Natural cement concrete and 312 cubic yards of Portland cement concrete were required to build the abutments. The bridge structure was finally installed in December 1903 after a year's work on the abutments.

Heading west, the canal and parkway trail pass through thick woods for the next two miles, all the way to Interstate 80.

22.2 RAILROAD BRIDGE #4 – This bridge, a one-span lattice through truss structure, was built across the canal area before the canal was completed. At 115 feet long, the bridge was built in 1905 by the American Bridge Company of New York for the Chicago & North Western Railway (C&NW). This is the only through truss railroad bridge built over the canal, the rest are deck and through plate girder spans.

Union Pacific (UP) acquired this line when it bought the C&NW in April 1995. When it was acquired, the line stretched from Nelson, Illinois, almost to St. Louis, Missouri. In reality, the line went south to DeCamp, Illinois, and got on the Litchfield & Madison (the C&NW had acquired the L&M in 1958) to Madison, Illinois, and the St. Louis area. UP soon negotiated rights over the Chicago & Illinois Midland from Barr to Springfield to get on their former Alton route. The line from Barr to Girard was abandoned in 1999. A new connection was built at Girard so trains from the Alton route could access the coal mine at Monterey. South of there, the line was sold to Norfolk Southern all the way to De-

Camp. On south, the line was mostly abandoned in 2000.

The former Chicago & North Western Railway bridge, known as Railroad Bridge #4, is shown with the remains of the telephone line east of the canal's visitor center. Photo by Barton Jennings.

Just west of the railroad and south of the canal is an old gravel pit. The barge company founded by LeRoy Mechling and Fred Wolf bought much of their gravel from this pit, shown at the time as being owned by the government. The gravel price was stated as being ten cents a yard. This was just one of several gravel pits used by the Corps of Engineers. The gravel was originally used for construction and to make improvements on roads and the canal towpath. Canal and road improvements made in 1915 used gravel from pits on miles 17, 22, 23 and 26 on the eastern section.

The Chicago & North Western built several tracks in this area to haul excess material from the canal, using it to fill in several railroad trestles in the area. Assistant Engineer James Long stated that "this arrangement was advantageous to the railroad company, and it enabled the United States to let the excavation at a very low figure."

22.3 BRIDGE #14A – The road is Illinois Highway 40, which connects East Peoria with Mt. Carroll, both in Illinois. The bridge was originally a steel Pratt truss span with concrete approach spans, but today it is a modern I-beam design with a concrete deck and seven-pile concrete bents. This was originally Illinois Highway 88, but it was renumbered when Interstate 88 opened. Interstate 80 is just to the north, and less than a mile to the south is the main highway entrance into the Hennepin Canal Parkway State Park visitor center.

22.6 VISITOR CENTER – The Hennepin Canal Visitor Center, located near Sheffield, Illinois, is a great place for a visit. The Visitor Center is located next to the Hennepin Canal Parkway Trail and features a number of displays about the construction and operation of the canal, as well as displays about area wildlife. Old photos, a display of tools used to build and maintain the canal, and a model of a lock system and an aqueduct, are some of the highlights. The area around the Visitor Center features a small wildflower prairie and several pavilions. There is plenty of parking in several lots, with restrooms in both the Visitor Center and the western parking lot. Just north of the Visitor Center is a canal boat basin.

Main Channel

This sign is located on Illinois Highway 40 and points the way to the Hennepin Canal Visitor Center. Photo by Barton Jennings.

To reach the complex, take Illinois Highway 40 (Exit 45) off of Interstate 80 and head south about a mile, then follow the signs. It is about the same distance north of U.S. Highway 6/34. Normally, the Hennepin Canal Visitor Center is only open on weekdays, but the grounds are generally open at all times.

The Hennepin Canal Visitor Center is shown from the canal trail as you approach from the east. It sits on a small hill overlooking a wide spot in the canal, and is an excellent rest stop with its many displays. Photo by Barton Jennings.

The location of the canal on this mile is in a small valley locally known as Hornby's Slough, according to the Corps of Engineers. The Hornby family moved to near here in the 1850s and acquired 160 acres, and their name was used to describe the area.

Sheffield

Several miles to the southwest, and officially where the visitor center is located, is the community of Sheffield. The Chicago & Rock Island built through the Sheffield area in early October, 1853. The town of Sheffield was founded by Joseph E. Sheffield and Henry Farnam in 1852. Both Sheffield and Farnam were involved with building the railroad and the town site was intended as a coaling station for trains. According to Farnam, he and Sheffield flipped a coin to see for whom the town would be named. Today, a monument to Joseph E. Sheffield, and the Rock Island Railroad, stands in Sheffield's town square. The frame CRI&P station also serves as a reminder of the rail line's history.

In 1932, Sheffield was a railroad town with a number of tracks; three tracks to the north of the depot and three to the south. South of the station were the B. S. Williams Grain & Coal and the Farmers Grain Company. Parts of the round Farmers elevator still stand. To the west were stockyards and the Wood, Howard & Company lumberyard. Less than a mile west of Sheffield was the Sheffield Shale Products Company, located just to the east of U.S. Highway 34 where it turns south.

While there were a number of companies at Sheffield, none of the industries were on the canal. In an attempt to serve the community, the A. L. Mechling

Main Channel

Gravel Company and their canal boats had a dock west of Sheffield during the 1920s. The facility measured 150'x100' and was located on the north bank.

Today, Sheffield has a population of about 1000, and features a gas station and convenience store for those looking for supplies.

23.0 BRIDGE #15 – This 110-foot long Pratt through truss bridge, built with riveted connections by Chicago Bridge & Iron, is used by the Hennepin Canal Parkway Trail to cross from the south side to the north side of the canal. The bridge was once used by a local road that is now closed, and the bridge design was the most common on the Hennepin Canal. This bridge was somewhat unique in that it was built with a wide eighteen-foot plank deck. The south bridge abutment is stamped "OCT 1902 SAYLOR'S". This means that the abutment was built in October 1902, and the concrete used was Saylor's brand of Portland cement. The bridge was installed in November 1903.

The Corps of Engineers produced volumes of information about the use of concrete as a part of the construction of the Hennepin Canal. To assist with the studies, many of the structures were stamped with the type used and the date. These markings can be found on the south concrete abutment of Bridge #15. Photo by Barton Jennings.

Near the south end of the bridge is plenty of parking, several of the typical signs about the canal, toilets, and a boat ramp. There are also several benches that can be used for a rest. During the canal's construction, there was an engineer's office southwest of Bridge #15.

Information signs about the Hennepin Canal and the modern Parkway Trail are found at a number of locations along the canal, including here at Bridge #15. Photo by Barton Jennings.

Emergency Gates

Just to the east of this bridge are the concrete remains of a set of wooden miter emergency gates, known in many canal documents as the Cecil's Slough Emergency Gate. These gates were designed to protect the east end of the canal's summit basin from a major failure of the Feeder Canal. The miter gates, aimed to the east, were kept closed, opened only for the passage of boats. There was a lock tender's house adjacent to the emergency gates.

Main Channel

The remains of the Cecil's Slough Emergency Gate can still be found just east of Bridge #15, where it was designed to protect the canal to the east from a break to the west. Photo by Barton Jennings.

From here west, the Hennepin Canal Parkway Trail will mainly be on the north bank of the canal, providing less shade during the summer months. The canal again turns to the northwest as it heads toward the Mississippi River.

23.2 BRIDGE #15A – The Hennepin Canal Parkway Trail passes under the two bridges of Interstate 80 on the north bank of the canal. Interstate 80 is a 2900-mile transcontinental highway that runs from downtown San Francisco, California, to Teaneck, New Jersey. It is the second longest Interstate Highway in the United States (after Interstate 90), and closely follows the route of the historic Lincoln Highway, the first road across America.

The trail under the highway is concrete, and it is located almost at the canal's water level. Heading west, the canal trail is again oil and chip paved, and it passes through a number of large farms planted with corn and soybeans.

After miles of quiet walking, users of the trail are suddenly thrown back into modern society as they pass under Interstate 80. However, it doesn't take long to leave the chaos and return to the woods and farms so typical of the canal. Photo by Barton Jennings.

24.1 HICKORY GROVE CAMPGROUND – Not far west of Interstate 80 is the Hickory Grove Campground, located immediately north of the canal. Campsites include those with full service such as water, electric, and septic, and also primitive camping sites. The campground has its own boat launch, ramp, and dock on the canal. Hot showers are available for registered guests. The canal turns to the west again for a short distance as it passes the campground.

Also to the north is the Hasbrook Lateral, a drainage canal that flows through the fields to the northeast. To the south of the canal is Devil's Slough Ditch. Both flow along sections of the canal in this area.

Main Channel

25.0 DEVIL'S SLOUGH CULVERT – Devil's Slough flows under the canal here using Arch Culvert #8. This is a large 12-foot concrete culvert, built with a large concrete flush basin on the south bank.

During the 1871 planning report on the proposed "ship-canal between the Illinois River, near Hennepin, and the Mississippi River, near Rock Island," Devil's Slough was the dividing line between the east and west ends of the canal. Even as the canal was built, Feeder Junction was often called the Feeder Junction at Devil's Slough. When Illinois was being settled, Devil's Slough was a major waterway. Today, it is a channelized drainage ditch.

On the south bank at Mile 25 is the flush basin for Devil's Slough. Photo by Barton Jennings.

25.1 BRIDGE #16 – The original Bridge #16 was ordered from the Lafayette Bridge Company, but some drawings from 1902 show that it was completed by the American Bridge Company's Detroit Plant. The Pratt through truss bridge was 98 feet long and had an eighteen-foot wide deck. It was installed during November 1903.

In 1971, Bridge #16 still stood, as shown looking to the northeast in this Corps of Engineers' photo. The photo shows a classic Pratt through truss span set on concrete headwalls. Illinois and Mississippi (Hennepin) Canal, "Photographic Files," Record Series 497.037, Illinois State Archives.

This bridge has been replaced by a causeway fill and culvert across the canal. The Hennepin Canal Parkway Trail also uses the fill to cross back to the south bank of the canal to use a passageway under the roadway, Bureau County Road 645 East. The trail then returns to the north bank. To the north on the east side of the fill is a parking lot, one of a number of official parking areas along the canal. Heading south, County Road 645 East crosses I-80 and ends at US Highway 6/34 on the east side of Sheffield, making it a popular parkway access point.

Heading west, the canal again turns to the northwest. In this area, the main walking and biking trail is on the north side of the canal while the equestrian trail is along the south bank.

Overseer's House

Bridge #16 features what is probably the most complete example of a canal house complex that still exists along the Hennepin Canal. It includes an overseer's house and farm, located to the southwest of the bridge. The house is boarded up, but the site still includes several barns and outbuildings. Note the concrete fence posts that surround the property. The Corps of Engineers built thirteen houses for overseers along the canal, and another was bought. Seven of them, including this one, were built as a two-story frame house. They sat on a 24-foot wide and 30-foot long foundation, and featured eight rooms.

Later reports show that there were eleven overseers on the canal – five on the east end of the canal, four on the west end, one on the Feeder Canal just north of Aqueduct #9, and one on the Milan section of the canal. Several of the Assistant Engineers and Superintendents also performed the job of overseer in addition to their regular tasks.

Bridge #16 features one of the most complete canal house complexes left along the canal. This is a view of the overseer's house, located just west of the bridge. Photo by Barton Jennings.

In addition to the house, the old barn still stands at Bridge #16. Photo by Barton Jennings.

Main Channel

Many of the canal housing areas also featured a warehouse. This one still stands near Bridge #16. Photo by Barton Jennings.

26.0 BRIDGE #17 – Bureau County Road 575 East crosses the canal on a fill which replaced the Lafayette Bridge Company structure that once was here. There used to be several Corps of Engineers support buildings here, including a blacksmith shop. A large farm complex still exists along the south canal bank. There is also a small parking lot at the north end of the causeway.

By 1910, there was also an ice house here. Ice was a big business for the Hennepin Canal, and both the Corps of Engineers and private companies built ice houses along the canal to handle the annual winter ice harvests, which lasted until manufactured ice became available. By 1914, more ice was made artificially than through field cutting, and the natural ice industry essentially ended during the early 1920s. According to the rules of the canal at the time, permits to cut ice were sold at a rate of one dollar per one thousand square feet of surface.

The trail crosses Bureau County Road 575 East at grade, and the trail is blocked by this post to keep motor vehicles off of it. Photo by Barton Jennings.

The canal has again turned to the west. During a summer day, ice would be nice to have while walking or biking this part of the canal. This is mostly open country with only a thin tree line to provide shade. With the trail on the north side of the canal, even less shade is available. Note that the canal bank is often much higher than the surrounding farmland. During late summer, the trails made by deer and other wildlife can easily be seen through the weeds and brush as they travel between the local corn and bean fields, and the water available from the canal.

Main Channel

Because the canal is above the surrounding land, there are some great views of the adjacent farms. Photo by Barton Jennings.

26.8   SAIN SLOUGH DITCH – This was Culvert #15 in the canal's construction plans, and was later assigned the name Arch Culvert #9. This 10-foot wide and 5'-9" tall concrete culvert also featured a flush duct. Notice the fenced area along the north bank where the canal narrows. This is the culvert under the canal for the Sain Slough Ditch, which drains fields to the south. It flows north and under the canal. To the north of the Hennepin Canal is the Hickory Creek Drainage Canal. Hickory Creek once wandered throughout the area, but was channeled first to drain area fields and then to avoid the route of the Hennepin Canal.

27.0   BRIDGE #18 – This causeway, also once a bridge, carries County Road 29, also known as Bureau County Road 475 East, across the canal. The Hennepin Canal Parkway Trail passes under the roadway using a large culvert on the north bank. The original bridge was a 98-foot long, 18-foot wide, Pratt through truss with a concrete deck. This was reportedly the third bridge design used on the canal.

With the trees and brush often found along the canal, the first view of some former bridge locations can be the culvert that the trail uses to pass under them. This view is from the east approaching former Bridge #18. Photo by Barton Jennings.

This bridge received special attention in a 1904 report by James C. Long, Assistant Engineer. "The abutments of bridge 18, due to having been built upon an unstable foundation, had tipped forward, the south abutment 12 inches and the north abutment 6 inches at the top. The earth was removed from behind the south abutment and the abutment pulled back to a vertical position and anchored to a heavy concrete deadman, constructed in the approach 52 feet behind the face of the abutment with rods and turnbuckles. The north abutment was anchored in a similar manner."

Highway bridges #16, #17 and #18 were built under contract by the Lafayette Bridge Company of Wallace Marshall, and all completed by 1903. The company later became the Lafayette Engineering Company. Wallace and his brother Henry ran the Lafayette Bridge Company, initially building bridges across Indiana and neighboring states. Henry Marshall was the powerful editor of the *Journal & Courier* of Lafayette, Indiana, and carried some political weight across the state. The Lafayette Bridge Company was later absorbed into the American Bridge Company, founded in April 1900 by J. P. Morgan as a consolidation of 28 of the largest U.S. steel fabricators and constructors.

While this is a fairly major county road, there is not an official parking lot here. Additionally, because of the height of the fill, there are safety railings alongside the roadway, making shoulder parking very limited. Not far west of this bridge, the canal has been taken over by water lilies. During the summer, the large surface leaves and blooms are a popular subject for photography.

The blooms of water lilies are a popular sight just west of Bridge #18. Photo by Barton Jennings.

27.8 BRIDGE #17A – This bridge, now a causeway across the canal, is noted for its numbering being out of order. It carries Bureau County Road 400 East across the east end of the Feeder Canal Junction. The trail passes under the road and then uses the fill to cross over to the south bank. From here west to Bridge #18A, the Hennepin Canal Parkway Trail is on the south bank of the canal, which heads to the southwest.

This Corps of Engineers photo from 1940 shows one of the big costs of maintaining the canal – bridges. Looking east, this canal barge is being used to sandblast and paint Bridge #17A. Illinois and Mississippi (Hennepin) Canal, "Photographic Files," Record Series 497.037, Illinois State Archives.

There is a small parking area at the north end of the fill. Not far to the north and located on the east bank of the Feeder Canal is the Lazy T Campground. The campground has both RV and tent camping. The campground features docks on the canal for fishing and boating, and most of the 28 sites in the campground are located within 100 feet of the Hennepin

Main Channel

Canal. While included on several lists of area campgrounds, signs at the entrance state "members only."

According to a 1903 Corps of Engineers report, the superstructures of highway bridges #17A and #18A were under contract with Wallace Marshall, with the date of contract expiration being December 31, 1902. The Lafayette Bridge Company delivered the 110-foot long Pratt truss structure, which was installed in December 1903.

27.9   FEEDER JUNCTION – The Feeder Canal flows in from the north, forming a large Y-shaped basin. The Feeder Canal, plus the Main Channel between Lock #21 and Lock #22, housed more than 100,000,000 cubic feet of water at normal depth. According to the writings of Major C. S. Riche, there was a fear of losing all of this water and the damage to the surrounding country it would produce. Therefore, several emergency gates were installed to limit the water loss should a break occur in this section of the canal.

Looking north at Feeder Junction, there is a view across the large pool here, and then the narrow Feeder Canal. Photo by Barton Jennings.

The main channel trail is on the south side of the Feeder Junction basin. Heading west toward the Mississippi River, the canal turns to the southwest.

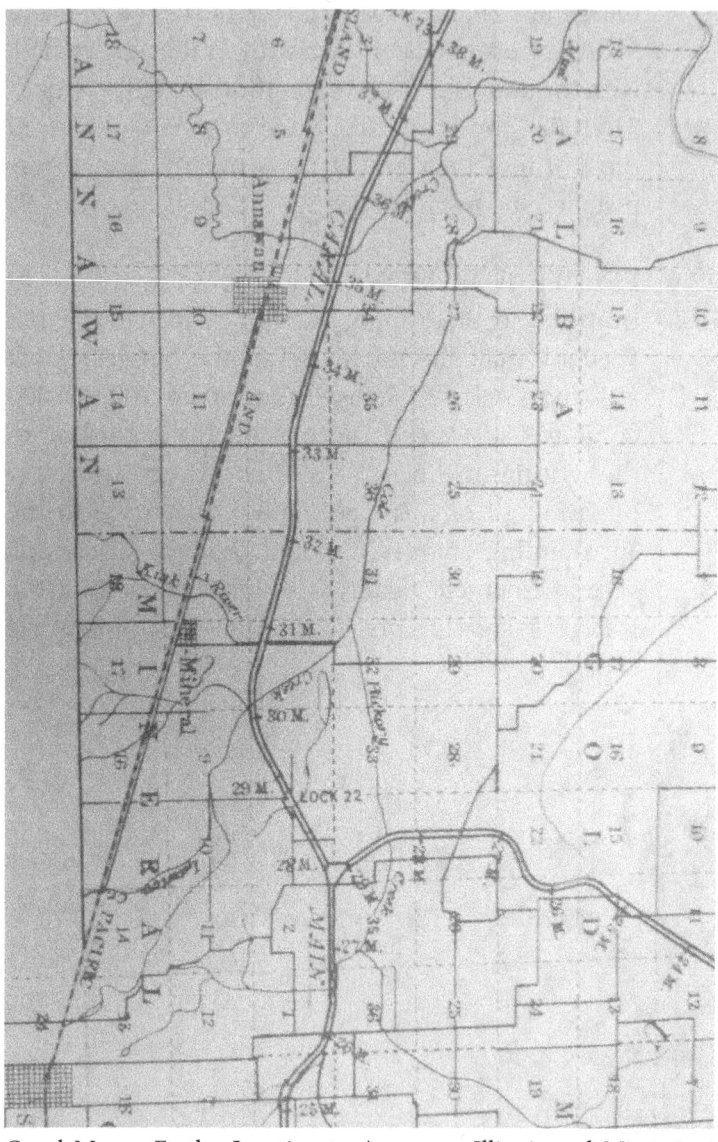

Canal Map – Feeder Junction to Annawan. Illinois and Mississippi (Hennepin) Canal, "Canal Route Plat Files," Record Series 497.008, Illinois State Archives.

Main Channel

28.3 BRIDGE #18A – This bridge, a 110-foot long Pratt truss structure that was installed in December 1903, has also been replaced by a fill, used by Bureau County Road 350 East. This was another bridge built by Wallace Marshall's Lafayette Bridge Company, using parts from the American Bridge Company's Detroit Plant. The county road serves several farm houses to the north, and connects with County Road 1750 North not far to the south. A small parking lot is located at the south end of the causeway.

Walking east, there is a stop sign for trail users warning them of the crossing with County Road 1750 North. In the background is a typical culvert used to allow water to flow through the canal. Photo by Barton Jennings.

The Hennepin Canal Parkway Trail and the county road both cross the fill. The Parkway Trail that follows the Feeder Canal comes in from the west side of that canal and joins the main channel trail at the north end of the fill. Information on the **Feeder Canal Trail** can be found starting on **page 323**.

Heading west along the main channel, the trail is on the north side of the canal.

28.8 LOCK #22 – Lock #22 is one of the locations along the canal that can be very busy as there are a number of facilities here, and access is relatively easy. There is parking on both sides of the canal, both accessible from Bureau County Road 300 East (310 East on some maps). To get to the road, head east on U.S. Highway 6 from Mineral. In about two miles, look for the signs that point you north, but don't get distracted by the beautiful private gardens to the south of the highway. The "Hennepin Canal Parkway Lock 22 Day Use Area" is about two miles north of there.

Look for this sign on U.S. Highway 6 east of Mineral, as it points you up Bureau County Road 300 East to get to Lock #22. Photo by Barton Jennings.

This lock marks the west end of the summit pool. Heading west, the canal and locks started lowering boats, a total of 93 feet to the Mississippi River. This lock had a nine-foot lift, and was the last lock whose construction was started (1905) and completed (1906). In 1961, the Corps of Engineers restored the wooden miter gate doors, returning the lock to operating condition. These is also a dam at the east end of the lock to keep the water level steady in the Feeder Junction area.

Main Channel

This westward view shows the restored wooden miter gates of Lock #22. Photo by Barton Jennings.

With the restored miter gates at Lock #22, the gate mechanisms have also been restored, showing the crank system once used to open and close them. Photo by Barton Jennings.

At the west end of the lock is another vertical lift bridge, almost identical to the one at Lock #21, known as **Bridge #19**. The bridge was installed in December 1905, months before work on the lock was completed. Bridge #19 was known as the Farmer's Bridge because it allowed area farmers to get across the canal with their farm equipment and wagons. For years, the road across the bridge was officially County Road 300 East. While automobile traffic is not allowed on the bridge today, it still retains its 18-foot wood plank deck, but with metal sheathing where traffic would wear the timbers.

Bridge #19 is another vertical lift bridge, identical to those at Locks #21 and #26. Photo by Barton Jennings.

A campground and toilets are available southwest of the lift bridge. The large amount of flat land is due to the many canal buildings that were once here. The lock tender's house was one of the first built, and by 1897 was being used by junior engineers as they supervised the construction of the canal. A 50'x20' warehouse was soon built directly south of the lock, and the lock house was to the west. To the north of the lock, drawings of the lock area show what was called Reider's House and Barn. One of the houses eventually burned. Today, much of the area is still surrounded by the distinctive concrete fence posts.

The Day Use Area at Lock #22 features the typical information signs and toilets, along with plenty of parking, picnic tables, and other facilities. Photo by Barton Jennings.

The second lock tender's house still exists, but was sold and moved off of canal property. Just northwest of the County Road 300 causeway is a private home, built from the Corps of Engineers house. This house has been restored, but it maintains the unique gambrel roof. According to the owner, when the house was rebuilt, a number of original Corps of Engineers markings were found on the timbers and window frames.

It is great to see a former canal house restored and in use, although it is now in private hands and not part of the canal property. Please respect the privacy of the owner and enjoy the house from a distance. Photo by Barton Jennings.

29.0 BRIDGE #19A – County Road 300 East crosses the canal on a fill that replaced the vertical lift bridge just to the east as the canal was being retired. The Parkway Trail passes under the county road on the canal's north bank. A concrete boat ramp and large parking lot is located just west of the road on the south side of the canal. Not far west of here, the canal turns to the west, and then the northwest. Heading west on the trail, there are few trees over the next mile, leaving the often grassy trail open to sun and wind.

Main Channel

The location of the road just west of Lock #22 is certainly easy to identify. Photo by Barton Jennings.

In 1912, there was a major break in the canal in this area that closed the canal. According to news reports, it took about two to three weeks and 1000 workers to put the canal back in service. In addition to losing some of the embankment, Aqueduct #4 had one pier and the wingwalls damaged.

30.7 AQUEDUCT #4 – Known as Coal Creek Aqueduct, this five-span concrete aqueduct crosses over this channelized stream, with the Hennepin Canal Parkway Trail crossing on the north side. Coal Creek, shown on some maps and documents as Cole Creek, forms just to the south with the merger of King Creek and Barbara Ditch. Coal Creek flows northward through its levee-protected channel until it merges with Hickory Creek. The stream then turns to the northwest and flows into the Green River, with maps showing this combined stream as both Mud Creek and Coal Creek. This is all part of a series of drainage canals built in the area to allow farming and mining. This aqueduct was damaged in 1912, as reported in the October 1912 issue of the *Bulletin of the Atlantic Deeper Waterways Association*, as discussed in the section entitled **Canal Navigation – Opening through World War I,** found on **page 43**.

For a short distance east of Aqueduct #4, the canal runs east-west. However, at the aqueduct, it turns to the northwest for more than a mile. For a number of years, there was a house at the northeast end of the aqueduct.

The sign says Coal Creek, but a few maps show it to be Cole Creek. Photo by Barton Jennings.

Main Channel

Aqueduct #4 is surrounded by large spoil piles which allows this photograph from the northeast. The aqueduct is still original, but additional handrails have been installed to prevent falls. Photo by Barton Jennings.

30.8 BRIDGE #20 – The historic Bridge #20, a 110-foot Pratt through truss with an eighteen-foot wide concrete deck, has been replaced by this modern concrete precast bridge, used by Bureau County Road 120 East, also known as County Highway 10. Mineral is about a mile south on the road, and there is limited parking available here.

According to early reports on the construction of the Hennepin Canal, the Chicago Bridge & Iron Company provided the superstructures of Highway Bridges #20 through #37, except for Bridge #36. These bridges all seemed to have been 110-foot-long Pratt through truss spans. The concrete deck was a unique early design, but other bridges later had their plank decks replaced by concrete.

The Chicago Bridge & Iron Company was founded in 1889 by Horace E. Horton in Chicago, Illinois. Known as CB&I, the firm was initially involved in bridge design and construction, but quickly moved to building bulk liquid storage facilities, especially after the discovery of oil in the Southwest. The company then concentrated on design engineering and field construction of elevated water storage tanks, above-ground tanks for storage of petroleum and refined products, refinery process vessels and other steel plate structures. During World War II, CB&I built Landing Ship Tanks (LSTs) to carry troops and supplies in both the European and Pacific theaters. Today, CB&I has its administrative headquarters in The Woodlands, Texas. A standard company joke is that Chicago Bridge & Iron isn't in Chicago, doesn't build bridges, and doesn't use iron.

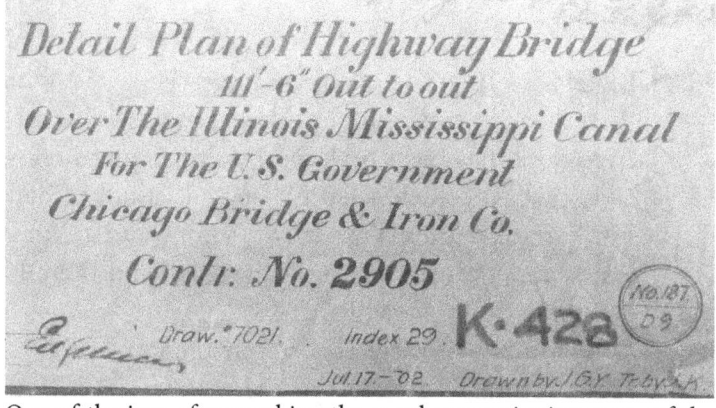

One of the joys of researching the canal was reviewing many of the original drawings of the canal. The beautiful work by draftsmen clearly came from a different era. Here is the title for the Chicago Bridge & Iron's bridges used on this part of the canal. Illinois and Mississippi (Hennepin) Canal, "Map, Drawing, and Plan Files, G-Q," Record Series 497.001, Illinois State Archives.

East of here, the trail is mostly a grassy route on fine stone. To the west, it is an oil and chip surface. The trail is still on the north bank.

Mineral

Not far to the south and across Interstate 80 is Mineral, Illinois. Coal was discovered near here in 1834 by John Green Reed, reportedly one of the first discoveries in the county. Soon, a number of small mines opened up south of Mineral and a community of 300 developed with the name Mineral. In 1850, Mineral was officially organized, and then later platted by William Riley in 1857. The part of town north of the Rock Island tracks became known as Riley's Addition due to his work. William Riley had other impacts upon the community as he was the first postmaster of the village, the first agent for the railroad, and he built and donated the first school at Mineral.

A second boom in coal mining took place in the late 1800s and early 1900s. This included the following coal mines: Forrest (1882-1895), Vanvelzer (1882-1895), Lester (1893-1894), Lloyd (1892-1893), Jensen (1894-1896), Brandt (1894-1926), Hodgett (1894-1929), Paul (1895-1900), Tucker & McFall (1897-1900), Tompkins (1900-1901), Higgins (1924), Good Luck (1925-1941), Johnson (1930), Mapes (1930-1934), and Jenkins & Crosland (1932-1943). The population of Mineral peaked in the 1940s and started to drop as the coal mines closed. Today, Mineral is a small farming community with a population of about 250, with a post office and a few businesses.

31.6 **BRIDGE #21** – As with many of these older bridges, this one has been replaced by a fill across the canal. A large culvert allows the waterway to pass through the modern fill, but the trail crosses the roadway at grade. Bureau County Road 45 East uses the fill to connect a number of farms in the area, and there is a small parking lot at the north end. Originally, this was another of the relatively common 110-foot Pratt through truss spans with an eighteen-foot-wide plank deck.

Note the drainage ditch which passes under the Hennepin Canal just west of this bridge, using Pipe #20. This ditch takes water north to the Elm Island Ditch, which then flows to the northwest to Coal Creek. The pipe was originally built using two 4-foot diameter cast iron pipes, while most originally used only one pipe.

32.0 COUNTY LINE – Look for the powerline where the canal makes a turn to the west. To the east is Bureau County while to the west is Henry County. **Bureau County** was organized out of Putnam County in 1837 with its county seat at Princeton. It was named for Michel or Pierre de Beuro, French Creoles, who ran a trading post from 1776 until 1790 near where Big Bureau Creek empties into the Illinois River. The county's population is less than 40,000.

Henry County was formed on January 13, 1825, from part of the existing Fulton County. It was named for Patrick Henry, the American Revolution spokesman who made the challenge "give me liberty, or give me death." With its county seat at Cambridge, the county's population is about 50,000. Most of the county is farmland, a profession celebrated each year at the Antique Engine & Tractor Association show in September.

33.1 BRIDGE #22 – This 110-foot steel Pratt truss bridge is gone and replaced by a fill across the canal. There is a small parking lot off the road, Henry County Road 2900 East, on the north side of the canal. Heading west, the canal turns to the west-northwest and is lined by a thin wall of trees as it passes through open farmland.

The Graddett Ditch passes under the canal just west of the bridge, using a 10-foot concrete arch culvert. The Graddett Ditch drains the fields to the south and takes the water to the north into the Elm Island Ditch, which then flows into Coal Creek. On the south bank is a concrete spillway and flush duct that allows excess water to flow out of the canal and into Gaddett Ditch. Care should be taken when exploring this spillway as it includes a drop of almost twenty feet.

On the south bank is the flush basin for Graddett Ditch. This flush basin is easy to explore, but watch the fall as it is a long way down to the stream. Photo by Barton Jennings.

Not far to the south, and just across Interstate 80, is the CHS ethanol plant. The plant opened in 2008 as Patriot Renewable Fuels, producing 125 million gallons of ethanol annually. It purchased and processed more than 200 million bushels of corn from area farmers in its first five years of production and created 550 million gallons of ethanol. On June 1, 2015, it was announced that CHS Inc. was buying the facility, the second ethanol plant that CHS has purchased. Their first was the former Illinois River Energy plant at Rochelle, Illinois, which they bought in June 2014.

With the canal sitting high and few surrounding trees, it is easy to see the CHS ethanol plant to the south. Photo by Barton Jennings.

CHS is one of those companies that few have ever heard of, but it is a Fortune 100 company. It is a global agribusiness founded in 1929 and is "owned by farmers, ranchers and cooperatives across the United States" and "supplies energy, crop nutrients, grain marketing services, animal feed, food and food ingredients, along with business solutions including insurance, financial and risk management services.

Main Channel

The company operates petroleum refineries/pipelines and manufactures, markets and distributes Cenex® brand refined fuels, lubricants, propane and renewable energy products," according to their website.

33.7 ANNAWAN DITCH – Another four-foot diameter cast iron pipe passes under the canal here, this one moving the water in the Annawan Ditch. This drainage ditch removes water from the east side of Annawan and takes it north and into the Graddett Ditch.

34.6 BRIDGE #23 – Illinois Highway 78, also known as East 2750 Street, crosses the canal on a large fill. The Hennepin Canal Parkway Trail uses a large culvert to pass under the north end of the fill. There are parking lots that can access the trail on both the north and south ends of the fill. A boat ramp, campground and toilets are located just west of the south end of the fill. This location is easily accessible as it is just north of Exit 33 of Interstate 80.

This was once another Chicago Bridge & Iron Company 110-foot Pratt through truss bridge, but it was replaced by September 1936 with a series of steel plate girder spans as part of the improvements on Illinois Highway 78. Early plats of the canal show a barn and a house along the south bank, west of Bridge #23.

Hennepin Canal Parkway: History Through the Miles

Those who live in farm country are used to tractors driving down the road. However, it is an interesting sight when one drives above the canal trail, as shown here at Bridge #23. Photo by Barton Jennings.

A noted characteristic of Illinois farms is how tidy they are. This farm on the north side of the Hennepin Canal at Bridge #23 certainly fits that description. Photo by Barton Jennings.

Annawan

Immediately to the south of the freeway is Annawan, Illinois. Annawan serves the local farming communities, hosting a post office, several convenience stores and gas stations, a farm co-op, a farm supply store, and a hotel. Its population was 878 in the 2010 census. There is an issue with the legal status of Annawan, as the community claims to be a village while the Secretary of State states that it is an incorporated town, not a village.

The first settlers arrived near Annawan in 1846 and their first efforts were to drain the local swamps so the land could be farmed. Mud Creek and the Green River were used to help drain the area, making land available. Efforts continued into the early 1900s to drain the land for farms. Today, a number of drainage canals lace the area making farming possible.

The Rock Island Railroad was building through this area in 1853, and landowners Charles Atkinson and James Grant plotted the Village of Annawan on some of the higher lands alongside the railroad. Some reports stated that the name came from a Winnebago Indian Chief.

Hennepin Canal Parkway: History Through the Miles

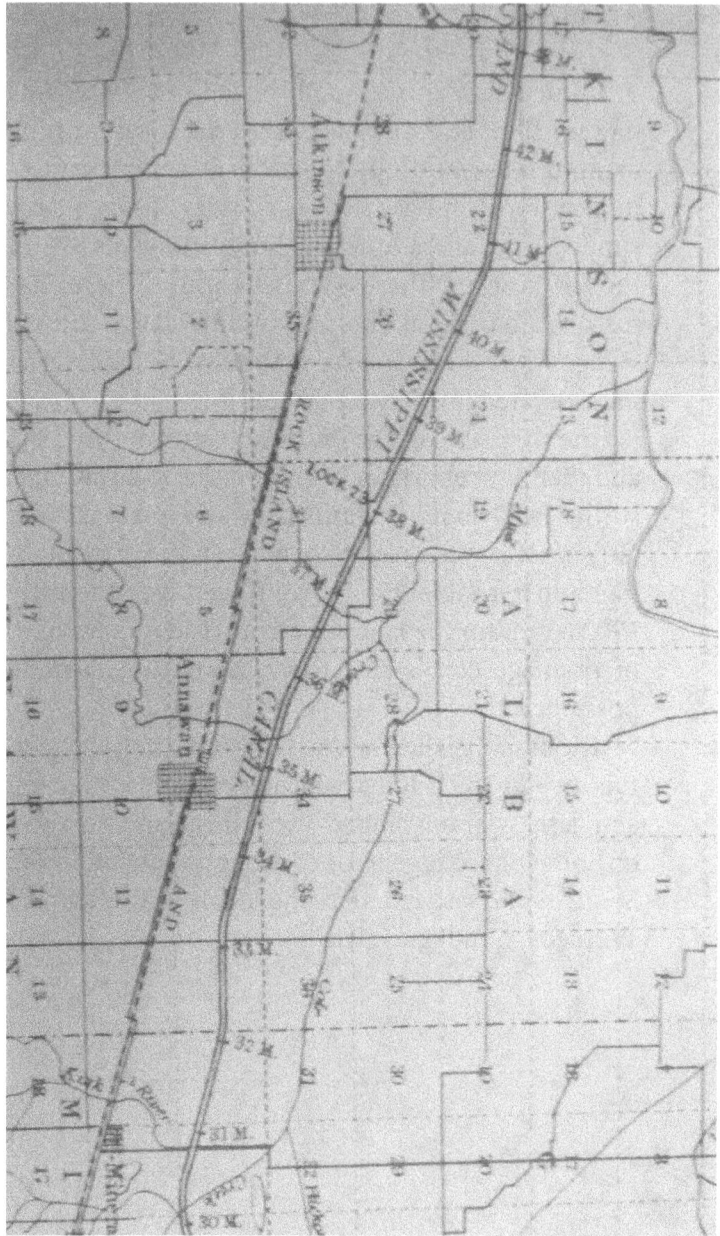

Canal Map – Annawan to Atkinson. Illinois and Mississippi (Hennepin) Canal, "Canal Route Plat Files," Record Series 497.008, Illinois State Archives.

Main Channel

35.3 AQUEDUCT #5 – This six-span, 240-foot-long concrete trough on concrete piers aqueduct crosses Mud Creek, thus its name Mud Creek Aqueduct. Mud Creek drains much of the area west of Annawan. It flows north, joins with Coal Creek, and then flows on to the northwest to enter the Green River. The area is covered with otter slides; trails they make while sliding down hills or across flat ground. If you keep quiet, it doesn't take long for an otter to pop out of the brush, Mud Creek, or the Hennepin Canal.

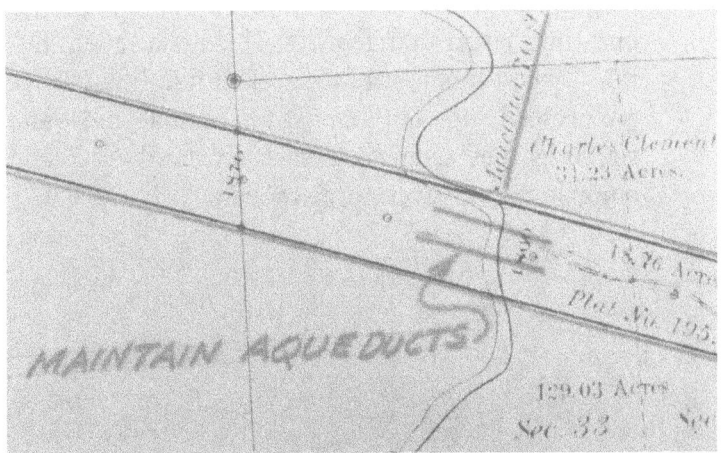

During the transfer of the canal to the State of Illinois, a number of studies were performed to determine what work should be done to maintain the canal. This drawing has Aqueduct #5 marked to maintain instead of replacing it with a siphon and footbridge. Illinois and Mississippi (Hennepin) Canal, "Map, Drawing, and Plan Files, G-Q," Record Series 497.001, Illinois State Archives.

The North American river otter lived all across Illinois during early European settlement, but fur hunting and the loss of habitat led to a great loss of population. By the early 1900s, seeing a river otter was a rare event, with the only significant populations existing along the Mississippi River and its backwaters in northwestern Illinois, where about 100 otter were believed to still live. The river otter was listed as a state threatened species in 1977, but the population began to grow and it was downgraded to state endangered in 1989. Efforts to increase the otter population included live-trapping and moving 346 otters from Louisiana to Illinois during the mid to late 1990s. With this, they were moved to state threatened in 1999, and were delisted in 2004. Otter can again be found in every Illinois county.

Adult otter measure three to almost five feet in length, and weigh 10 to 25 pounds. Males are about one-third larger than females. This makes them Illinois' largest member of the weasel family, and they are probably one of the most fun animals to sit and watch as they seem to almost constantly play and enjoy just about everything they do.

The pedestrian bridge across Aqueduct #5 really provides a close-up view of the canal. It is not unusual to see otter playing on the slopes around the aqueduct. Photo by Barton Jennings.

Main Channel

Not far west of Aqueduct #5, the Hennepin Canal comes next to Interstate 80 and curves to the northwest as the highway curves to the southwest. The trail swings away from the canal for a short distance. At about Milepost 36, a fence alongside the north side of the trail marks the location of another stream that passes under the canal using a large culvert. Throughout this area, the canal is full of water lilies.

36.5 **BRIDGE #24** – This bridge is crossed by what is sometimes identified as County Road 2570 East, which ends just to the south in a farm field. County Road 2750 East turns off of Baker School Road west of Illinois Highway 78. This bridge consists of an original 110-foot single-span Pratt through truss, built by the Chicago Bridge & Iron Company. It was the most common design on the canal and was eighteen feet wide and had a plank deck. The Hennepin Canal Parkway Trail passes under the north end, with a grassy riding path on the south bank. Access roads connect with the canal embankments on the northeast and southwest ends of the bridge, making it easy to explore the bridge. All of these roads are lined with concrete fence posts.

Sitting in the middle of several farm fields is this 110-foot single-span Pratt through truss bridge, known as Bridge #24. Photo by Barton Jennings.

The bridge is still used by some farm and canal equipment, and a curving dirt road can be used to reach the bridge and cross over the canal. Photo by Barton Jennings.

Main Channel

Bridge #24 is circled by a large collection of concrete fence posts, all manufactured at the Post House near Lock #17. Photo by Barton Jennings.

36.9 SHABBONA SPECIAL DITCH – Not far west of Bridge #24, the Shabbona Special Ditch passes under the Hennepin Canal, using a 12-foot arched concrete culvert. This ditch is part of the Shabbona Special Drainage District. The Ditch connects the former coal strip mines southeast of Atkinson to Mud Creek, located to the north. The word Shabbona comes from the name of an old Pottawattamie chief, Shabbona, who once lived in the area. Shabbona was actually from the Ottawa tribe and was born about 1775, reportedly a grandnephew of Pontiac, the famous Ottawa leader. The name Shabbona means "indomitable" or "hardy" in several of the regional languages. Several English translations show his name to mean "built strong like a bear" or "built like a bear." The Ottawa had been driven out of the Ontario, Canada, area by the Iroquois, and had joined with The Council of Three Fires (Ojibwa, Odawa and Potawatomi tribes) scattered across Michigan, Ohio, Indiana and Illinois.

Shabbona had fought beside Pontiac during Pontiac's War, and later with the Shawnee chieftain Tecumseh during the War of 1812. Both of these efforts were designed to prevent white settlement in the original Northwest Territory of the Ohio Valley. After the war, different chiefs were chosen by different Indian Agents, and Shabbona was recognized only by the Indian Agent at Peoria, Illinois, creating some challenges to his leadership. During the Winnebagos' Red Bird uprising of 1825, Shabbona attempted to keep the Potawatomi (spelled Pottawattamie in some of the reports from that time) out of the conflict, and was quickly labeled a whiteman spy. Shabbona did receive a large land grant for his assistance during the war, a land grant that is legally debated today as to whether the Potawatomi still own it. He later also resisted the Black Hawk War in the early 1830s, recognizing that it was useless to resist white settlement. Shabbona participated in the movement of the Potawatomi to Nebraska in 1836, but returned to Illinois to settle, where he died in 1859.

37.4 BRIDGE #25 – A fill has replaced the former bridge for East 2500th Street. The original bridge was the 110-foot Pratt through truss that the Corps of Engineers used frequently on the Hennepin Canal. This one had a plank deck that was eighteen feet wide.

Today, the Hennepin Canal Parkway Trail crosses the road at grade, while a large culvert allows the waterway to flow through the fill. There is limited parking available here. The canal heads northwest, passing several farms before arriving at Lock #23.

Main Channel

37.9 BRIDGE #26 – This location is signed as being the "Hennepin Canal Parkway Lock 23 Day Use Area". Henry County Highway 22, Road 1920 North, crosses the canal on a large fill. This road runs east-west and crosses the canal at a sharp angle, while the original Bridge #26, a 110-foot steel Pratt truss installed in November 1903, crossed the canal at a right angle.

A number of facilities are located at what is known as the Hennepin Canal Parkway Lock 23 Day Use Area. Photo by Barton Jennings.

This road can be reached from just north of Atkinson, Illinois, and this is a popular fishing and recreational park. On the west end of the fill, there is a parking lot with toilets, information signs and a small campground. A paved trail runs along the north side of the roadway to cross the canal. There are several traditional farms visible from the trail here, which uses a culvert with a concrete floor to pass through the east end of the fill.

Pritchard Elevator Company

Plat maps of the canal show that the land that the canal sits on was acquired through condemnation from Samuel Pritchard in September 1899. There were several branches of the Pritchard family in the area, and actually several Samuel Pritchards lived nearby. At the west end of this bridge, on the south side of the canal, was the Pritchard Elevator Company. The company leased two tracts of land (0.19 and 0.14 acres) on each side of the road, which today would be south of the current road. The first lease was dated August 1, 1914, for $5 per year. The last contract in the Illinois State Archives is dated August 1, 1929. However, a contract dated August 1, 1934, shows that Turner-Hudnut had a lease on the site by that time.

38.0 LOCK #23 – This lock has had its miter gate doors rebuilt and restored, done in 1961 by the Corps of Engineers. There is no bridge across the lock, but the east gates have had a handrail installed to allow people to cross the gates. The east gates are closed and the water flows through the lock's bypass. When in service, the lock provided an eleven-foot lift. Access to the lock area is from a parking area on the south side of the canal, where toilets are also available. The paved Pathway Trail is on the north bank of the canal. A trail connects the two on the north side of County Road 22.

Main Channel

The miter gates at Lock #23 were restored a number of years ago, and this gate at the west end demonstrates how they would fit into the lock's walls to clear boats. Photo by Barton Jennings.

The west end of Lock #23, the downstream end, features these large stairways which are often used for fishing. Photo by Barton Jennings.

Lock #23 had a number of canal structures, all once located in the wooded area on the south side of the lock. Near where the parking lot is now located was a warehouse, and then a gambrel-roofed house to its west. South of the lock and along the road was another house, with a barn to its north. A photograph from 1934 shows that there was a small dock and fuel pump at the southeast end of the lock for boats operated by the Corps of Engineers.

This photo from the files of the Corps of Engineers, found in the Illinois State Archives, looks east from Lock #23 on March 22, 1934. It shows a gambrel-roofed canal house, a warehouse, the Pritchard Elevator Company facility, and Bridge #26. Note that the canal is still drained as it is being prepared for the 1934 shipping season. Illinois and Mississippi (Hennepin) Canal, "Photographic Files," Record Series 497.037, Illinois State Archives.

The Corps of Engineers Telephone System

An early report stated that the "telephone line was hastily constructed in 1896 by stringing the wires on 2 by 4 inch pine scantling nailed to posts of the right of way fence. These supports have become rotten and not suitable for the purpose. The line is now being repaired and wire suspended on cedar posts along the towpath where it can be easily cared for and where it is not liable to come in contact with trees, etc." The cedar posts didn't last much longer, and soon the Corps of Engineers began to manufacture concrete telephone poles, which were used along much of the Hennepin Canal.

Heading west from Lock #23, there are several concrete telephone poles alongside the towpath, and a large number of concrete fence posts separating the canal property from local fields. All along the canal will be found the remains of the telephone system that once connected the entire Hennepin Canal. This network was used to alert employees and management of emergencies, notify the lockkeepers when boats were moving through the canal, and to exchange news. Originally, the system was mounted on wooden posts, trees, and even fence posts. As the canal was completed, the system was modernized and stretched along both sides of the canal. A 1932 report on the telephone system included a map and description of the various pole lines along the canal. It noted that copper and iron wire was used, as well as concrete and wooden poles. This report broke the system into six lines, with a basic description of the materials used.

Line #1	This was on the north side of the east end of the canal's main channel. It was primarily iron wire, but had stretches of both concrete and wood poles.
Line #2	This was on the west side of the Feeder Canal, and consisted of copper wire on concrete poles.
Line #3	This line was on the east side of the Feeder Canal and used iron wire on concrete poles.
Line #4	This telephone line was on the south side of the main channel on the east end of the canal. Most of the line was copper wire on concrete poles, but there were several stretches where it was copper wire on wood poles, and iron wire on concrete poles. Most of these short stretches seemed to be where floods had taken out the original line and canal embankments.
Line #5	This line was on the north side of the west end of the main channel. It used iron wire on concrete telephone poles.
Line #6	This line was on the south side of the west end of the canal and consisted of copper wires on concrete poles.

Main Channel

The remains of the Corps of Engineers telephone system can be found all along the canal. These poles can be seen just west of Lock #23. Photo by Barton Jennings.

38.5 BRIDGE #27 – This is East 2400th Street, and has very limited parking. This new concrete deck bridge has replaced the historic structure that once stood here. This bridge was originally a 110-foot Pratt through truss span, supplied by the Chicago Bridge & Iron Company and installed in November 1903. Like most of these bridges, it had a plank deck that was eighteen feet wide. These bridges were wider than the first bridges built to cross the canal, possibly because of the changing standards for roadways that happened at the time of the canal's construction.

Heading west, the canal and trail passes through miles of farm fields, but often with large spoil banks on the edge of the canal property. The canal property is lined by a thin row of brush and trees. There are also a number of large culverts that pass under the canal to allow streams to drain area fields. With the trail on the north side of the canal, hikers and bikers are in the sun much of the day.

In many places along the canal are stands of large trees. During the early days, walnut, elm, and catalpa were the most commonly planted. Examples of all of these can still be found today. The catalpa trees bloom and have long bean-like pods, while the walnut trees have their baseball-size nuts which drop in late summer though fall. For the elm, most mature elms have died from Dutch elm disease. Photo by Barton Jennings.

38.7 PIPE CULVERT – Along the north bank of the canal is a small flush box, used with the four-foot diameter cast iron pipe culvert that passes under the canal. The waterway that uses the culvert helps to drain farmland northeast of Atkinson, Illinois.

39.6 BRIDGE #28 – East 2300th Street crosses the canal on a large fill, with the trail passing under it through a large culvert on the north end. There is a parking lot and boat ramp on the south side of the canal, just east of 2300th Street. This was originally another

Main Channel

110-foot Pratt through truss span built by the Chicago Bridge & Iron Company in December 1903.

In a number of locations, the canal is at a higher elevation than the area fields. This can raise the water table in the area. To keep fields from being too wet, drainage canals line each side of the Hennepin Canal, as can be found here.

40.7 **BRIDGE #29** – East 2200th Street also now uses a fill to cross the canal instead of the original steel bridge, also built with culverts for both the waterway and the Parkway Trail. The original bridge was a standard 110-foot Pratt through truss span, provided by the Chicago Bridge & Iron Company. However, this bridge was one of four known to have been built for the Corps of Engineers with an eighteen-foot-wide concrete deck. After tests, a number of the other bridges lost their wooden decks and had them replaced with concrete panels. This is another example of how the Hennepin Canal was a test for many new engineering and construction techniques and materials.

There is a parking lot on the north side of the canal, near where the Hennepin Canal Parkway Trail passes under the fill. The canal turns to the west-northwest for about two miles until East 2000th Street.

Atkinson

Less than two miles to the south is the community of Atkinson. Atkinson is named for Charles Atkinson, an eastern capitalist who arrived here in 1843 and began buying land. Just as he did at Annawan, Charles Atkinson platted a town on the new Chicago & Rock Island Railroad. Atkinson advertised the community (and others) across Europe and brought a number of new immigrants from Belgium and Holland to settle here during the 1860s. In 1867, Atkinson was incorporated.

Atkinson was one of the communities that the Hennepin Canal counted on for freight traffic. There were coal mines in the area, and coal was needed for the factories and houses in Rock Island. Mines began to open here by 1883, including the Weatherspoon Coal Mine (1883-1885, a slope mine 15 to 40 feet deep), Frew Coal Mine (1883-1896, a slope mine 15 to 38 feet), Mowbray Coal Mine (1883-1903, described as a slope mine at a depth of 10 to 44 feet with a coal seam of 3 feet in thickness), and the Kay Coal Mine (1883-1907, a shaft mine 28 to 40 feet deep). Other mines quickly opened, including the Armstrong & Welch Coal Mine and the Campbell Coal Mine, both slope mines that opened in 1884 and closed soon after; the Atkinson Coal Mine (1891-1920), an underground slope and drift mine at a depth of 15 to 50 feet with a coal seam of 4 feet in thickness; the Riley Coal Mine (1893-1902), a shaft mine going to a depth of 30 to 40 feet with a 3-foot coal seam; and the Marley Coal Mine (1894-1898), a shaft mine 20 to 45 feet deep.

Other mines opened in the late 1890s and early 1900s, including the Coull Coal Mine (1896), Loy Coal Mine (1897-1900), Waine Coal Mine (1898-1904), Stiner Coal Mine (1901-1911), Rumla Coal Mine (1903), Hartman Coal Mine (1904-1911), Omel Coal Mine (1906-1907), Collins Coal Mine (1907), and the Atkinson Coal Mine (1923-1927). All mined a coal seam of about three feet thick approximately forty feet below ground level.

Main Channel

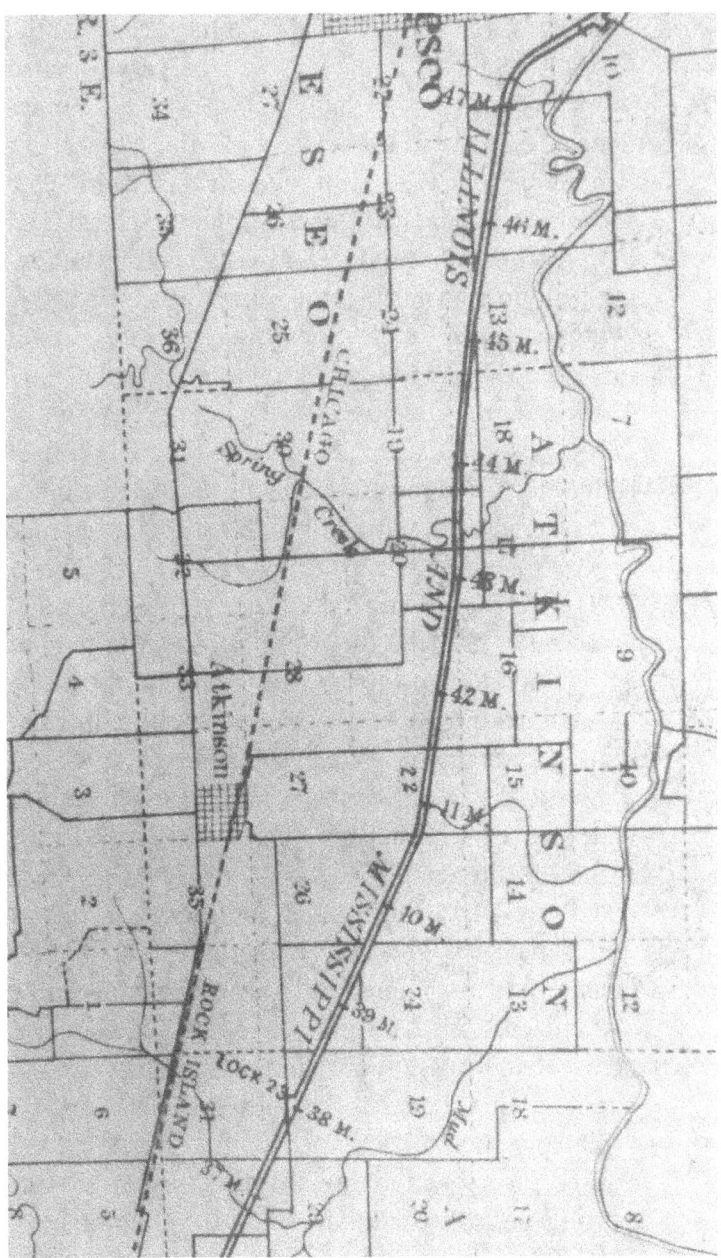

Canal Map – Atkinson to Geneseo. Illinois and Mississippi (Hennepin) Canal, "Canal Route Plat Files," Record Series 497.008, Illinois State Archives.

Major surface mining began in the area when the Midland Electric Company No. 1 Coal Mine opened in 1929, with the 125 to 150 local workers immediately represented by the United Mine Workers of America. From 1934 until the mine closed in 1953, the mine was operated by the Midland Electric Coal Corporation. With modern mining and earth moving equipment available, the mine was a strip mine, going as deep as fifty feet. The area east and south of town still shows the scars of the mining activities.

Much of the community's history can be found at the Atkinson Museum. Atkinson Grain & Fertilizer is busy in town, and Atkinson also has a post office and several stores serving the almost 1000 residents.

41.5 **BRIDGE #30** – East 2120th Street crosses the canal using a low fill. The canal trail crosses the road at grade while the waterway uses a large culvert. The original bridge was a 110-foot Pratt through truss span. Like many others along the Hennepin Canal, the plank deck of the bridge measured eighteen feet wide. There is a limited amount of unofficial parking at this location.

Just west of Bridge #30 is another pipe culvert under the canal. This culvert used two four-foot diameter cast iron pipes, and had rock headwalls to prevent erosion. A number of the bridges in this area have culverts on one side or the other, used to handle drainage ditches that keep area fields dry.

During the winter, much of the Parkway Trail is used for snowmobiling. To direct riders to other trails and communities, signs are often erected. Signs for "ATK" are placed here to point people to Atkinson.

Main Channel

Not long after the snow has melted in early 2019, this sign points towards Atkinson from Bridge #30. Photo by Barton Jennings.

42.5 BRIDGE #31 – Not far east of Bridge #31, the trail moves several feet away from the canal, allowing trees and brush to grow between the trail and canal. Bridge #31 is another low fill that crosses the Hennepin Canal, which turns to the west not far west of here. This fill carries East 2000th Street, and the trail simply crosses the road. There is a parking lot on the south side of the canal, to the west of the street. The original Bridge #31 was identical to Bridge #30.

About Milepost 43, the canal turns due west. Through this area, the canal still passes through open farmland with just a narrow line of trees at the edge of the property line.

43.3 BRIDGE #32 – The Hennepin Canal Parkway Trail passes under the north end of a high fill that carries

East 1950th Street across the canal. Heading south on the road will take you to U.S. Highway 6, several miles west of Atkinson. Heading north to North 2120th Avenue, you will be at the historic location of the Spring Creek School. Note the concrete telephone poles in this area on the north side of the canal. Parking is limited at this location.

43.5   AQUEDUCT #6 – The Hennepin Canal Parkway Trail crosses the north side of this five-span concrete trough on concrete piers aqueduct. The aqueduct crosses Spring Creek, giving it the name Spring Creek Aqueduct. Spring Creek forms east of Osco, and north of Cambridge, both in Illinois. The stream flows generally east, gathering a number of small streams that drain area farmland. At one time, much of this land was swamp, and Spring Creek is one of many area streams used to drain the land to allow farming. It eventually turns north, flows under the Hennepin Canal, and on north into the Green River.

Because the only walkway across Spring Creek is on the north side of the aqueduct, the equestrian trail uses this route between Bridge #32 and Bridge #33. However, because the south bank is used for maintenance, it can be walked as far as the aqueduct for those who want a ground-level view of it.

Not far west of Aqueduct #6, several Kinder Morgan natural gas pipelines pass under the canal. Kinder Morgan operates approximately 70,000 miles of natural gas pipelines, moving approximately 40 percent of the natural gas consumed in the United States. This pipeline breaks off of the major line to Chicago not far southwest of here, and supplies natural gas to very northeast Illinois.

Main Channel

This photo shows many of the details of a Hennepin Canal aqueduct. This is the south side of Aqueduct #6 – note the upstream batter (pointed end) of the concrete piers, built to break up ice floating down the stream. You can also see the mix of steel and concrete that supported the structure. Photo by Barton Jennings.

43.7 BRIDGE #33 – This low fill across the canal carries County Road East 1900th Street. There was once a 110-foot Pratt through truss span here, eighteen feet wide with a plank deck. The trail crosses the road at grade at the north end of the fill, but parking is very limited. Just to the west, the canal again turns to the west-northwest. This leaves hikers and bikers exposed to the sun on most afternoons.

Before the corn grows tall, and after it is harvested, there can be great views of area farms. This farm is to the north just west of Bridge #33. Photo by Barton Jennings.

45.2 DANNY MARTINS MEMORIAL SITE – This green bench, a great place to spend a few minutes sitting beside the canal, is a memorial to Danny Martins, someone who loved the canal. To the north of the bench is a canal survey benchmark, as well as a number of concrete fence posts. There are a number of memorial benches along the canal, but most are at cities like Milan and Rock Falls.

Main Channel

The Danny Martins Memorial Site is just one of a number of benches that have been installed along the Hennepin Canal as a memorial to someone who has appreciated the canal and trail. Photo by Barton Jennings.

45.7 BRIDGE #34 – East 1700th Street crosses the canal on a low fill, and the trail crosses the road at grade. There is a small parking lot on the north end of the fill. The 110-foot Pratt through truss bridge that once stood here had a unique concrete deck. On the north side of the canal, N. 2120th Avenue is located next to the Parkway Trail. Note that the road is on canal property and that the Corps of Engineers' concrete fence posts are located on both sides of the road.

In 1911, this was a busy location with roads in all directions, connecting farms owned by people with the names Bollen (to the northeast), Johnson (northwest), Nelson (southeast) and Pritchard (southwest). To serve the local farmers and their children, there was a local school on the Pritchard property, located just southwest of here on today's N. 2120th Avenue.

Heading west, the canal and trail passes over several culverts for local waterways, which merge just to the north and flow into the Green River. The original culverts have been replaced by modern steel corrugated culverts. Notice how a number of trees alongside these smaller streams show the presence of beavers.

46.2 **ARCH CULVERT** – There is a 12-foot concrete arch culvert under the canal at this location. It handles another drainage ditch that helps make it possible to plant area fields. The culvert can be found due to the sound of running water.

47.0 **BRIDGE #35** – This low fill across the canal carries County Road East 1570th Street. The original bridge built for the Corps of Engineers by the Chicago Bridge & Iron Company was a Pratt through truss that measured 110 feet long and eighteen feet wide. The trail crosses the road at grade. Just west of this bridge, the canal turns to the northwest to pass north of Geneseo. In the same area, a housing subdivision backs onto the south side of the canal, with several streams passing under the canal. Note the rock used to stabilize the grade and the large spoil banks in the area.

This area was one of the busier along the canal, both historically and today. There were several newspaper articles about the ice business on the Hennepin Canal that mentioned an ice house on the canal north of Geneseo.

Geneseo

Geneseo is home to the famous gun manufacturing company, Springfield Armory, Inc., which is located on Main Street, about two miles to the southwest. It was founded in 1974 by the Reese family. Also in Geneseo is Armalite, owned by Strategic Armory Corps of Phoenix, Arizona, but all manufacturing is still conducted in Geneseo. The gun manufacturing in Geneseo is unusual based upon how the community was founded. In 1827, members of a Congregationalist church in Geneseo, New York, started planning a new community in the "Old Northwest" – Illinois. In May 1836, a delegation (the "New York Committee" or "New York Group") visited the area and surveyed the property. Soon, members of the seven founding families departed to create a "church in the wilderness," naming the community after the city in New York where they started. The trip took much of the year as the group was not prepared for country without roads, or the harsh winter weather.

After building a few crude cabins, the first act of the new settlers was reportedly to create a temperance society and then start construction on the original First Congregationalist Church. Its first communion was held on April 18, 1838, with those in attendance having to fight a large hail storm which broke out almost all of the windows in town. Next came the creation of the Geneseo Seminary, which closed in 1857 due to considerable debt.

The arrival of the Rock Island Railroad on Christmas Day, 1853, reportedly helped the community's situation. The editor of the *Rock Islander* reported that there were "one hundred new buildings erected in Geneseo" in 1854 alone and "seventy [more] built in the present year [1855]." This boom allowed Geneseo to become a town in 1855 and a city in 1865. This is the era that gives Geneseo its nickname of "Victorian Geneseo" as the new wealth was often spent on large and impressive homes. Most remain and are featured during the annual Christmas Walk. Geneseo's population today is about 7000, and there are numerous stores, restaurants and gas stations in town.

There were once a number of coal mines in the Geneseo area. The Aldrich Coal Mine opened during the 1870s, and was open until about 1902 in some form. The Winer Coal Mine was open 1904-1905. There was a sudden boom in coal mining here in 1934 with the Bennett & Crist Coal Mine, Briar Bluff Coal Mine, Milan Coal Mine, and Munsen No. 1 and No. 2 Coal Mines opening that year. The Spring Creek Coal Mine (1935), West Geneseo Coal Mine (1938), and Shady Beach Coal Mine (1939) opened over the next few years, but none lasted long or shipped on the canal.

Main Channel

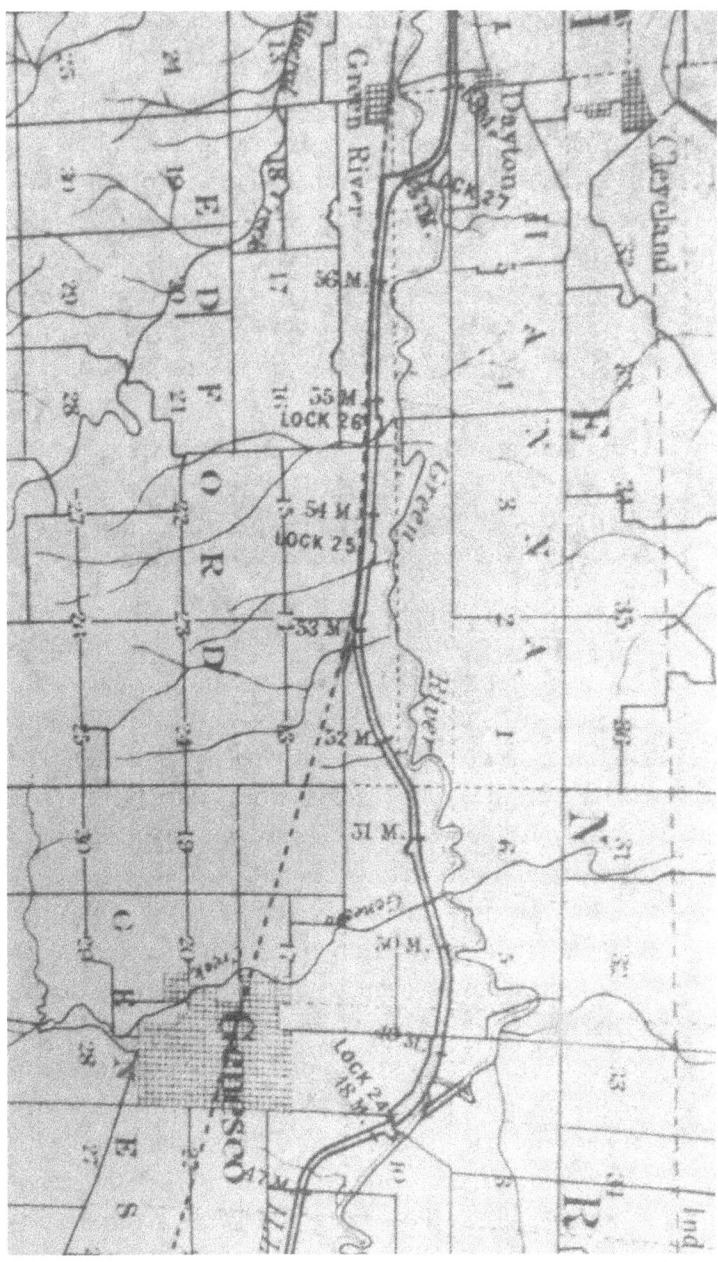

Canal Map – Geneseo to Green River. Illinois and Mississippi (Hennepin) Canal, "Canal Route Plat Files," Record Series 497.008, Illinois State Archives.

47.9 GENESEO FISH HATCHERY – Located between the canal and the Green River to the north was once the Geneseo State Fish Hatchery. Like the fish hatchery at Lock #21, this one was authorized on June 26, 1925, as one of a series of hatcheries across the State of Illinois. According to the December 4, 1927, *Daily Illini*, the Geneseo Fish Hatchery was near completion. The short article stated: "Covering an area of eight acres, the state fish hatchery at Geneseo, designed to produce more than 1,000,000 fish a year, is rapidly nearing completion. Only construction of a dam between the two ponds, completion of the outlet gate and laying of a six inch pipe from the canal to the ponds needs be done before the hatchery will be ready for use."

Reportedly, the entire facility eventually covered fourteen acres and consisted of six small ponds. Water was supplied from the canal and expelled into the Green River. The hatchery was still open and holding events in 1959, but closed soon after. The brick entrance and fencing around the facility still stands, visible from the original Grange Road near the Green River, just north of Lock #24.

Approaching Lock #24, the 22-foot wide and 28-foot long foundation of the former lockkeeper's house can be seen in the woods to the north. There were thirty-eight houses built for lockmen or patrolmen along the canal, with thirty of them being a common design featuring two stories with a gambrel roof (symmetrical two-sided roof with two slopes on each side, like many barns) and seven rooms. During the spring and summer, the foundation is easy to find due to all of the daylilies that grow around the site.

Main Channel

If you look in the woods east of Lock #24, you can find this foundation, the remains of one of many houses that once stood alongside the canal. Photo by Barton Jennings.

Across the canal to the south, located 500 feet east of Lock #24, was a warehouse and dock owned by the Sterling, Dixon & Rock Falls Packet Company. The lease for this property was part of the agreement for the land at Rock Falls. Corps of Engineers' records indicate that a 16'x20' warehouse was built here, and that the leases were cancelled in 1910.

48.1 LOCK #24 AND BRIDGE #36 – The area around Lock #24 is a busy tourist destination, being just north of Geneseo. There are several parking lots and toilets related to the Hennepin Canal Parkway Trail. A covered pavilion, picnic tables, barbeque grills, benches, information signs and a boat ramp are also at the location. Note the Friends of the Hennepin Canal bench on the north side of the lock, and the Clyde H. Neumann bench to the south. Neumann lived almost all of his life in Geneseo and owned several businesses, and was a frequent fisherman along the canal.

The Lock #24 area is a popular and busy one, and an official snowmobile access area. This sign clearly marks the location. Photo by Barton Jennings.

During the days that the canal was in operation, a number of buildings stood around Lock #24. There was a house just north of the east gate, with a barn further to the east. About 200 feet east of the barn was an ice house and another barn. Finally, there was the lockkeeper's house whose foundation has already been mentioned.

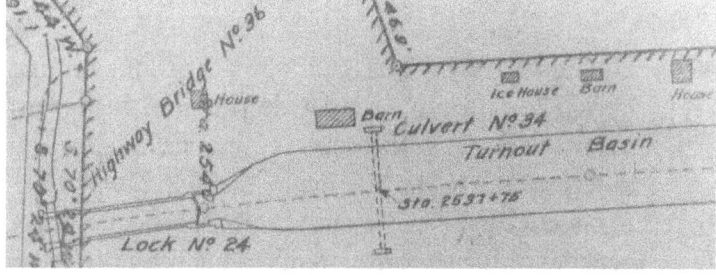

Lock #24 has always been a busy area, and several canal houses and barns once stood here. Illinois and Mississippi (Hennepin) Canal, "Map, Drawing, and Plan Files, G-Q," Record Series 497.001, Illinois State Archives.

Main Channel

To the north is the Green River, and to the west is the Geneseo Country Club and its golf course. The Hennepin Canal forms a large lake just to the west, a large turning basin once used for local freight business and to hold barges awaiting their turn through Lock #24. When in operation, Lock #24 provided a lift of eleven feet. The lock had its wooden gates restored in 1961 by the Corps of Engineers. Grange Road used to cross the canal just outside the west gates, using a through plate girder bridge (**Bridge #36**) built by the Pittsburg Steel Construction Company in January 1905, using steel from Carnegie Steel. The south approach used a part of the lock's concrete wall, then a 40-foot through plate girder span, and then a 25-foot steel girder span over the parkway trail. While still in place, the bridge is only open to pedestrian traffic and a new Grange Road has been built to the west.

The miter gates at Lock #24 were restored in 1961 by the Corps of Engineers. This view of the west gate also includes Bridge #36, which crosses the canal just west of the gates. Photo by Barton Jennings.

This Pittsburg Steel Construction Co. drawing title for Bridge #36 is dated August 26, 1904. Illinois and Mississippi (Hennepin) Canal, "Map, Drawing, and Plan Files, G-Q," Record Series 497.001, Illinois State Archives.

The Pittsburg Steel Construction Company advertised that it provided "steel buildings, bridges, plate and tank work" and the firm was based in Allegheny, Pennsylvania. In 1904, Alexander Laughlin purchased the company, and later merged it into his Central Tube Company. Meanwhile, the erection business became part of J. S. Hunter & Company. Note the spelling of "Pittsburg" in the company's name on the builders plate. When the City of Pittsburgh was originally founded, the "h" was used in the name, but not when it was incorporated in 1816. There are a number of stories about why, including a printer's error and a cultural battle between those who used an "h" and those who didn't. However, the "h" was returned to the spelling on July 19, 1911, when a special meeting of the United States Geographic Board officially adopted the spelling "Pittsburgh".

48.2 GRANGE ROAD CAUSEWAY – Grange Road now crosses the Hennepin Canal, and nearby Green River, on a new alignment. To cross the canal, the road uses a high causeway fill that includes a large culvert for the Hennepin Canal Parkway Trail, and another for the waterway. Grange Road curves east and north and eventually connects Geneseo with Illinois Highway 92. It has long been a significant road in the area.

To the south is Olson Acres, the home of Olson Show Cattle. Olson breeds and trains cattle that "excel at all levels from county fairs to prospect shows to major shows and state fairs." The firm sells show cattle throughout the year and also has a Private Treaty sale in the fall.

Heading west, the canal makes a slow turn to the west. This wide canal basin is covered in water lilies, and is a beautiful area during late summer as the blooms cover the waterway. The canal was made wider here with several turning basins, former dock locations, and areas for canal boats to pass. A number of recreational boat docks still exist on the south bank, used by the homeowners located on the low ridge south of the canal.

For the hiker and biker, the woods are pretty thick on each side of the canal until Aqueduct #7, providing morning and late afternoon shade. Additionally, there are parks and campgrounds throughout the area. This is probably one of the most scenic parts of the entire Hennepin Canal, and is a popular recreational route. The Dean Gotthardt bench provides an excellent spot to sit and enjoy the view. Gotthardt was a freight car mechanic for the Rock Island Railroad, and was an avid fisherman along the canal.

The area west of Lock #24 is one of the most scenic on the canal, and the water lilies are a big reason why. Photo by Barton Jennings.

The area west of Lock #24 has always been popular, with several private clubs and homes lining the south bank of the canal. Photo by Barton Jennings.

Main Channel

49.2 BRIDGE #37 – A modern three-span beam bridge carries Illinois Highway 82 across the canal. Highway 82 connects Nekoma, Illinois, to Joslin, Illinois, towns less than thirty miles apart. There is a parking lot for the trail on the north shore of the canal. Also to the north is the Geneseo Campground. The campground promotes its location on the canal and provides camping spots for RVs and tents. There are restrooms, showers and a laundry for the users of the campground, which also rents cabins and a yurt. On the south bank of the Hennepin Canal is the Geneseo Izaak Walton League park and campground.

Bridge #37 has parks and campgrounds both to the north and the south. To the south of the canal is the Geneseo Izaak Walton League Park, where this welcome sign can be found. Photo by Sarah Jennings.

One of the most interesting signs along the canal is this one about water skiing. It can be found along the south shore at the Izaak Walton Geneseo Park. Photo by Sarah Jennings.

Also to the south is the Geneseo Prairie Park, once the Geneseo Outing Club site. The park is located at the northern boundary of Geneseo next to the Hennepin Canal. The park includes almost 60 acres of forested and restored prairie land, with a number of hiking and bike trails. When the Outing Club was created, Captain L. L. Wheeler assisted with the project by providing boats and barges to help build a beach and stabilize the shoreline. According to several reports from the time, Wheeler considered the location of the club to be the best and prettiest on the canal.

The original bridge, built for the Corps of Engineers, was a 110-foot Pratt through truss span with a concrete deck. In 1931-1932, the bridge was moved and rebuilt to fit a new road alignment, and it was reconstructed in 1973 with a new superstructure. However, heavier traffic volumes and vehicle weights led to the need for a new bridge. The new seven-steel-beam, concrete deck bridge, built during the early 2010s with some details to make it look like a park bridge – "aesthetically pleasing" – was designed by Maurer-Stutz, Inc. The design of the new bridge had to meet the standards of both the Illinois Department of Transportation and the Illinois Department of Natural Resources.

50.3 **AQUEDUCT #7** – This aqueduct is known as the Geneseo Creek Aqueduct since it crosses the Geneseo Creek. Geneseo Creek forms from a number of small streams on the southwest side of Geneseo. It flows north around the west side of town, under the Hennepin Canal, and then into the Green River just north of here. The Hennepin Canal Parkway Trail crosses the creek on the north side of the four-span aqueduct.

Note the wide turning basins just east and west of the aqueduct, designed to hold barges awaiting their turn through the aqueduct. According to the 1911 *Report of the Chief of Engineer, U.S. Army*, a serious break occurred at the east end of Aqueduct #7 on September 27, 1910. The report stated that the "banks were broken on both sides of the canal for about 50 feet. Repairs were made with some difficulty and no further trouble is expected at this locality."

Heading west toward the Mississippi River, the canal is now heading west-southwest. The trees alongside the Parkway Trail get thinner again as farms line the canal. Additionally, the canal is often at a higher elevation than the surrounding land, providing some nice views.

Like all of the aqueducts, Aqueduct #7 is less than forty feet wide, meaning only one boat could cross it at a time. This required the construction of timber moorings, also known as dolphins, at each end of the aqueducts. The timber moorings protected the end of the aqueducts from out-of-control boats, and also allowed boats to safely dock when necessary. Photo by Barton Jennings.

51.5 BRIDGE #38 – This bridge has been replaced by a low fill that carries East 1200th Street across the canal. There is a small parking lot for the canal to the northeast, near where the trail crosses the roadway at grade. The original bridge was a typical 110-foot Pratt truss, installed in January 1904, but with an unusual 16-foot-wide concrete deck. As the bridges aged, several had their wooden decks replaced by concrete based upon the Corps of Engineers' experience.

Main Channel

At Bridge #38, the canal curves to head to the southwest. Not far west of here at Mile 51.8, a 12-foot concrete arch culvert moves water from the south northward under the canal towards the Green River, which is located less than a mile to the north.

52.6 **BRIDGE #39** – A small farm road, shown as County Road 1100 East on some maps, crosses the canal on a fill to reach a number of farms and houses on the north side of the Hennepin Canal. The Hennepin Canal Parkway Trail is on the north bank to the east of the bridge, and then on the south bank to the west. Heading west, the north side towpath is used as an access road (2225 North) to reach a number of homes. The Parkway Trail on the south side of the canal is in the shade almost all day.

The canal trail uses the fill at Bridge #39 to cross the canal. Look for the signs like this that point the way. Photo by Barton Jennings.

There is a small informal parking lot and boat ramp on the north shore of the canal, just west of where Bridge #39 once stood. Bridge #39 was identical to Bridge #38 when built, and was also installed in January 1904. Just west of the parking lot, the canal turns to head west-northwest.

Maps created by the Corps of Engineers show that there was once a barn and a house to the southwest of the bridge. Today, to the south of the canal and on the west side of County Road 1100 East is a former canal house, much rebuilt. There are also several other buildings, such as a barn and small shed. Note the concrete fence posts used to fence the property. To complete the scene, there is also a Hennepin Canal State Trail sign alongside the road.

53.6　**LOCK #25** – This lock once lifted or lowered barges eight feet. Today, its gates are gone, removed in 1965 by the Corps of Engineers, and a small dam has been built at its east (upper) end. There is a small pedestrian bridge across the lock at the east end that connects to the parking area to the north along the local road. Almost immediately to the south is the Iowa Interstate Railroad's Chicago to Rock Island mainline, once the Chicago, Rock Island & Pacific Railroad that the canal was supposed to successfully compete against.

Like most of the locks, the gates are gone and a small pedestrian bridge crosses Lock #25. Photo by Barton Jennings.

There were two canal houses and at least one barn at Lock #25. The lock tender's house at Lock #25 was completed by early 1903 and was initially used "by junior engineers in charge of works in those vicinities," according to a Corps of Engineers report from the time. Housing along the canal route was scarce during the construction of the canal, an issue cited several times as making it hard to attract labor. This also made it essential that houses for the lock tenders, supervisors, and others who worked for the canal be provided by the Corps of Engineers. A later report by the Corps of Engineers seemed to contradict some of this information, as it stated that a number of lock tender's houses, overseer's houses, and patrolmen's houses were still being built in 1907 and 1908. Among these were houses at Locks #25, #26, #27, #28, and #29. However, some locks featured two houses, one for the lock tender and one for a patrolman/inspector or overseer.

At Lock #25, there was a patrol house north of the west gate, a lockkeeper's house to its west, and then a barn further west. The patrol house, according to a 1926 drawing, was a small two-bedroom, two-story house. The lockkeeper's house was a larger version designed in March 1900, with an office, kitchen, dining room, and reception room on the first floor. There were four bedrooms on the second floor, as well as a full basement. Both the patrol house and the lock house received central heat from the Rock Island Stove Company in 1926.

Heading west, the canal trail swings to the south, away from the canal, and stays close to the railroad until it reaches Lock #26. Between the trail and canal are often spoil piles, creating an embankment between the two. Much of this part of the trail passes through a replanted prairie area that is an official Illinois Nature Preserve. Note the many signs about not mowing or spraying. Along the road on the north side of the canal, which has better views of the canal through here, are several houses.

Much of the area west of Lock #25 is an official Illinois Nature Preserve, as noted by several signs like this. Photo by Barton Jennings.

Main Channel

54.6 HENRY COUNTY ROAD 235 – This road, also known as E. 900th Street, crosses the canal on a low fill, and the trail crosses the road at grade. The route carries the designation of **Bridge #40A**, but was not a bridge when the Corps of Engineers was planning the retirement of the canal. County Road 235 connects U.S. Highway 6 to the south, northward to a series of small subdivisions along the south side of the Rock River.

On both sides of the canal there are roads to the west to parking lots at Lock #26. The trail shares its route with the access road on the south bank, so watch for highway traffic.

54.7 LOCK #26 AND LIFT BRIDGE #40 – This can be a busy place, and there are parking lots on both the north and south sides of the lock. A campground with toilets is located on the south bank. When the Corps of Engineers and the State of Illinois were promoting the canal as a recreational facility, a number of promotional photos were taken here of families enjoying the canal.

Lock #26 once provided a nine-foot lift for barges. The gates are now gone and a dam has been installed on the east end of the lock. As with most of the locks, the Corps of Engineers made the changes about 1965. To the north is a former lock tender's house, now part of a private residence and much modified. Originally, there was a gambrel-roofed lockkeeper's house on the southeast corner of Lift Bridge #40, plus a barn south of the east gate of the lock. This area is now open lawn used for recreation, so the earlier promotional effort here must have worked.

This photo from the files of the Corps of Engineers, found in the Illinois State Archives, looks east at Lock #26, showing a number of features of the lock area. Bridge #40 and the lockkeeper's house both can be seen at the west gates. This photo was one of many taken to promote recreational use of the canal, and fishing appears to be popular. Illinois and Mississippi (Hennepin) Canal, "Photographic Files," Record Series 497.037, Illinois State Archives.

At the west end of Lock #26 is a vertical lift bridge, once known as **Bridge #40**. This bridge, like many others on the canal, was built in 1904 by the Pittsburg Steel Construction Company, under the supervision of Major C. S. Riche of the Army Corps of Engineers. The bridge has a plank deck eighteen feet wide, and is used by pedestrians as the Hennepin Canal Parkway Trail has a paved route on the north bank and a gravel and grassy route on the south bank west of here.

Builders plates such as this are located on the three lift bridges, including the one at Bridge #40. Photo by Barton Jennings.

Just west of Lock #26, look for the MidAmerican Energy Pipeline, easily found due to the "do not anchor or dredge" sign. MidAmerican Energy provides electricity and natural gas to customers in Iowa, Illinois and South Dakota, in addition to natural gas customers in Nebraska. Many energy users in the Quad Cities rely upon the company.

The roads that follow the canal end here. About two miles west of Lock #26, the canal turns to the northwest, leaving the railroad and crossing the Green River on what was once Aqueduct #8. Much of this area is wetland hardwood forest, with the canal at a slightly higher elevation. Note the concrete fence posts in the woods, showing how wide the canal right-of-way was in this area.

56.9 AQUEDUCT #8 – This aqueduct is gone and was replaced by a 36-inch inverted siphon during the 1960s by the Corps of Engineers. The siphon is required to allow the canal to stay watered, and takes water from one side of the Green River to the other in a controlled manner. The aqueduct was, like the others, a concrete trough set on concrete piers. With the aqueduct gone, a pedestrian bridge has been built on the north towpath. Both the north and south trails join together at the east end of the aqueduct to allow hikers, bikers, and horseback riders to use this replacement bridge.

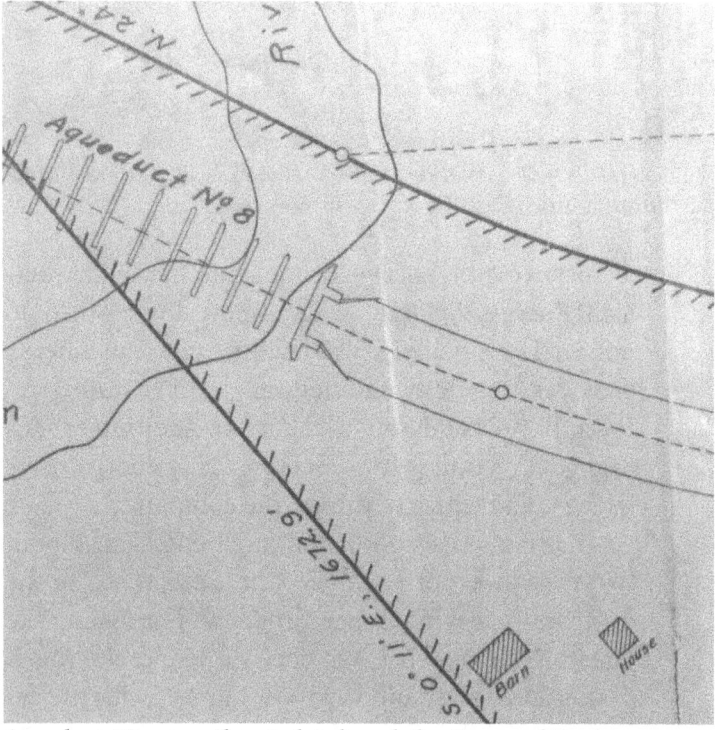

Aqueduct #8 was rather isolated, and the Corps of Engineers once had a house and barn here, located compass south of the structure, as shown in this plat of the area. Illinois and Mississippi (Hennepin) Canal, "Map, Drawing, and Plan Files, G-Q," Record Series 497.001, Illinois State Archives.

Main Channel

Aqueduct #8 was also known as the Green River Aqueduct. The Green River has closely followed the Hennepin Canal to the north. When Henry County was drained, the Green River was straightened and channelized as part of the work. The river flows a few miles further south and west before entering the Rock River south of Carbon Cliff.

57.0   LOCK #27 – This lock was once located at the west end of Aqueduct #8 and the Corps of Engineers placed full walls at the upper (east) end of the lock chamber to replace the removed gates. The east end has been incorporated in the siphon that replaced the aqueduct, while the gates on the west end have been removed. When the lock was in operation, it had a lift of eight feet.

Lock #27 serves as the west side of the siphon, required since Aqueduct #8 is gone. Because of this, the gates have been removed and the east end has been sealed with a new wall, shaped like the original miter gates. Photo by Barton Jennings.

Just west of Lock #27, the north canal embankment washed out during Spring 2019 flooding, putting a large breach in the parkway trail but leaving the horse trail on the south bank undamaged. There has been a great deal of work involved in building a levee along the Green River and restoring the farmland and embankment north of the canal.

Further west, the canal turns to the west towards Colona, Illinois. The Hennepin Canal Parkway Trail continues on the north bank, while a grassy route is available to the south.

58.1 BRIDGE #41 – The original Bridge #41 was installed in January 1904, and the 110-foot steel Pratt truss structure was built by the Chicago Bridge & Iron Company. It was replaced by this large fill, which carries Green River Road, also known as County Road 600 East, across the Hennepin Canal. There is a parking lot along the south bank of the canal. From here west, the trail is used as a community walking trail as it passes through a series of residential areas.

Many references show this area to be named Dayton Corners. Located not far north of here, Dayton was laid out in October 1836, and is considered to be one of the oldest towns in Henry County. In 1837, the first election, which created the Henry County government, was conducted at Brandenburg's Tavern in Dayton Corners. At the time, Brandenburg's Tavern was basically the area's mall with a hotel, horse stable, post office, and other businesses. A small stone monument marks its location today, and Dayton Corners is simply an unincorporated community in Henry County.

Green River

Not far to the southwest is the small unincorporated community of Green River, Illinois, located on the mainline of the former Rock Island Railroad. The community was named after the river to its north. However, the town was originally named Oakley after Charles Oakley, a local landowner who built a dam at the site in 1837. As the town grew, it was discovered that there was another Oakley, Illinois, that already had a post office. In 1889, the town was renamed Green River to avoid the name conflict. About this time, a number of coal mines operated here, including the Cable & Keator Coal Mine (1870s-1883), Campbell Coal Mine (1879-1880), Wilson Coal Mine (1879-1880), Peacock Coal Mine (1886-1894), and Woodbury Coal Mine (1898-1903).

During the late 1930s, the community of Green River was the site of the creation of the Dairy Queen chain. Actually, it was the location of the invention that made Dairy Queen possible. During the late 1930s, John Fremont (J. F.) McCullough purchased a former cheese factory near the railroad depot in Green River. McCullough and his son Alex became involved with a number of projects, including creating a machine that could make and dispense soft-serve ice cream. They also invented the various mixes that would work with the machine. The machine and mixes soon led to the creation of Dairy Queen when Sherb Noble, a customer of McCullough, served the ice cream at his Kankakee, Illinois, ice cream store. In 1940, Noble and McCullough opened the first Dairy Queen in Joliet, Illinois.

Hennepin Canal Parkway: History Through the Miles

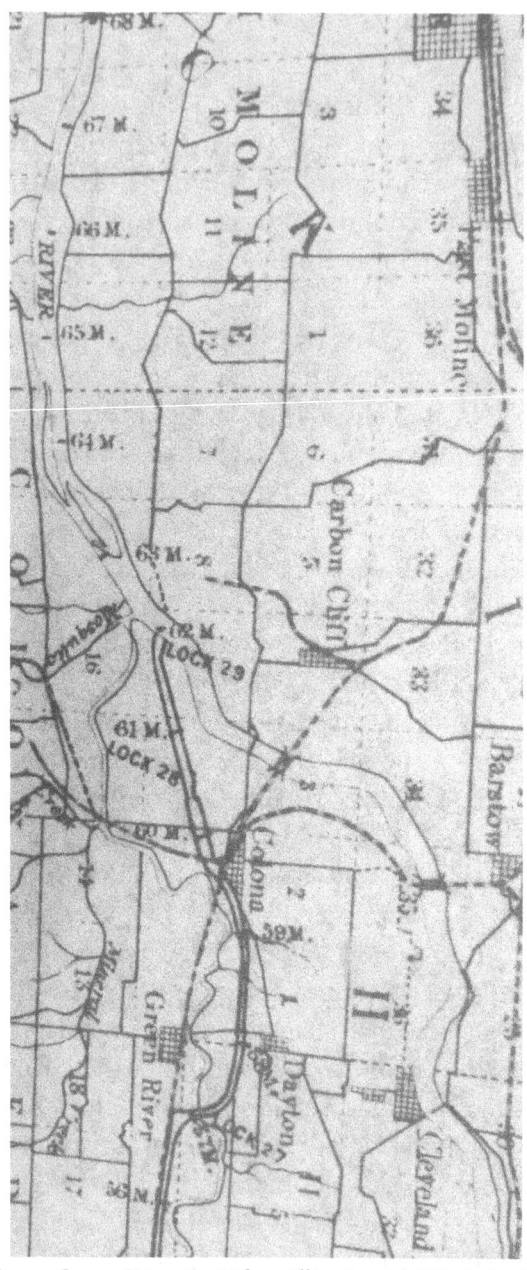

Canal Map – Green River to Milan. Illinois and Mississippi (Hennepin) Canal, "Canal Route Plat Files," Record Series 497.008, Illinois State Archives.

Main Channel

For the hiker, neither Dayton to the north, or Green River to the south, have convenience stores close by. Heading west to Colona, the canal is still lined with trees, with farms to the south and housing to the north.

58.9 INTERSTATE 80 – Some charts show this I-80 to be at Milepost 59.2, while others show it to be at 59.5. However, it is less than a mile from Bridge #41. The canal again crosses under this interstate highway, which passes around the east and north side of the Quad Cities region. The canal trail uses a concrete box culvert to pass through the highway's fill, just south of Exit 7. The canal itself is blocked by the highway grade, and the former canal channel is filled for about 600 feet.

The canal passes under Interstate 80 for the second time, and truck traffic again disturbs the peaceful experience that the canal trail provides. Photo by Barton Jennings.

The construction of I-80 created a number of issues with the canal. To the west of I-80, the Illinois Department of Transportation (DOT) lowered the elevation of the south canal embankment, allowing flood waters from the Green River to enter the canal. Additionally, the DOT installed a drainage ditch from the I-80 interchange to the north into the original Culvert #40, originally a four-foot diameter cast iron pipe located at Mile 59.0. This culvert allowed water to move under the canal to the Green River. However, the additional water flow and sediment from the highway soon blocked the culvert, breaching the north canal embankment. To correct this, the runoff was directed into the canal through a 36-inch corrugated metal pipe, adding to water level issues in the canal.

A series of projects in the 1980s were conducted to fix all of these problems. Notice where a drainage canal now enters the Hennepin Canal just west of I-80. The preserved canal was once closer to I-80, but the area had a culvert installed and the canal filled for several hundred feet to reduce the amount of water that can flow in from the elevated highway. Further to the west is a concrete spillway on the north bank that allows overflow water to enter Culvert #40.

Heading west to Lock #28, the canal turns to the west-southwest and passes through a cut which required a great deal of work to open. Just east of Lock #28, the canal turns to the southwest. In this area, the north side of the canal is residential while the south side is wooded, with the Green River less than 500 feet away to the south.

59.3 WOODRUFF STREET – Ignore the Milepost 58.9 shown on the small green location sign, as this is another location with an incorrect milepost. Woodruff Street is a local access point to the trail, and features a very unique concrete post that has been modified as a hitching post. Heading north on Woodruff Street will get you to Cleveland Road in less than two blocks. About three blocks to the east on Cleveland Road is Exit 7 of Interstate 80.

Every time the author walked the Hennepin Canal, he found something new. After walking this part of the trail several times, he finally realized that this fence post at Woodruff Street also had a ring on it so it could serve as a hitching post. Photo by Barton Jennings.

59.4 SPRING STREET – Look for the small green sign which notes this access point to the canal trail. Spring Street comes south and curves west here, becoming Warren Street. South of Warren Street is the Old Colona Park. As the road curves west, the canal turns to the southwest to pass through Lock #28 and under Railroad Bridge #5.

59.5 LOCK #28 – This lock, located in Old Colona Park, once provided a lift of eight feet. Like most other locks on the Hennepin Canal, it had its gates and machinery removed by the Corps of Engineers in 1965, and a concrete breastwall installed to maintain five feet of water upstream. This lock was originally designed to be further west, but it was moved to here so that the canal would be at a lower level, requiring less work to raise the Rock Island and Burlington railroad bridges just to the west.

Looking to the east, Lock #28 provides a quiet scene with shade and a waterfall where a small dam has replaced the east miter gates. Photo by Barton Jennings.

There was a great deal of work required in this area to build the canal. Corps of Engineers reports from 1903 stated that the "deep cut at and below Colona, and the embankments to Rock River, miles 60, 61, and 62, are being executed by hired labor and plant owned by the United States, consisting of steam shovel and railway equipment." During the previous years, several of the contractors had failed and quit work on the canal project. Much of this was due to the Panic of 1901, which is recognized as the first stock market crash on the New York Stock Exchange. This crash involved many of the who's who of the time, including Standard Oil, William Rockefeller's First National City Bank, J. P. Morgan, James J. Hill, E. H. Harriman and Jacob Schiff. All were involved in a bidding war for the Northern Pacific Railway, and when a compromise was reached, stock values dropped in many related fields. A number of banks closed, taking the money of their investors and depositors with them, preventing many firms from paying their bills. During this time, there were numerous reports of contractors having their equipment and supplies seized, preventing them from working and being paid.

Because of this, the Corps of Engineers began to supervise parts of the Hennepin Canal project, hiring their own laborers and using their own equipment. While some work was always planned to be conducted this way, much more was done than was ever planned. To house the Corps of Engineers managers, efforts were made to quickly build the lock tender and supervisor houses along the canal. By early 1903, the houses at Lock #28 were built and were being used as housing and offices by the junior engineers in charge of the canal and bridge construction projects in the area.

According to plans dated March 1902, the overseer's house featured a kitchen, dining room, living room, and office on the first floor. On the second floor were a number of bedrooms, with some used as offices or a living room during the canal's construction. Later documents from the 1920s include plans to add a heating plant to the houses.

Colona

Colona is a community created by the merger of the City of Green Rock and the Village of Colona in 1997, reportedly the first communities in Illinois to merge by popular vote. According to the Henry County Tourism Bureau, Colona was named after its founding family, Eric and Natasha Colona, and their children Abdul and Elaine. Colona is located where the Green River and Hennepin Canal flow into the Rock River.

The Hennepin Canal wanders through Colona, and a number of street signs like this one at 1st Avenue and Cleveland Road point you in the right direction. Photo by Sarah Jennings.

Today, Colona is at the east edge of the Quad Cities region, and has a population of a bit more than 5000. The Hennepin Canal Parkway Trail is a popular walking trail in this area, especially as it passes

Main Channel

through a number of residential communities and parks. The Old Colona Park features a pavilion and playground for families, as well as parking.

59.5   RAILROAD BRIDGE #5 – The canal passes under this former Chicago, Rock Island & Pacific Railroad bridge, now used by the Iowa Interstate Railroad. This Iowa Interstate line connects Chicago with Rock Island, Illinois, and then further west to Council Bluffs, Iowa.

The Iowa Interstate operates several trains a day across Railroad Bridge #5, so scenes like this are not uncommon. Photo by Barton Jennings.

A new railroad bridge was required to provide sufficient clearance for boats on the canal. Instead of doing the work itself, the Corps of Engineers contracted with the Rock Island Railroad to raise the tracks, build the new abutments, and to install the new bridge. The new bridge was built for the Corps of Engineers in 1900 by the American Bridge Company of New York, and was designed to carry two tracks. The bridge consists of a 70-foot-long through plate girder span, a popular railroad design that provides few clearance restrictions.

Just west of Railroad Bridge #5, the canal turns back to the west-southwest and heads straight to the Rock River. For almost a mile, the canal continues to pass through residential areas, lined with a series of small parks.

59.7 RAILROAD BRIDGE #6 – The Chicago, Burlington & Quincy Railroad (CB&Q), today's BNSF, bridges over the canal with this single-track 80-foot through plate girder span, opened in 1904. This is the Barstow Subdivision which connects Galesburg, Illinois, with Plum River near Savanna, Illinois. This is another bridge that had to be built for the Corps of Engineers as a part of the Hennepin Canal project. Note that the canal sign in 2019 shows this to be Railroad Bridge #5, another sign error as this is Railroad Bridge #6.

This railroad traces its history back to the Rockford, Rock Island & St. Louis Railroad, which in 1868 began building a railroad northward from Beardstown, Illinois. The Rockford, Rock Island & St. Louis Railroad was organized with a board on May 17, 1865, and construction and several line purchases followed. On October 8, 1868, the railroad purchased the St. Louis, Alton & Rock Island Railroad Company, acquiring its surveys and properties. With funding coming from multiple sources, the railroad built approximately 200 miles of track from Orion, Illinois, south to East Alton by March 1, 1870. East Alton provided connections with several railroads in the St. Louis area, while Orion provided a junction with the Rock Island & Peoria Railroad, a line between the two cities in its name.

To save their investment, many of the stock and bond holders created the St. Louis, Rock Island & Chicago Railroad Company on April 21, 1876, to acquire the Rockford, Rock Island & St. Louis Railroad Company. On May 18, 1876, the sale took place, but the railroad was quickly leased to the CB&Q on October 1, 1876. Construction northward through Colona and on to Barstow also took place that year by the new St. Louis, Rock Island & Chicago Railroad. The company was deeded to the Chicago, Burlington & Quincy on June 1, 1899, leading to the line's ownership by BNSF today.

BNSF operates a large number of trains across Railroad Bridge #6, as shown here. The Iowa Interstate and BNSF railroads cross just north of here in Colona, so if one train is moving, the other railroad likely has a train stopped nearby. Photo by Barton Jennings.

60.1 BRIDGE #42 – This bridge, originally a 110-foot steel Pratt truss structure installed in July 1904, is now long gone. Today, in this general area, there are three fills across the former Hennepin Canal. The first is used by a paved trail that follows the general route of South 3rd Street (Milepost 59.9) and connects the Hennepin Canal Parkway Trail with homes to the south. Not far to the west is the 2nd Street access point at Milepost 60.0.

The second fill is the main highway that serves as Illinois Highway 84, also known as First Avenue. The canal trail passes through the north end of this fill using a concrete box culvert. Just west of Bridge #42 is a popular local park with several pavilions, picnic tables, restrooms, parking, and other facilities. A few concrete fence posts can still be seen in the area.

Illinois Highway 84 can be busy, so look for the sign and be sure to use the concrete box culvert to pass under the highway. Photo by Barton Jennings.

The third fill is a curving fill that connects 5th and 6th Streets at Milepost 60.3. Hennepin Canal Bridge #42 was located approximately where Illinois Highway 84 now sits. The Hennepin Canal Parkway Trail crosses over from the north canal bank to the south canal bank using the 5th/6th Street fill. There is a parking lot on the northwest corner of the fill with a paved trail that connects to the Parkway Trail. There is also a nice park just west of the parking lot that includes tennis courts, a baseball field, pavilion, and a playground. Heading west, the towpath on the north bank is now used as Hennepin Drive, shown as Hennepin Canal Parkway Street on some maps.

Continuing west, the canal trail is on the south side of the canal, generally on top of an embankment in full sunshine. There are few buildings along this route and again it has the feel of being in the country. There are a number of benches along the trail, as well as several covered picnic tables.

61.3 **PICNIC TABLE** – This is one of the covered picnic tables along the trail in this area. To the north along the canal are several signs warning about the Mid-American Energy natural gas pipeline, a part of their local distribution system.

61.7 **LOCK #29** – This lock controlled movements between the Rock River and the Hennepin Canal. It provided a lift of eleven feet when it was in service. The upstream end of the lock now includes a dam, installed about 1965 when the Corps of Engineers removed the old gates and machinery. A pedestrian bridge also crosses the east end of the lock. There are the three typical signs here about the parkway trail, the canal engineering, and the anatomy of the canal. This is a very popular fishing area, and the lock is often lined with people, filling the many benches here.

The Hennepin Canal Parkway Trail uses the south towpath while a road to a large parking lot is on the north side of the canal. A boat ramp provides access to the Rock River and there is the Timbrook Field baseball field to the north. There is a large parking lot designed for vehicles with boat trailers. This area marks the end of the main channel trail.

Lock #29 was one of last locks built, starting in 1904. To the north was a lockkeeper's house, with a barn further north. These structures were located about where the right field in the ball park is today.

Lock #29 is where the canal flows into the Rock River. As seen here, it is a very popular place, with people fishing at almost all times of the day and night. Photo by Barton Jennings.

61.8 ROCK RIVER – Heading west, canal traffic entered the Rock River and used the river for more than nine miles before again using a short canal to reach the Mississippi River. Just across the Rock River is the TPC Deere Run golf course. This is the home of the annual John Deere Classic, a part of the PGA golf tour.

Rock River Pool of Hennepin Canal

The Rock River, approximately 300 miles long, starts in Fond du Lac County, Wisconsin, and wanders along the Wisconsin-Illinois border before entering the Mississippi River in the Quad Cities area, just a few miles downstream from here. Sources say that the Sauk and Fox Indians called the river "Sinnissippi", meaning "rocky waters."

The Rock River was dredged between Colona and Milan to provide a channel for boat movement as a part of the Hennepin Canal. The Corps of Engineers knew the Rock River area between Lock #29 and Lock #30 as the Rock River Pool. In the United States, the area between locks on a canal or river is known as a level or pool, since the water is held up by the lock and dam. An early plan for the canal was to use more of the Rock River to allow the canal to be located further north than its final location. There were also some suggestions that the Rock River be made navigable as far north as Wisconsin, and numerous studies were conducted by the Corps of Engineers.

The files of the Illinois State Archive are full of dredging reports about the Rock River, and several dredges owned and operated by the Corps of Engineers routinely worked the channel to keep it open. For example, in 1910-1911, the dredges *Geyser*, *Phoenix*, and *Apache* worked the Rock River Pool to keep the channel deep enough for boat traffic. Additionally, several bridges across the Rock River were impacted by the navigation plans, however, they were not numbered in the canal's series of bridges, and were not built by the Corps of Engineers.

61.8 ROCK RIVER – Heading west from Lock #29, canal traffic entered the Rock River and then used the river for almost nine miles before again using a short canal to reach the Mississippi River. Several miles of dredging, and even some blasting below Lock #29 and at the upper end of Anderson Island, occurred in 1907. Interstates 74 and 280 are generally just a short distance south of the Rock River from here to the Mississippi River.

Almost immediately to the south (west on the canal), the Green River flows into the Rock River. The Hennepin Canal and the Green River have followed each other for the past thirty miles. The Green River forms ninety miles to the northeast in northern Lee County, and flows south to Bureau County and then west to here. Much of the river has been straightened and channelized to help drain northwestern Illinois to allow farming.

Heading west, the main navigation channel of the Rock River passed south of Anderson Island and north of Indian Island. As the river turned westward, the channel was south of the Mansill Islands, several small islands that could be one island during low water levels. The channel then passed north of the Hilliers Islands, another set of small islands that at times formed one large island. The navigation channel then passed north of Clam Island and south of Sinn Island, before passing under the Moline Wagon Bridge. From there, the channel headed west, passing just north of Swanson and Vetter Islands, where there was an ice house on the south shore of the Rock River. The channel crossed to the north shoreline and passed just south of Hoskins Island before turning to the southwest to enter Lock #30.

64.3 COUNTY LINE – East of here, the Rock River serves as the county line between Henry County (to the east) and Rock Island County (to the west). However, at this location (approximately where the westbound weigh station is located on Interstate 74), the county line heads south along the fourth principal meridian. The fourth principal meridian, established and located in 1815, is the principal base line for land surveys in northwestern and west-central Illinois. In 1831, the line was extended as a base line for land surveys in Wisconsin and northeastern Minnesota.

Henry County was formed on January 13, 1825, from part of the existing Fulton County. It was named for Patrick Henry, the American Revolution spokesman who made the challenge "give me liberty, or give me death." With its county seat at Cambridge, the county's population is about 50,000. Most of the county is farmland, a profession celebrated each year at the Antique Engine & Tractor Association show in September.

Rock Island County was established by an act of the Illinois Legislature on February 9, 1831. The county was formed out of parts of Jo Davies county and named for an island located in the Mississippi River. Almost immediately, the arrival of new settlers threatened a war with the several area tribes, such as the Black Hawks and Sacs. The resulting small battles and political maneuvers basically prevented the county from being organized until 1833. George Davenport, for whom Davenport, Iowa, is named, was elected as one of the first three county commissioners. The City of Rock Island is the county seat, and the county's population is approximately 150,000.

To the north are several backwater sloughs, including from east to west, Bowles Slough, Coaltown Slough, and Greenwood Slough. Much of this land is flood plain, with little development due to the almost annual flooding.

Kiwanis Trail

Not far west of the county line is Greenvalley Park, located on the north side of the Rock River in Moline, Illinois. Here, the Kiwanis Trail starts and generally follows the Rock River westward to Ben Williamson Park. The trail is currently 6.5 miles long, but there are plans to extend it to connect into the Great River Trail, American Discovery Trail, and the Hennepin Canal State Parkway Trail in Colona. While parts of the route are trails in the woods, much of the route is down streets with no sidewalks, passing through suburban neighborhoods.

Signs for the Kiwanis Trail can be found at several of the access points. This one is located at 36th Street. Photo by Barton Jennings.

The Kiwanis Trail follows the Rock River Pool on the north bank, and starts at the Greenvalley Park in Moline, Illinois. Photo by Barton Jennings.

From Greenvalley Park, often listed as Green Valley Park, the trail heads south along 60th Street to 75th Avenue at Veterans Memorial Park, close to the Rock River. It then follows 75th Avenue and the river westward to 48th Street, turns briefly northward, and then heads west again on 55th Avenue. Part of this route is closed to vehicular traffic, and bikers must maneuver their bikes around closed gates, at least after the floods of 2019. There are several parking areas along this route, and the Old Green Valley Park, located at the west end of 75th Avenue, features a boat ramp, picnic tables, and the Quad Cities Skyraiders Model Aircraft airfield. This is also the east end of the Green Valley Nature Preserve.

Heading west, there are numerous views of the Rock River, like this one from the Veterans Memorial Park area. Photo by Barton Jennings.

The short stretch along 55th Avenue features a number of houses located along the river. A block to the west, the Kiwanis Trail actually becomes a trail as it loops through woods westward and then northward to 49th Avenue. This area includes much of the Green Valley Nature Preserve. Once at 49th Avenue, the trail turns west, again through neighborhoods without sidewalks. After a long block, the trail follows 36th Street back south to the river. It then follows North Shore Drive westward, passing under Interstate 74, and then becomes a trail to pass under 27th Street, the former Moline Wagon Bridge.

Just west of the 27th Street bridge is the Harold's Landing Park. This park features a boat ramp and dock, picnic tables, plenty of parking, and flush toilets with running water sinks. There is plenty of shade and access to the Rock River. This is a great place to stop and spend a few minutes. It should

Rock River Pool

be noted that this park was built after several local businesses experienced repeated flooding, as many as seventeen floods in seven years. The name Harold's comes from a restaurant that stood here for years, and closed in 2000. The park has been flooded a number of times, most recently in 2019.

Harolds Landing Park is an improved park with benches, restrooms, and a dock on the Rock River, a good stop while walking the Kiwanis Trail. Photo by Barton Jennings.

From here, the trail follows North Shore Drive to the North Shore Inn & Marina at 7th Street, where it turns north to 52nd Avenue. There, a newly paved route heads west and then southwest to pass under the Milan Beltway, and then a short distance further west to Ben Williamson Park. At the Milan Beltway Bridge, the Kiwanis Trail connects to a walkway on the west side of the highway bridge that crosses the Rock River. This route then connects to a trail that follows much of the Milan Section of the Hennepin Canal.

67.8 INTERSTATE 74 BRIDGE – I-74 was built between I-80 at Davenport, Iowa, and I-75 at Cincinnati, Ohio. It basically provides a 415-mile shortcut around Chicago for traffic from the Southeast to the upper Midwest. There are also a few stretches of I-74 in North Carolina. The road was built in the late 1960s and early 1970s, so the bridge was never listed in the Hennepin Canal documents.

68.0 MOLINE WAGON BRIDGE – The State of Illinois Rivers and Lakes Commission Bulletin 1, dated October 1, 1911, titled *The Conservation of Water Power in the Des Plaines and Illinois Rivers and the improvement of these rivers for navigation*, listed this bridge as a part of its description of the Hennepin Canal. Today, 27th Street stands approximately at this location.

The first bridge here was built in 1872 by four Moline businessmen. Their plan was to create a trade route that would attract business to the area. Later, there was a city-owned toll road. Newspaper articles show that the tolls were: cattle, 4 cents; hog or sheep, 2 cents; horses without riders or wagons, 5 cents; horse with rider, 10 cents; one-horse vehicle, 15 cents; and a two-horse vehicle, 20 cents.

While called the Moline Wagon Bridge by the Corps of Engineers, most other documents show it to be the Moline High Bridge, indicating that the bridge was much more than a simple wagon bridge. *The Engineering Record*, dated February 11, 1905, had a large article about "The Moline Bridge." The article stated that a new bridge was built in 1904 to replace an older county bridge, because of "the desire to utilize a stretch of the Rock River as part of the Illinois and Mississippi Canal." The federal government provided $25,000 so that a bridge could be built that would allow barges and boats to pass under. The J. G. Wagner Co. of Milwaukee, Wisconsin, known as the Milwaukee Bridge & Iron Works, was chosen as the bridge designer, but the firm was acquired by the American Bridge Company before construction was completed. The new bridge was described as a 710-foot-long riveted through steel truss that used the original bridge substructure, except for one new pier. The bridge had a deck 18 feet wide, and provided a 35-foot clearance for boats. The bridge had an interesting look to it as both ends were ramped up, meeting at a peak with the main span over the river channel. The channel span was a typical through truss, but the two approach spans (called side spans by the designers) all had truss structures both above and below the highway deck. For those interested, the three-page article provides photos and engineering drawings of the unique design.

For those wanting even more details, the March 25, 1905, issue of *The Engineering Record* had a two-page article on building the bridge. The article noted that the bridge metal was shipped to Davenport, Iowa, where it was placed on barges for movement to the construction site. The construction article stated that the bridge was built for the federal government, with Major William Louis Marshall serving as the government's supervisor.

Records show that the bridge was replaced in 1938, necessary due to the increased weight of highway vehicles. At that time, the 1904 bridge was called "rickety" and the hump-back design was considered a menace to vehicular traffic. The need for more bridge capacity also came about because U.S. Highway 6 was rerouted through Moline, using the bridge to cross the Rock River. The new bridge used steel beams and a concrete deck, as well as various Art Deco features. Most of this detail has been removed as it has been rebuilt over the years for use by 27th Street. Today, U.S. Highway 6 uses the I-74 bridge just to the east.

70.0 MILAN BELTWAY BRIDGE – The Hennepin Canal Parkway Trail connects to a parkway that crosses the Rock River on the Milan Beltway, also known as the Veterans Memorial Bridge. The walkway crosses the river to the north and then connects to the Kiwanis Trail that heads both east and west on the north bank of the river. The route west heads only a short distance to the Ben Williamson Park, a popular boat ramp and fishing area, and the home of the Backwater Gamblers Water Ski Shows. To the east, the Kiwanis Trail heads all the way to Greenvalley Park.

This bridge opened in 2006 and is a fairly typical beam-girder bridge, using steel beams with a concrete deck. The bridge is almost 1700 feet long. The trail on the south bank that connects the bridge with Lock #30 is well-paved and features benches at regular intervals, many of them dedicated to local residents. The trail primarily uses the top of the flood levee that protects Milan.

70.6 LOCK #30 – This lock allowed westbound river traffic to enter the Milan section of the Hennepin Canal, and documents stated that it had no standard lift between the canal and the Rock River. Instead, the lock's primary purpose was to protect the canal from flooding on the Rock River. This type of lock is generally known as a guard lock, as it is as high as the guard wall that protects the canal. The lock today has a low dam on the east end, holding water in a short stretch of the canal to the west. There is a large parking lot located on the south side of the lock, accessible from 14th Street NE in Milan. A number of signs explain the engineering of the canal and provide information about the canal parkway.

The paved trail over the Milan Beltway Bridge and west along the Hennepin Canal is shared with the Rock River Trail, and is a popular exercise and recreation trail in the Milan area. Numerous signs point the way. Photo by Barton Jennings.

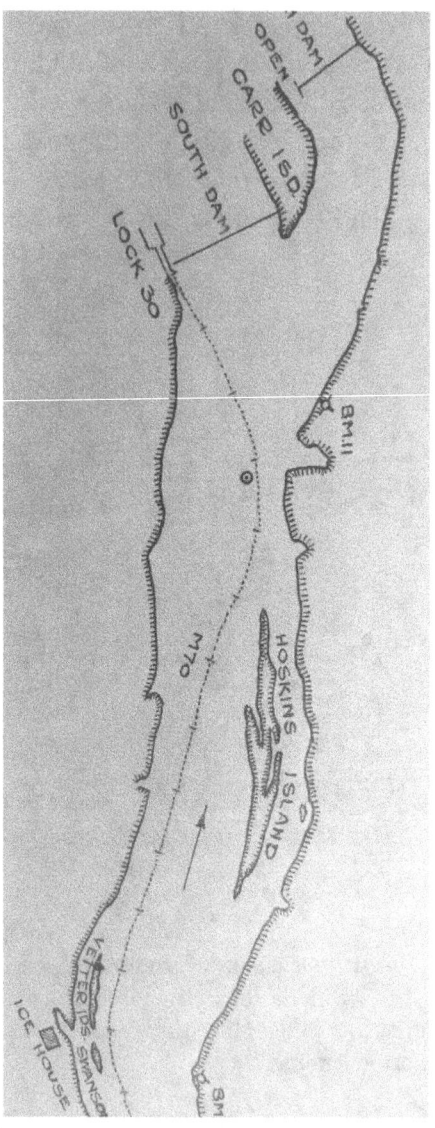

This map of the Rock River Pool shows Lock #30 and the dams to the left, Hoskins Island near the center, and the ice house at Swanson and Vetter Islands to the right. The Milan Beltway Bridge now crosses the west end of Hoskins Island, while Swanson and Vetter Islands have been filled in and connected to the south shoreline to provide land for Interstate 280. Illinois and Mississippi (Hennepin) Canal, "Map, Drawing, and Plan Files, G-Q," Record Series 497.001, Illinois State Archives.

Milan Section of Hennepin Canal

The Milan Section of the Hennepin Canal was the first part of the canal funded and built. *The River and Harbors Act of September 19, 1890*, provided $500,000 to pay for construction of about five miles of canal just above the mouth of the Rock River near Milan, Illinois. This part of the canal had priority due to the area's population and the need to move coal from mines to the east to the industries around Rock Island. Rock Island had also become the primary steamboat coaling station on the Mississippi River, and heavy coal movements were projected for this business.

Construction began on the Milan Section during July 1892, and the shovel used to turn the first dirt is today displayed at the Historical Society of Davenport. By the time work began, the Corps of Engineers had decided to use concrete for the locks instead of the traditional cut and sized stone, so the locks in this area are some of the first ever built using that construction method. According to the Illinois Department of Natural Resources and the Corps of Engineers, this part of the canal included 4.5 miles of canal, two dams 1392 feet long across the arms of the Rock River, one guard lock, two lift locks, seven sluiceways and gates, one arch culvert, one railway swing bridge, one wagon swing bridge, one pontoon bridge, three lockkeeper's houses, and one office building. It was stated that the Milan Section was designed to provide 18 feet of elevation difference between the normal water level in the Rock River pool, and the low water level on the Mississippi River for the year 1864.

Construction was reported to be complete by November 1894, and the canal was watered starting on November 29, 1894. Because winter almost immediately set in and the water froze, the canal was drained for the winter and officially opened for traffic on April 17, 1895. An interesting note from the grand opening was that a river captain in attendance commented that the canal was already out-of-date based upon the new design of ships then being built.

While it would be another decade before the main channel of the Hennepin Canal was active, by fall of 1895 coal from Central Illinois was being shipped down the Milan and Rock River sections of the canal. However, this traffic would mostly be gone by the time the entire canal was active.

A detailed Corps of Engineers report for the period of July 1, 1903, through June 30, 1904, stated that the canal was open for two hundred and thirty-two days (closed from November 21 through April 1 due to the winter freeze), but that Lock #32 was closed for twenty-one days due to flooding. During the remaining two hundred and eleven days, a total of 997 boats and barges passed through the Milan Section of the canal. The boats carried 2621 passengers and 514 tons of merchandise. The next year the canal was open for navigation two hundred and forty-seven days. 1261 boats and barges moved through the canal, hauling 10,555 tons of freight and 2310 passengers. The Corps of Engineers stated that the freight traffic volumes were up "due to the carrying of rock used by the United States in revetting the canal banks." The term revetting means to face with a layer of stone or concrete.

The lock gates on this part of the canal were rebuilt in 1910-1911, and were the subject of the article *Rebuilding Lock Gates, Milan Section of Illinois and Mississippi Canal, During Seasons of 1910-1911* by Assistant Engineer J. C. McElherne. The article provided a detailed description of the construction process and the materials used for the gates. The article stated that the lumber used in construction was oak with pine sheathing, and it was creosoted at the Milan boatyard.

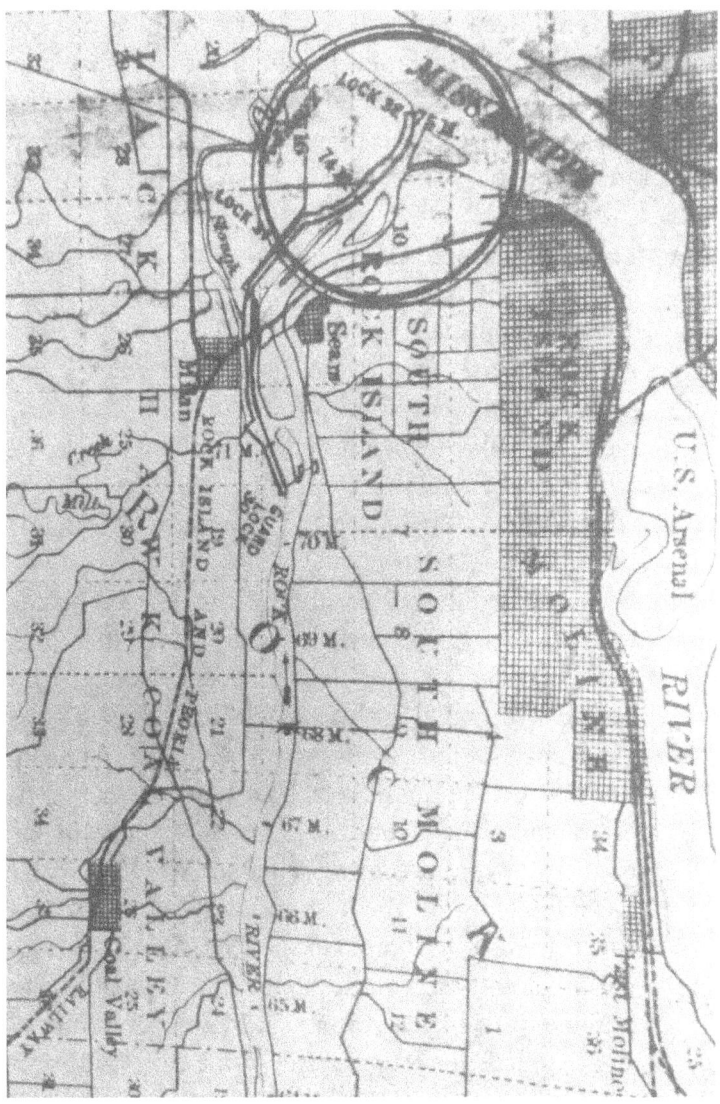

Map of the canal route from Milan to the Mississippi River. Illinois and Mississippi (Hennepin) Canal, "Canal Route Plat Files," Record Series 497.008, Illinois State Archives.

This part of the canal is not an official part of the Hennepin Canal Parkway State Park, although it is part of the original Hennepin Canal. However, much of this part of the canal is followed by a walkway, and information about the Milan Section is included for its historic importance, providing information about how to view the system. The mileages used are from the Illinois River at the very east end of the Hennepin Canal.

70.6 LOCK #30 – According to the State of Illinois Rivers and Lakes Commission Bulletin 1, dated October 1, 1911, and entitled *The Conservation of Water Power in the Des Plaines and Illinois Rivers and the improvement of these rivers for navigation*, this was Canal Lock #35. The lock number was changed when a new Feeder Canal route was chosen and fewer locks were required. Locks #36 and #37 were also renumbered as Locks #31 and #32.

This lock allowed westbound Rock River traffic to enter the Milan section of the Hennepin Canal, and documents stated that it had no standard lift between the canal and the Rock River. Instead, the lock's primary purpose was to protect the canal from flooding on the Rock River. This type of lock is generally known as a guard lock, as it is as high as the guard wall that protects the canal. The lock today has a low dam on the east end, holding water in a short stretch of the canal to the west. There is a large parking lot located on the south side of the lock, accessible from 14th Street NE in Milan. A number of signs explain the engineering of the canal and provide information about the canal parkway.

This was the first lock built, with construction starting in 1892. To supervise and operate the lock, staffing was required and they were provided a house, built in 1894 and located south of the east end of the lock. A barn was located further south. Central heat was added to the house by the Rock Island Stove Company in 1926. As recreation increased along the canal, a plan for a chain fence was produced on June 11, 1941.

The Lock #30 area is another busy location, and is popular with those fishing, walking and biking as it provides terrific access and views of the Rock River. Photo by Barton Jennings.

This old photo shows the Lock #30 area soon after the canal opened. The Tainter Gates are to the left. To the right is Lock #30, a canal house and a barn. Note the ice skaters on the canal. Illinois and Mississippi (Hennepin) Canal, "Photographic Files," Record Series 497.037, Illinois State Archives.

Hennepin Canal Parkway: History Through the Miles

The Lock #30 canal house still stood in 1936, but the trees had grown greatly. Illinois and Mississippi (Hennepin) Canal, "Photographic Files," Record Series 497.037, Illinois State Archives.

The Corps of Engineers built some nice houses along the canal, and this drawing shows the south and north elevations of the house at Lock #30. Illinois and Mississippi (Hennepin) Canal, "Map, Drawing, and Plan Files, G-Q," Record Series 497.001, Illinois State Archives.

Milan Section

To the north in the Rock River is the Milan Steel Dam, originally known as Dam #2 (Dam #1 was on the north side of Carr Island). This dam blocks the south channel of the Rock River, connecting the south shore with Carr Island. Carr Island was once a separate island just east of Vandruff Island, but with changing water levels and some fill material, the two islands are now one, but each part still carries its original name.

This low water dam is one of several that once existed on the Rock River. Several structures that were used on the old Feeder Canal to provide water for the Hennepin Canal's Milan Section also still stand. One of the structures here is a series of three Tainter Gates, used to supply water for the canal. This type of gate is described as a "type of radial arm floodgate used in dams and canal locks to control water flow." The gate has a curved face that can be swung up and down to open or close the waterway. The gate is named for Wisconsin structural engineer Jeremiah Burnham Tainter. Tainter worked for Knapp, Stout & Co., the largest lumber manufacturer in the United States in the late 1800s. He had eight patents involving dam and canal gate designs, and patented the Tainter Gate in 1886.

Fans of engineering or of old machinery will find the Tainter Gates at Lock #30 worth a visit. These gates were raised and lowered by this machine, which operated on rails on top of the feeder dam. The large rounded shields behind the machine are the actual Tainter Gates, and good views of how they operated are also possible. Photo by Barton Jennings.

At one time, Kickapoo Slough headed south from the Rock River here, and then headed west to the Mississippi River, basically an overflow route during high water. The western part of this slough still exists, although channeled in many places and used to drain water away from the west side of Milan. Signs on Illinois Highway 92 show that it is named Mill Creek, but Kickapoo Slough is the name still shown on many maps. Part of the channelized Mill Creek at Canal Milepost 71.3 uses the former route of Kickapoo Slough through downtown Milan.

QC Trails – Hennepin Canal Parkway Trail: Milan Section

This is the east end of the hiking trail along the Milan Section of the Hennepin Canal. QC (Quad Cities) Trails is an organization that promotes the use of trails in the Quad Cities area, and their website provides information about this and other regional trails. The organization states that the "scenic Milan section of the Hennepin Canal Trail follows along both sides of the canal as it runs next to the Rock River and passes by three historic locks."

The trail head and parking lot can be reached off of 14th Street NE. The paved trail follows the south side of the canal while a grassy trail, often un-mowed, is on the north side. A sign at Lock #30 states that the north trail has had its "mowing reduced to encourage wildlife nesting habitat." The paved trail features a number of benches and generally runs along the top of the Milan flood levee instead of along the old towpath. The trail is well-paved until the site of the Milan Wagon Bridge. West of there the trail is oil and chip paved until near Milepost 73.6. From there to Lock #32, the trail uses the former towpath on the north canal embankment. This part of the trail is not paved and is described as a "primitive" trail. Don't be surprised by knee-deep vegetation and a sometimes rocky trail. Bug spray is recommended.

Hennepin Canal Parkway: History Through the Miles

The paved trail along the Milan Section of the Hennepin Canal is generally located on the top of the flood levee. This provides great views and generally a breeze, but also lots of sun. Photo by Barton Jennings.

71.3 MILL CREEK – Heading west, the paved Hennepin Canal Parkway Trail follows the top of a levee on the south side of the old canal. This levee turns south to protect the area from floods on Mill Creek, and the trail loops to the south, using a bridge on Airport Road to cross the stream. The grassy trail also turns south and joins the paved route. Mill Creek drains the hills to the south of Milan, and flows into the Rock River here.

In this area, the Hennepin Canal is blocked off, allowing Mill Creek to directly flow into the Rock River. On the west side of Mill Creek, the paved trail is again on the south side of the canal while a grassy route works through the brush on the north side to near the former Rock Island Railroad bridge. This area has a unique urban feel to the south, but country to the north, as the trail passes downtown Milan.

Milan Section

72.1 MILAN WAGON BRIDGE – Today, a bridge for U.S. Highway 67 stands near this location. U.S. 67 is 1560 miles long. Its south end is at the U.S.-Mexico border at Presidio, Texas, while its north end is at Sabula, Iowa. This bridge is 700 feet long and features a 300-foot steel through arch span, built in 1948 and rehabilitated in 1985. It crosses the south channel of the Rock River between Vandruff Island and Milan.

A through arch span is probably one of the most beautiful bridge designs, and the current Milan Wagon Bridge uses that design. In 2019, the bridge was receiving a new coat of paint and some deck work, but the trail still passed under the south end. Photo by Barton Jennings.

Manufacturing of the original Milan Wagon Bridge was finished on August 22, 1894, and it was shipped on September 1, 1894. Erection of the bridge was finished by 1896 and it was located west of the current U.S. Highway 67 bridge. The approaches and turn span base in the canal are still visible. The original bridge was built by the King Bridge Company of Cleveland, Ohio. The company started in 1858 as the King Iron Bridge & Manufacturing Company of

Cleveland, Ohio, founded by Zenas King. Many of the bridges built near Cleveland came from King, and he apparently also had strong connections in the Chicago area. Many of the King bridges were used along navigable waterways, thus the bridges here. The company was not part of the new American Bridge Company, so it faced stiffer competition over the next few years. The company was managed by Zenas's sons from the 1890s until the company closed in 1922.

This early photo shows the Milan Wagon Swing Bridge, soon after it was built. Illinois and Mississippi (Hennepin) Canal, "Photographic Files," Record Series 497.037, Illinois State Archives.

The office for the turn span was to the north, located between the highway and railroad. Further to the north was the oil house, used to house the lubricants for the turn span. The highway turn span was a through truss span that carried both the road and the Tri-City Railway & Light Co. (TCR&L). The TriCity Railway was a street trolley system created in the early 1890s when a number of smaller sys-

Milan Section

tems were merged together. In 1899, the system was taken over by a local company headed by Samuel S. Davis, who is credited with bringing electricity to the area. Streetcars continued to operate across the Quad Cities region until 1936, when all the streetcar lines, except for the one using the Government Bridge, were converted to bus lines. Trolley tracks can still be seen in the pavement on the south bank of the canal.

The remains of the foundations of the Milan Wagon Bridge can still be found in the canal, including the bridge's turn span base. The rails of the long-gone Tri-City Railway & Light Company can also still be found. Photo by Barton Jennings.

The original swing bridge was replaced in 1948 by the larger bridge to the east. This became necessary when the part of the bridge north of Vandruff Island collapsed on March 18, 1946. Approximately 150 feet of the 200-foot bridge fell into the river under the load of one automobile, taking power and telephone lines with it. The driver and passenger were both rescued. Some blame was placed upon a heavy truck which had crossed minutes earlier, as well as ice jams in the river. However, the new bridge to the east was already under construction as it was recognized that the old bridge needed to be replaced.

Sears

To the north of the river was once a community named Sears. This community had a much larger impact on the Quad Cities region than its small population would indicate. David Benton Sears arrived in the Moline area in 1836 and built a dam and mill on Sylvan Slough along the Mississippi River. Mr. Sears was busy over the next decade, having platted both Rock Island and Moline. His work and development reportedly attracted John Deere to the community. After the federal government took over his Sylvan Slough property for their military complex along the river, Sears moved to the Rock River and built four dams on the river. One was here where the railroad would eventually cross the river, and Sears built a five-story flour mill on the south side of the dam and river channel by 1868. Nearby, a number of other industries developed along 1½ miles of riverfront controlled by Sears, including paper mills, sawmills, woolen mills, and a cotton mill. With this development, a town grew up known as Sears, or Searstown. Searstown was annexed by the City of Rock Island in 1915.

By 1907, most of the Sears mill complex was gone and a new project was underway. In that year, Samuel S. Davis established the Rock River Navigation and Water Power Company to build a hydroelectric dam on the Rock River. While never as large as originally planned, the S. S. Davis Water Power Company and its Sears Powerhouse was the third largest electric company of 63 waterpower dams on the Rock River in 1949. In 1958, the family heirs donated the powerhouse to Augustana College, which operated it until 1966. The powerhouse was then closed and stripped, and donated to the State of Illinois.

In 1980, Mitchell and Melba White leased the real estate and water rights from the State of Illinois through their White Hydropower Company with plans to rehabilitate the powerhouse and again produce electrical power. This was accomplished by 1985. In 2008, the City of Rock Island bought the power plant and upgraded it for local use.

72.1 CHICAGO, ROCK ISLAND & PACIFIC RAILROAD BRIDGE – The former Rock Island Railroad bridge across the Hennepin Canal has been replaced by a fill, but the bridges across the Rock River remain. The original railroad bridge was extended with the construction of the Hennepin Canal, with a turn-span bridge built in 1895 by the King Bridge Company of Cleveland, Ohio, to cross the canal. This made the new railroad bridge very similar to the road bridge to the east.

Over the years, the weight and size of freight trains increased, and about 1930, the Rock Island rebuilt its Rock River Bridge. The spans used were not new, having been manufactured in 1894 by Lassig Bridge & Iron Works of Chicago, Illinois. They had originally been part of the approaches to the Government Bridge that crossed the Mississippi River at Rock Island. This bridge was on the mainline between Chicago, Illinois, and Omaha, Nebraska, and also served the Rock Island Arsenal.

Hennepin Canal Parkway: History Through the Miles

This photo shows the Rock Island Railroad swing bridge at Milan. In the background is the local Corps of Engineers office, located north of the canal. Illinois and Mississippi (Hennepin) Canal, "Photographic Files," Record Series 497.037, Illinois State Archives.

Some of the construction drawings for the Hennepin Canal can be considered as art. This drawing shows the pivot table for the Rock Island Railroad swing bridge at Milan. Illinois and Mississippi (Hennepin) Canal, "Map, Drawing, and Plan Files, G-Q," Record Series 497.001, Illinois State Archives.

Milan Section

The rail line that crossed this bridge started life as the Rock Island & Mercer County Railroad Company, chartered on April 29, 1876, to construct a railroad "from the village of Milan, in Rock Island County and State of Illinois to Section sixteen (16) in Richland Grove Township in Mercer County in said State." This placed the end of the line at the various coal mines then developing near Sherrard and Cable, Illinois. Over the next few years, the railroad expanded to serve more coal mines, but came under the control of the Rock Island & Peoria Railway (RI&P) by the late 1890s. The Rock Island & Peoria Railway had been chartered on October 9, 1877, to build a rail line "from the City of Rock Island in the State of Illinois, to the City of Peoria in said State." On June 10, 1903, the Rock Island & Mercer County Railroad (RI&MC) was fully purchased by the Rock Island & Peoria Railway. The two railroads connected at Milan and the RI&P was able to use the tracks of the RI&MC between there and Rock Island.

The next day, June 11, 1903, the Chicago, Rock Island & Pacific bought the Rock Island & Peoria and brought both railroads into its system. However, the Rock Island wasn't interested in much of the rural line and leased the original Rock Island & Mercer County route to the Rock Island Southern (incorporated on April 25, 1905). The Rock Island Southern (RIS) was designed to be an interurban company, and it already owned the former Western Illinois Traction line from Monmouth to Galesburg.

According to the February 1, 1910, *Rock Island Lines List of Officers, Station Agents, Etc.*, the line from Rock Island to Peoria was the Peoria Line, while the former Rock Island & Mercer County west of Milan was the Sherrard Branch, even with it under lease to the Rock Island Southern. By 1910, the RIS had built a connecting line from Southern Junction southward to Monmouth to consolidate the system. As with most interurban railroads, its business declined during the middle of the 1900s. It was shut down in February 1952, and abandoned on June 30, 1952.

The former Rock Island & Peoria route was also mostly abandoned, with the route between Coal Valley (a few miles east of Milan) and Orion being removed in 1941. The route between Milan and Coal Valley remained to serve the coal mines in that area. The remaining track in the Rock Island and Milan area remained a part of the Chicago, Rock Island & Pacific until the company folded and was eventually sold to the Iowa Interstate Railroad.

Hennepin Canal Parkway Trail

The north canal trail follows the east side of the tracks to connect to the paved trail at a paved parking lot alongside Big Island Road. Identified as an official trailhead, there is parking and generally a portable toilet. Both the Illinois Department of Natural Resources and the Big Island River Conservancy District have information boards here with information about upcoming events and rules of the trail.

Heading west, the Hennepin Canal Parkway Trail stays on the levee and eventually crosses over to the north side of the canal's remains. East of here, the trail is paved asphalt or concrete. To the west, it is oil and chip. On the south side of the canal is Big Island Road, which eventually leads to Lock #32.

Milan Section

Not far west of the railroad, the flood levee and trail curves across the canal. In this area is a bench and a number of concrete structures that are a mystery to many who walk the trail. The devices are actually control gates which allow water to flow through the flood levee and into the Rock River. During major flooding, the gates can be closed and pumps used to move water into the Rock River without having flood waters back up into Milan. Photo by Barton Jennings.

73.2 **LOCK #31** – The State of Illinois Rivers and Lakes Commission called this Lock #36 in 1911. The Commission stated that the lock had a six-foot lift. Today, the lock has had its gates removed and water flows straight through the lock. There is a large parking lot to the south, with a pedestrian bridge across the lock to a covered picnic shelter. There is often a portable toilet located in the parking lot. A prairie flower garden is located on the north side of the lock, adding some color to the scene.

Lock #31, being one of the oldest locks on the Hennepin Canal, is also one that shows the most deterioration. Photo by Barton Jennings.

Just east of the lock was a pontoon bridge across the canal, replaced with a new pontoon about 1934. The concrete docks at each end are still in place, hidden in the brush. A pontoon bridge is actually a floating bridge, basically a barge, that could be floated in and out of position. As canal traffic dropped, there was less need to move the bridge.

The area to the south of the lock was once the site of a lockkeeper's house. The house was located alongside the public road directly south of the west gates of the lock. Drawings show that the house was two stories and included a covered front porch. The second floor featured four bedrooms, a store room, and several closets. The first floor included a kitchen and pantry, a dining room and sitting room, and an office directly off the front porch. The basement eventually featured a coal-fired furnace, and there were plans created for wiring the lock house for elec-

Milan Section

tricity in May 1934. There was also a barn west of the house. Much of the area was fenced and shown as a lawn by Corps of Engineers maps.

Lock #31 had lawns and gardens since almost the time of its construction, so the Pollinator Prairie Garden is very appropriate here. Photo by Barton Jennings.

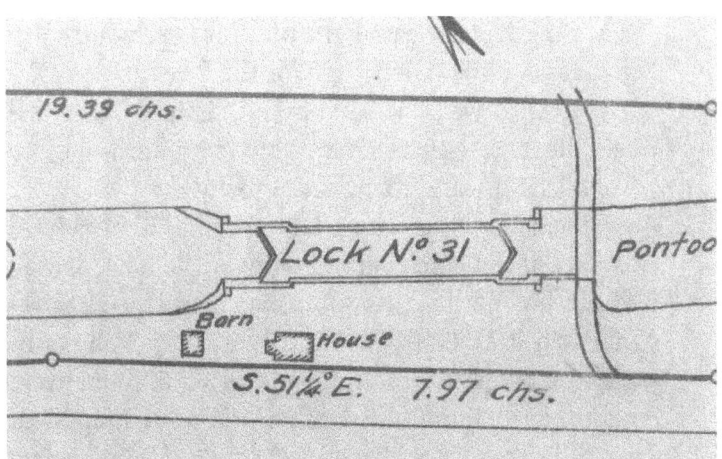

This Corps of Engineers drawing shows the layout around Lock #31 years after the canal was constructed. Note the pontoon bridge at the east end of the lock. Illinois and Mississippi (Hennepin) Canal, "Map, Drawing, and Plan Files, G-Q," Record Series 497.001, Illinois State Archives.

The land to the north of the canal, squeezed between the canal and the Rock River, is known as Indian Island, Smith's Island, and Beaver Island. The area is actually a slough area where the amount of land depends upon the water level in the Mississippi River and the Rock River. The land to the west and south is known as Big Island by many locals. This area is noted as a viewing area for water fowl, including herons, egrets, ducks and geese, and even bald eagles. Heading west, the canal was built through the previously existing Silver Lake.

Silver Lake Boat Yard

Not far west of Lock #31 was the Silver Lake Boat Yard, also known as the Milan Boat Yard. The boatyard was owned by the Corps of Engineers to build and maintain the barges and ships used on the Hennepin Canal and Mississippi River. Located on the south bank of the canal, the boatyard included a dry dock and a boat anchorage for the Rock Island District fleet. It was also used by Mississippi River vessels, plus Mississippi River buoys from Burlington to Rock Island were stored here in winter.

Silver Lake was a long lake that was channelized as part of the canal's construction. The lake, as well as the boatyard on its south bank, was used to repair and store Corps of Engineers crafts. For example, during 1909, many pieces of equipment were repaired, including towboats *Ruth*, *Mac*, *Emily* and *Fox*; dredges *Ajax*, *Apache*, *Vulcan*, *Phoenix*, *Boom Dredge* and *Geyser*; drill boats No. 6 and No. 103; plus 44 more smaller boats such as barges, quarter boats, office boats, dump scows, pontoons, and launches. They also built 8 barges and 1 houseboat

Milan Section

for the Hennepin Canal, plus 1 barge for the Vicksburg District and 3 for the Kansas City District. In the winter of 1911-1912, 76 boats, barges and pontoons were stored here.

The Milan Boat Yard was a very important Corps of Engineers facility for a few years during the early 1900s, producing work for all parts of the Mississippi River system. The boat yard featured, from west to east, a large lumber yard, a mill building, a series of stores and warehouse buildings, a boatway for moving craft in and out of the water, an ice house, and a cook house. All of the facilities were connected by a private Corps of Engineers railroad. Many of these facilities were still here during the mid-1930s.

This Corps of Engineers photo from 1936 shows how an ice house was set up to receive ice. This ice house was located at the Silver Lake Boat Yard and was owned by the Corps of Engineers. Illinois and Mississippi (Hennepin) Canal, "Photographic Files," Record Series 497.037, Illinois State Archives.

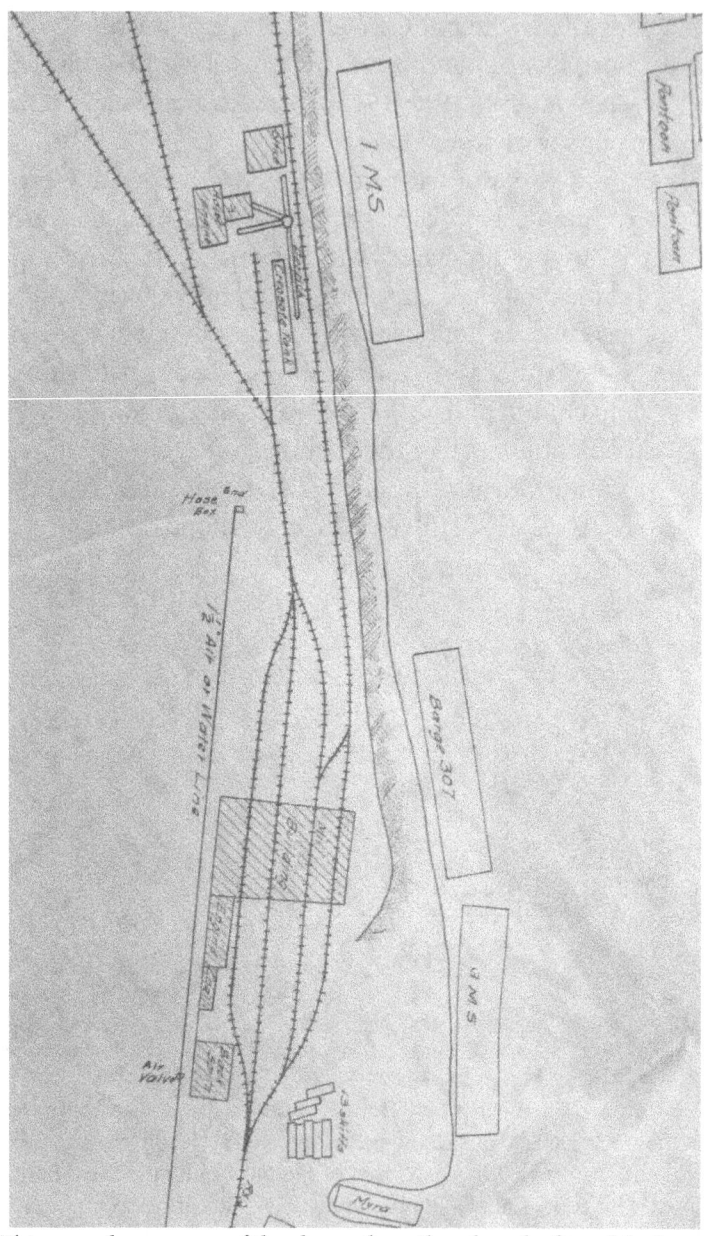

This map shows some of the shops, the railroad, and a few of the boats stored at the Milan Boat Yard during the winter of 1911-1912. Illinois and Mississippi (Hennepin) Canal, "Photographic Files," Record Series 497.037, Illinois State Archives.

Milan Section

73.5 LEVEE AND TRAILHEAD – The Hennepin Canal Parkway Trail continues to follow the river levee to the northwest before looping back to connect to a parking lot and trailhead along Big Island Road. There are a number of benches and information signs here. The levee again blocks the Hennepin Canal, which the trailhead route follows. The canal trail continues on the north side of the canal, changing from the open levee to a heavily wooded route along the north embankment's tow path. This part of the trail is not paved and is minimally maintained. However, it is some of the most interesting of the route and is certainly worth the time to walk.

These benches, signs and information boards mark the west end of the developed trail, and point the way to the "primitive" trail to Lock #32. Photo by Barton Jennings.

The canal and trail is now heading north-northwest. Just to the northwest of the trailhead parking lot is the 110-acre Rock Island Conservation Club (RICC) which has a road and trail that loops through the woods and closely follows the canal for a short distance. The RICC stocks their own lake for fishing and hosts a number of events for its members.

To follow the canal and reach Lock #32, those interested can drive 27th Street West off of Big Island Road. Heading north, the road eventually reaches the canal and then turns to the northwest to follow it to the Mississippi River. There it becomes Canal Road.

For those who want to drive to Lock #32, signs like these point the way. Photo by Sarah Jennings.

74.4 ILLINOIS HIGHWAY 92 – Approaching Highway 92, the canal curves to the northwest to follow the Rock River to the Mississippi River. The trail is through hardwood wetlands, providing an almost jungle-like experience. Because the area is not developed, birds and wildlife are commonly seen. There are also great views into the wetlands and of the Rock River to the north.

Milan Section

The last part of the canal and trail passes through wetlands, and walking the trail can provide some very unique views not normally available. Photo by Barton Jennings.

The overhead bridge serves Highway 92, also known as the Centennial Expressway. This road has been upgraded to freeway standards to help move traffic in and out of the Rock Island area. The canal trail uses the east side of the highway grade to cross to the south side of the canal. On the west side of the bridge, an access road that is often used as a trail loops to the north side of the remains of the Hennepin Canal and follows it west to Lock #32. Canal Road continues to stay on the south side. The Rock River is immediately to the north.

75.1 **LOCK #32** – The State of Illinois Rivers and Lakes Commission called this Lock #37 in 1911. This is the westernmost lock on the Hennepin Canal. It provided a twelve-foot lift and controlled the movement of boats between the canal and the Mississippi River. The east gates have been replaced by a dam to hold water in the canal. There is a large parking lot on the south side of the lock, and a pedestrian bridge across it.

The gates are gone at Lock #32, and a small dam and pedestrian bridge have been installed at the east end. Note how close the Mississippi River is to the lock. Photo by Barton Jennings.

Just north of the lock is where the Rock River also flows into the Mississippi River. This is a very scenic area with the two rivers and the heavy woods. At the west gate area, there are several sandy beaches that are popular for fishing.

Lock #32 was an important location since it was the connection to the boat traffic on the Mississippi River. There was a lock house south of the lock, with a barn to the west. A loop road came in from the east that connected with a local road to the south. Surrounding the buildings and drive were a series of lawns and gardens, with more on the north side of the lock. A powder magazine was also placed here in April 1929, designed to store explosives used to break up river ice.

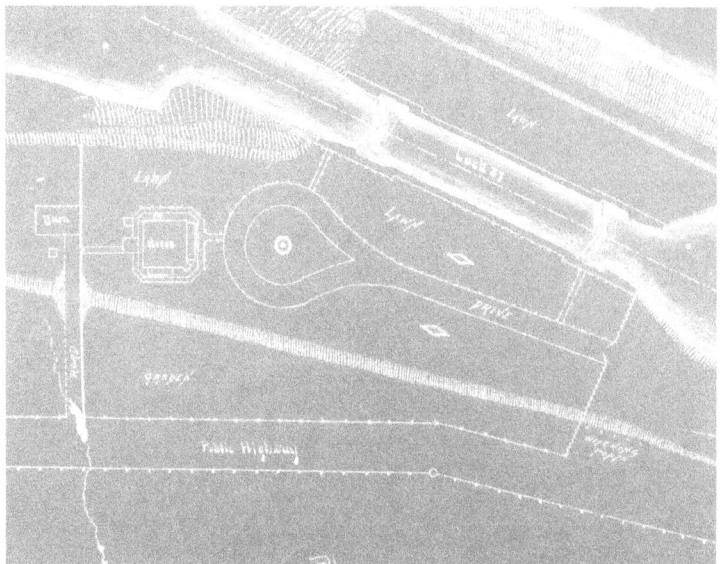

This plat shows the layout of the buildings and roads at Lock #32, known originally as Lock #37. Illinois and Mississippi (Hennepin) Canal, "Map, Drawing, and Plan Files, G-Q," Record Series 497.001, Illinois State Archives.

For visitors, the views here are wonderful, with views up and down the Mississippi River and the Rock River. There are several sandy beaches here that are commonly used for fishing or cookouts.

75.2 **MISSISSIPPI RIVER** – The Mississippi River separates Rock Island County in Illinois, and Scott County in Iowa. The Mississippi River starts in northern Minnesota and flows south to the Gulf of Mexico below New Orleans, more than 2300 miles in total length. It is the main stem of the largest American inland waterway for barge service. Even after the railroads arrived, it still was an important transportation artery. Today, the river sees regular barge service, primarily moving bulk products such as grain, fertilizers, coal, salts, and similar products. This was the goal of the Hennepin Canal, to connect Chicago with the Mississippi River, and provide a shorter waterway to the grain and other products from the northern plains.

A southbound barge tow on the Mississippi River passes Lock #32, a great example of how the Hennepin Canal was too small for modern barge traffic. Photo by Sarah Jennings.

To protect the canal, over the years the river has been lined with stone, and wooden pier protection systems were used around the lock's west gate. Most of this work has been buried or damaged by years of flooding and harsh winters, but some of it remains to be explored.

Milan Section

For those starting their walk at Lock #32, this sign points the way. Photo by Barton Jennings.

Hennepin Canal Parkway: History Through the Miles

Feeder Canal of Hennepin Canal

The Feeder Canal of the Hennepin Canal was the last part of the system built. Its design and location was changed several times before it was completed. When originally planned, its north end was to be at the Rock River at Dixon, Illinois. However, after several years of political campaigning and new surveys, it was moved to the Rock River in the Rock Falls-Sterling area. This placed the source of water for the canal at a lower elevation, which also lowered the elevation of the summit section of the Main Channel of the Hennepin Canal.

The Feeder Canal of the Hennepin Canal is well marked in Rock Falls. Photo by Sarah Jennings.

While the first half mile of the Feeder Canal was dug through solid rock, much of the Feeder Canal was built at an elevation higher than the surrounding farmland. Thanks to the new route of the canal, water drops only 2.3

feet over the 29 miles of the canal. This required a great deal of embankment work and raised bridges to get roads over the canal. Another major project was the construction of a 1335-foot-long dam across the Rock River, creating Lake Sinnissippi. Corps of Engineers reports stated that a 3-foot gauge railroad was used to build the first eight miles of the Feeder Canal, and other reports show that it was used all along the Feeder Canal.

Construction on the Hennepin Canal officially ended on October 21, 1907, and water was sent into the canal from the Rock River on October 24, 1907. It took weeks for the water to fill the canal, and more than a year for all of the leaks to seal from silt in the water. This means that the Feeder Canal was the last part of the Hennepin Canal to be built, but except for the Milan Section, was the first to be in service.

The distances shown for each location are from the Rock River at Rock Falls, Illinois. The canal, and the trail that follows it, basically runs north-south through miles of some of the richest farmland in the United States. The canal and trail is much less developed than the main channel, with fewer parking lots and facilities, partly because of the lack of canal locks. There are miles of heavily wooded right-of-way, plus a number of private fishing, camping and recreational camps. Except for the Rock River area where it is used heavily by locals, traveling over the Feeder Canal Parkway Trail can result in a quiet and private adventure. This guide is written for a walk from Rock Falls south to the main canal, following the mileposts assigned to the canal.

Feeder Canal

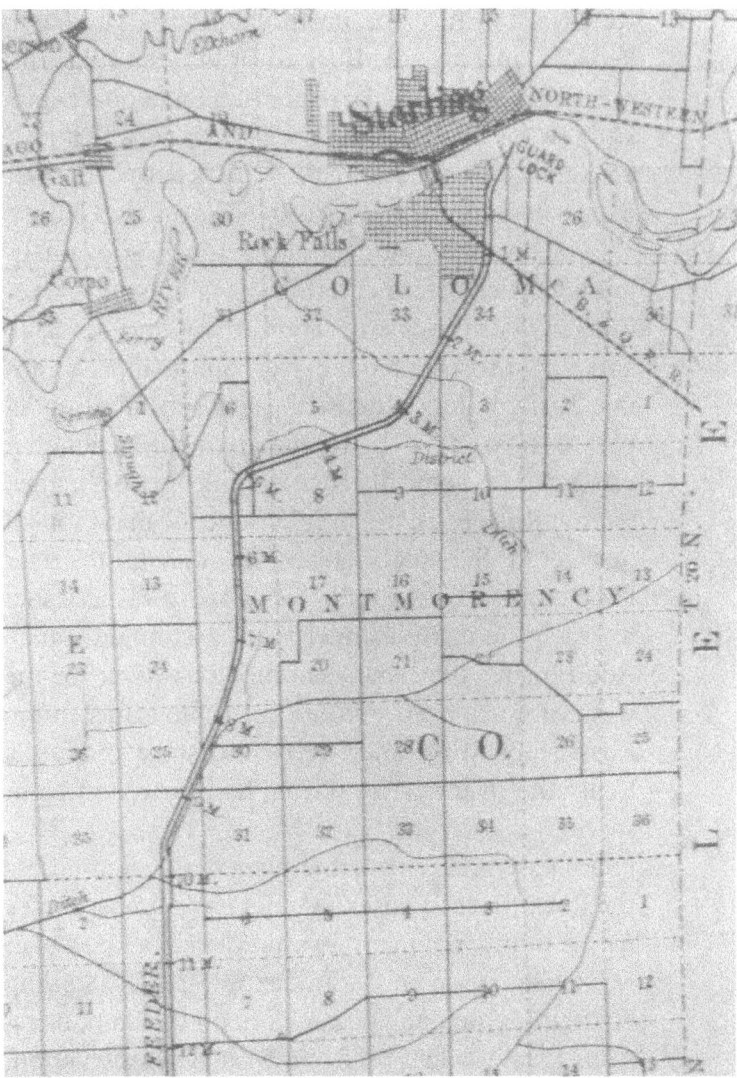

Feeder Canal Map – Rock Falls South. Illinois and Mississippi (Hennepin) Canal, "Canal Route Plat Files," Record Series 497.008, Illinois State Archives.

0.0 ROCK RIVER – The north end of the Hennepin Feeder Canal is at the Rock River in Rock Falls, Illinois. There is a park, large parking lot, a boat ramp, and several small floating docks to the east that provide great views of the area. The Rock River, approximately 300 miles long, starts in Fond du Lac County, Wisconsin, and wanders along the Wisconsin-Illinois border before entering the Mississippi River in the Quad Cities area. Sources say that the Sauk and Fox Indians called the river "Sinnissippi", meaning "rocky waters". The Rock River was an essential part of the plan for the Hennepin Canal, although it was generally some distance from the main channel. Here at Rock Falls, the river became the main source of water for the canal system. Plans were for the river to be dammed, with water sent down a feeder canal to reach the main channel of the Hennepin Canal. Additionally, the canal used the Rock River for the westernmost dozen miles of the route to get to the Mississippi River. There were also some proposals to use the river upstream from here for river freight service.

An essential part of the plan was a dam across the Rock River to raise the water level almost twelve feet. A number of plans were produced before a plan was agreed upon on December 6, 1906. The Sterling Hydraulic Company began work on the dam, using stone from the first mile of the canal's construction. The dam was completed by October 1907, and service on the Hennepin Canal began almost immediately, requiring some ice to be broken around various locks.

The Sinnissippi Dam was designed to include a hydroelectric plant, but it wasn't until 1914 that the Rock River Light & Power Company opened their

Feeder Canal

plant on the north bank. This hydroelectric power plant was decommissioned in 1955, and finally demolished in 1977. Today, the area is a small park at the north end of the walkway on the dam. On the south end of the dam is the Rock Falls Hydroelectric Power Generating Plant, owned by The City of Rock Falls Electric Department. This is a rather new facility, having been built in 1988 where a lock once existed. Today, the dam also features a pedestrian walkway, built in 2006. This trail is part of the Rock River Trail, a system of recreational trails on and along the Rock River that goes through 11 counties in Wisconsin and Illinois. The trail system was created in 2010 with the goal of promoting the recreational use of the entire Rock River system.

A pedestrian bridge has been built across the Sinnissippi Dam as part of the Rock River Trail, allowing even more of the Hennepin Canal project to be explored. Photo by Sarah Jennings.

Rock Falls

Rock Falls, Illinois, with a population of just more than 9000, sits on the south bank of the Rock River, opposite the larger community of Sterling, Illinois, with 15,000 residents. After the Black Hawk War of 1832, the Sauk and Fox Indians left the area and white settlement soon began. Reportedly, Hezekiah Brink, formerly of Indiana, was the first settler in the Sterling-Rock Falls area. Development began on the north shore of the Rock River first, and little was built on the south shore until A. P. Smith bought the rights to the water power on the south side in 1867. Smith soon platted the town of Rock Falls to support his industrial development.

Stering, located on the north bank of the Rock River, was already an industrial city when the canal was built. However, railroads already served Sterling and little business moved to the canal. Photo by Barton Jennings.

Feeder Canal

Rock Falls was always the second city when compared with Sterling, which was on the Chicago-Omaha mainline of the Chicago & North Western Railway. Therefore, the construction of the Hennepin Feeder Canal through the east side of town was considered to be a big plus for the community. Reports from the time state that the opening of the canal on October 24, 1907, resulted in one of the largest crowds and celebrations ever in the community.

The ceremony attracted thousands of people from across the region, and featured Illinois Governor Charles S. Deneen, former Minnesota Governor Samuel R. Van Sant, and Congressman Frank Orren Lowden. Grace Wheeler, the daughter of the canal's chief engineer, Captain L. L. Wheeler, had the honor of opening the gates for the first time. Following the ceremony, Rock Falls held a parade that was reportedly two and a half miles long, and it was followed by a boat parade on the canal.

For a number of years, a series of manufacturing plants operated alongside the river. Today, Rock Falls is primarily a residential community with a small business district, plus a series of parks alongside the Rock River. Almost all of the city is located west of the canal.

0.1 **BRIDGE #43** – Almost immediately after leaving the river, a boat would meet Lock #33, the only lock on the Feeder Canal, and Bridge #43, which crosses the north end of the lock. On March 26, 1909, the Sterling, Dixon & Rock Falls Packet Company signed a lease with the Corps of Engineers for a piece of property on the northeast corner of Highway Bridge #43. This property went 250 feet north, and was 115 feet deep to the east. For $5 a year, the packet company used the location as a dock and warehouse location. This property is essentially the current parking lot to the east. An attachment to the lease stated that it was cancelled on September 29, 1910.

The bridge #43 area is a busy but scenic location, with the bridge, lock, several parks, and a number of historical structures. Photo by Barton Jennings.

East 2nd Street uses the bridge to cross the lock, and it was known as **Bridge #43** by the canal. The original bridge, designed in 1906 and installed by July 1907, consisted of a 46'-6" through plate girder span over the guard lock, set on concrete piers. There were then two steel beam spans over the two Tainter Gates, also set on concrete piers. The bridge was manufactured by the American Bridge Company's Toledo Plant, through a contract with Wallace Marshall. Today, two modern concrete spans are used, one across the Guard Lock and one across the Tainter Gates.

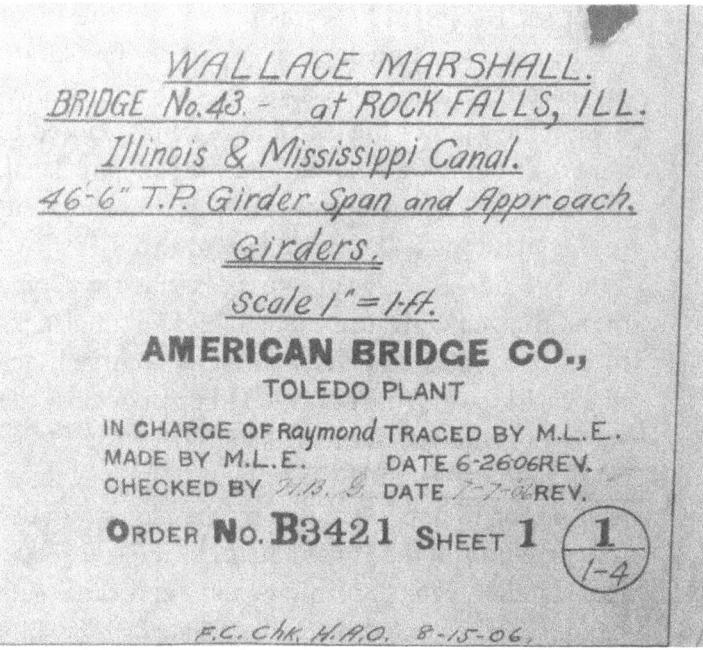

Many of the projects along the canal were contracted to one firm, which then used subcontractors for parts of the job. This blueprint shows that Bridge #43 was contracted to Wallace Marshall and his Lafayette Bridge Company, but much of the manufacturing was done by the American Bridge Company. Illinois and Mississippi (Hennepin) Canal, "Map, Drawing, and Plan Files, G-Q," Record Series 497.001, Illinois State Archives.

0.1 LOCK #33 – The water from the Rock River was essential for the canal since it was downhill to both the Mississippi and Illinois Rivers from the summit area, but the Corps of Engineers was also afraid of too much water from the Rock River. Located on the west side of the canal is Lock #33. This lock served as a guard lock, preventing flood waters from entering the canal and damaging the locks and levees along its route. The lock also allowed boats to move between the canal and the Rock River, and could hold water for slight differences in the river level and canal level. The guard lock was restored in the 1960s by the Corps of Engineers as a part of the plan to preserve the Hennepin Canal for recreational purposes. The gates of the guard lock remain closed to help control the water levels in the Hennepin Canal.

Besides the guard lock, there was a sluice adjacent to the guard lock. The sluice was controlled by two Tainter Gates. This type of gate is described as a "type of radial arm floodgate used in dams and canal locks to control water flow." The gate has a curved face that can be swung up and down to open or close the waterway. The gate is named for Wisconsin structural engineer Jeremiah Burnham Tainter. Tainter worked for Knapp, Stout & Co., the largest lumber manufacturer in the United States in the late 1800s. He had eight patents involving dam and canal gate designs, and patented the Tainter Gate in 1886. The Tainter Gates fed more than 100 cubic feet of water per second into the Hennepin Canal to maintain the original seven foot depth required for navigation.

As is typical at many locations along the line, there are three signs that explain the engineering of the canal, its impact on the area, and information about the Hennepin Canal Parkway Trail.

Structures at Lock #33

The lock area includes parking, restrooms, a lock tender's house, and other facilities. This area once included a large number of other Corps of Engineers structures and buildings, designed to operate and maintain the Feeder Canal. There was an overseer's house, a repair shop, warehouses, a railroad shop, a barge construction yard, an ice house, a grain warehouse, and many other facilities.

Feeder Canal

Located east of the lock on East 2nd Street is a **lock tender's house**, built in 1905. The lock tender's house was one of thirty built to a common design with a gambrel roof (symmetrical two-sided roof with two slopes on each side, like many barns) on a two-story house with seven rooms. The foundation measured 22 feet wide and 28 feet long. The lock tender's house has been rehabilitated, but is boarded up for protection from vandals.

A gambrel-roofed lock tender's house is located just east of Lock #33. Photo by Barton Jennings.

To the west of Lock #33 is the former office and residence of the canal Superintendent. This large house has been known by a number of different names. Construction drawings show it to be the "office and residence at the feeder guard lock," while later reports call it the "Big Government House" or the "**Superintendent's House**." Construction drawings show that the first story was built using concrete blocks, while the second floor featured wooden shingles. Drawings also show that the house was built on both floors so that the eastern half was offices while the western half was residential. The east half featured offices on both floors, while the west half featured a parlor, dining room and kitchen on the first floor, and three bedrooms, a sewing room and a bath on the second floor. There were no internal doors connecting the east and west sections by design, and a person would have to step outside to walk between the two halves of the building.

The Superintendent's House at Rock Falls is an impressive structure, and a large number of drawings were made to reflect various changes and the final design. This is a drawing of the front of the structure, with offices to the left and the residence area to the right. Illinois and Mississippi (Hennepin) Canal, "Map, Drawing, and Plan Files, G-Q," Record Series 497.001, Illinois State Archives.

Feeder Canal

Records show that central heating was installed in 1929 by the Rock Island Stove Company, which had earlier installed heating systems in a number of other canal houses. The Rock Island Stove Company dates back to 1868 when several individuals decided to manufacture stoves locally instead of bringing them from plants in New York. The firm officially became the Rock Island Stove Company when it located in that city in 1870. While it originally manufactured only stoves, it added centralized furnaces in 1911. In 1923, it began to sell enameled jacketed heaters for small homes. The firm lasted until the Depression of the 1930s.

This large and impressive building stands just west of Lock #33, and once provided both office and living space for administrators of the Hennepin Canal. Photo by Barton Jennings.

The area behind the Big Government House features several fenced spaces using the typical concrete fence posts, protecting what were once gardens and chicken houses for the families living in the house. A small tool shed and a Stevenson screen stand behind the house. For those unfamiliar with the term Stevenson screen, it is an enclosure for a weather station. The wooden box protects the meteorological instruments from precipitation and direct sun, while still allowing air to circulate freely around the weather devices. Today, this canal house is occupied by an employee of the Department of Natural Resources.

Alongside the canal trail just south of the lock is a tall white **ice house** building, set on a concrete foundation. This building clearly shows as a dark building in photos from 1908. Next to this building is a square 17' by 17' concrete building, located at the top of the concrete steps from the canal. This structure, the **pump house**, isn't an original building, but was instead built in 1909 with the installation of a 41-foot tall water tower, with a 10' by 10' tank on top. A February 4, 1909, Corps of Engineers drawing shows the plan for the tower to stand on the top of this concrete building. Plans dated April 23, 1909, show the design proposed by the U.S. Wind Engine & Pump Company of Batavia, Illinois.

Feeder Canal

This building has the traditional look of a Hennepin Canal ice house – tall and thin with small access doors at different levels. Photo by Barton Jennings.

The square concrete building just south of Lock #33 was once the base of the water tower, and housed the water pump house for the facilities of the Corps of Engineers at Rock Falls. Photo by Barton Jennings.

The U.S. Wind Engine & Pump Company was an Illinois business with a Connecticut connection. During the 1850s, windmills designed by Daniel Halladay were manufactured by the Halladay Windmill Company in Ellington, Connecticut. John Burnham, the company's general sales agent, was based in Chicago and sold windmills across the region. Halladay and Burnham got together and decided to manufacture the windmills nearer the major market of Illinois, and the first meeting of the new U. S. Wind Engine & Pump Company was held in the Chicago office of the Chicago, Burlington & Quincy Railroad on March 25, 1857. Stone buildings were built at Batavia by 1863 to house parts and to build the windmills and related devices, and by 1881, the U.S. Wind Engine & Pump Company was the largest windmill company in the world. Catalogs showed windmills, water tanks, pumps, and other related items, all sold by traveling salesmen across the Midwest. The company made Batavia the Windmill Capital of the World, and at its peak, six windmill companies operated out of the city. U.S. Wind Engine & Pump Company became a part of the Batavia Metal Products Company by the end of World War II, and windmills were made in Batavia until 1951.

Further south, but still alongside the canal, is a **warehouse** building. This one is rectangular (30'x100') and aligned along the canal. To the west are several small sheds. Further west are the backyards of neighboring homes.

Feeder Canal

Warehouses such as this one were located at a number of places alongside the Hennepin Canal. They held tools, machinery, parts, and other supplies required for the operation and maintenance of the canal. Photo by Barton Jennings.

During the construction of the Feeder Canal, there were even more facilities in this area. One of these was a three-stall **railroad engine house**. This wooden shop was located just west of the ice house, with a small yard just to its south. In 1908, photos showed at least three steam locomotives based here, all lettered for the U.S. Engineering Department. The tracks went south, dropping down to the grade of today's Parkway Trail near the warehouse.

Just to the south was a **boatyard** where barges were built. A photo from 1908 shows two barges under construction at the time. Between the boatyard and the railroad engine house were piles of parts, timber piles, rail and ties, steel beams, machinery, and almost anything else needed to build and maintain the canal, the railroad, or the boatyard. In 1908, there were also at least three buildings along the **east side of the canal**. These looked like worker's homes and docks for barges working the canal. All of these structures are now gone.

Besides the canal buildings, there were also several independent facilities here. Early reports mention a **grain warehouse** at Rock Falls. Records also indicate that Adelbert Spencer leased a "tract of land comprised within right of way of the Illinois & Mississippi Canal near Rock Falls, Illinois," on April 1, 1915. Spencer used the property for his **boat and barge operation**, and the consideration for the five-year lease was $5 per year.

The Hennepin Canal Parkway Trail

The Hennepin Canal Parkway Trail is on the west side of the Feeder Canal and is paved as far south as Bridge #46. Alongside the trail is Nims Park, a small community park. On April 15, 1947, the Coloma Township Park District leased the canal property from the U.S. Corps of Engineers at Nims Park to use for recreational purposes. The Hennepin Canal Parkway is today an important part of the series of recreational trails and parks in Rock Falls, and it is hard to walk it here without seeing others out for a walk, run or bike ride.

Along the canal, and especially near Rock Falls, are a number of benches that have been dedicated to various people. At the south end of Lock #33 is a bench dedicated to Orville and Mary Thome, both of whom were active in various events in Rock Falls. For example, Orville Thome was the Chair of the

Feeder Canal

Guidance Committee for the centennial of Rock Falls. Both Orville and Mary are buried in the former Odd Fellows Cemetery, now the Coloma Township Cemetery, across the canal to the east. The cemetery started in October 1883 when the Odd Fellows organization purchased ten acres for $125 per acre. Many of the pioneers of Coloma township are buried there.

The first mile of the Feeder Canal was dug through a low rock ridge that forced the Rock River to the north and west. According to the Corps of Engineers, an estimated 75,000 cubic feet of rock was excavated over the first mile, using a steam shovel and several narrow gauge trains of dump cars. Almost all of the rock was used for canal construction, including rip-rap in several areas where washouts were possible. Several hundred yards of stone were also crushed and used to make concrete.

0.4 **SPILLWAY** – On the west bank is a concrete spillway or flush duct that allows excess water to flow out of the canal, or to use water to clean out the culvert. There are a number of these spillways along the canal, and they play an important role in preventing the canal from washing out, or locks and embankments from being damaged. Water can flow into these spillways when the water level exceeds the canal's design. The water can also be used to flush out debris from the culvert, helping to keep it clean.

0.6 **BRIDGE #44** – Just north of this three-span concrete bridge the canal turns due south, a direction that it will follow until it again turns to the southwest at Railroad Bridge #7. The canal and Hennepin Canal Parkway Trail pass under Dixon Avenue, which heads east as County Road 16, also known as Rock Island Road. Located between 4th and 5th Streets, the original bridge, known as the Dixon Road bridge, was one of the few built while awaiting a court ruling on what standards to use in their design. The court case took more than three years and greatly delayed construction of parts of the canal as a final canal design could not be created until the standards for the bridges that crossed the canal were known. The case was dismissed in May 1903, but threats of new litigation had the Corps of Engineers recommend that no bridge work be done until the issue was fully settled.

The bridge here was originally a 98-foot steel Pratt truss built by Wallace Marshall and his Lafayette Bridge Company. It was installed in July 1901, and since it had a clearance of almost nineteen feet, and was 18 feet wide, there were no concerns that it would not meet the new proposed Illinois highway standards. Thus, it was one of the first bridges installed on the canal. Most of the rest of the bridges on the Feeder Canal weren't installed until Summer 1907.

The bridges through Rock Falls are clearly marked by their street name, so it is not easy to get lost while walking this busy part of the trail. Photo by Barton Jennings.

0.8 SPILLWAY – On the west bank is another concrete spillway that allows excess water to flow out of the canal, or can be used to clean out the culvert that passes below the canal.

1.0 RAILROAD BRIDGE #7 – The almost 100-foot-long through plate girder span above the canal and trail was once the Chicago, Burlington & Quincy Railroad (CB&Q). The Chicago facility of Lassig Bridge & Iron, a part of the American Bridge Company, supplied this bridge structure in 1900. The Lassig Bridge & Iron Company of Chicago was founded by Moritz Lassig in 1881. Lassig originally partnered with John Alden, but the partnership split in 1886. Being located in Chicago, and with Lassig providing great service to his customers, most Midwestern railroads bought his bridges. The business boomed during the 1890s, making it a target for acquisition by the recently created American Bridge Company. In May 1900, Lassig sold his company, and the Chicago Lassig plant was used by the American Bridge Company until early 1902.

This bridge was built for the Corps of Engineers, while the railroad was built as the Chicago & Rock River Railroad, chartered on March 21, 1869. Construction started between Shabbona and Rock Falls during July 1870. When completed, the line was immediately leased to the Chicago, Burlington & Quincy Railroad Company on October 9, 1872. Train service over the line began a week later on October 16th. In 1884, a bridge across the Rock River was completed, located where the new hotel now stands on East 2nd Street. The line became fully a part of the CB&Q on June 1, 1899. The line began to be abandoned during the 1930s, and the last part was abandoned by the 1980s. The abandoned grade is being turned into a trail and there are several informal trails that connect the canal trail with this rail-trail.

While abandoned, Railroad Bridge #7 is well maintained and is also used as part of another trail system. Photo by Barton Jennings.

Not many of the bridges still have their builders plate, but Railroad Bridge #7 still displays its American Bridge Company plate with a date of 1900 clearly visible on it. Photo by Barton Jennings.

Feeder Canal

To the southwest is the traditional Whiteside Grain & Storage facility. This grain elevator sits where it could use either rail or water for grain movements. A 1912 property map showed that the land that the elevator sits on was owned by the CB&Q. The foundation of the old railroad roundhouse can be found just south of the elevator.

Near the canal is the traditional Whiteside Grain & Storage facility, a landmark for decades that was found at the junction of the Hennepin Canal and the Chicago, Burlington & Quincy Railroad at Rock Falls. Photo by Barton Jennings.

Alongside the canal was a tract about 400 feet long and 100 feet deep that was leased to J. L. McKinney on April 1, 1938. Unfortunately, few of the leases stated the planned use for the property. However, in the January 27, 1946, issue of *The Observer* of Rockford, Illinois, there was an advertisement for Mac's Garden Shop, "The Seediest Place in Town." J. L. McKinney was listed as the proprietor.

Hennepin Canal Parkway: History Through the Miles

1.1 BRIDGE #44B – The canal and trail pass under Eleventh Street, another three-span concrete bridge. Signs identify the road as Industrial Road. There are connecting trails up to the street because the Parkway Trail is a popular local walking trail. The 1912 Whiteside County map by George A. Ogle and Company shows that Tenth Street bridged across the canal, but that there was no Eleventh Street at the time.

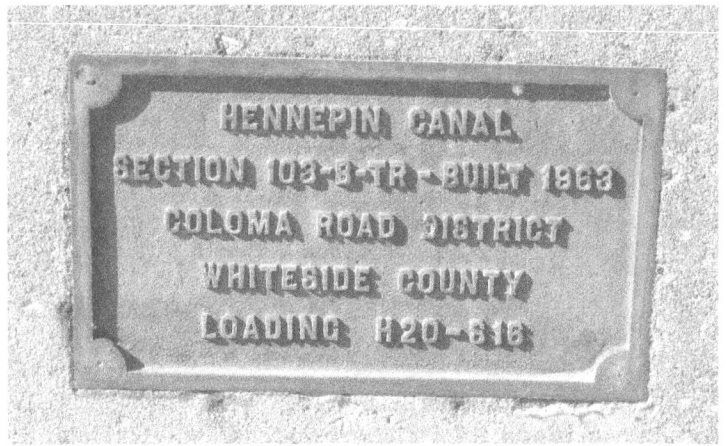

This plate on Bridge #44B clearly states that it was built to cross the Hennepin Canal in 1963. Photo by Barton Jennings.

Heading south, there is the Linda (McGonigle) Wiederaenders bench, and then the Parkway Trail passes next to Centennial Park, named for Rock Falls' 100th anniversary. The park covers 50 acres and is the largest and most developed of the Rock Falls parks. The park includes a lake with paddleboats, three baseball diamonds, concessions, restrooms, a restored schoolhouse, and a Rock Island Railroad caboose. There are several pathways that connect the canal with Centennial Park.

Feeder Canal

Toward the south end of the park is the Ralph (Tom) Zigler bench.

1.7   **BRIDGE #44A** – The Hennepin Canal and trail passes under East Rock Falls Road, also designated as U.S. Highway 30, the Lincoln Highway. The Lincoln Highway was one of the first transcontinental roadways designed for cars. Built from Times Square in New York City, to Lincoln Park in San Francisco, the planning started in 1912 and the roadway was formally dedicated on October 31, 1913. The Lincoln Highway, often known as "The Main Street Across America," was the first national memorial to President Abraham Lincoln. Its success attracted interest in other roadways, helping to create a boom in road construction.

This bridge was not an original part of the canal, thus the designation of Bridge #44A. The milepost of 2.0 is assigned to the bridge, but mileposts along the canal show it to be about Milepost 1.7. Corps of Engineers records show that the bridge was installed in November 1939. It was 227 feet long and consisted of three steel girder and concrete spans. The span over the canal was 100 feet long.

Not far south of Highway 30, located at the Milepost 2.0 sign, is another bench where you can sit and relax alongside the canal. This one is labeled as having been installed by the Rock River Development Authority (RRDA) and Jedi Amusement, a local toy store. The RRDA was established in September of 1984 as a group of local volunteers under the sponsorship of Blackhawk Hills Resource Conservation and Development. Their basic mission is to enhance and preserve the recreational areas in and around the Rock River and Hennepin Canal Feeder. Members of the RRDA help to maintain the Hennepin Canal parkway by cleaning up litter, removing graffiti, and sponsoring various projects.

2.2 **BRIDGE #45** – This major new bridge carries north-south running Illinois Highway 40 across the canal and trail. The roadway has its south end at Interstate 74 in East Peoria, and its north end is at Illinois Route 78 at Mt. Carroll, Illinois. This bridge has always been an important one on the canal and saw many early improvements. For example, the original concrete block floor was removed in 1915, and the bridge received a solid concrete floor. It was one of a dozen canal bridges that received a solid concrete deck that year.

With the construction of a new Bridge #45, the trail has been paved and changed to loop under the bridge right at water level. Photo by Barton Jennings.

Feeder Canal

The bridge was installed in October 1907, and was described as a 98-foot steel Pratt truss with two steel beam extensions, measuring 152 feet in total length. It was manufactured by the American Bridge Company. The bridge seemed to be a problem location for the canal, and there were several truck wrecks that involved the bridge. On January 1, 1944, a Keeshin Motor Express Company vehicle wrecked and damaged the bridge enough that the Corps of Engineers had to immediately make repairs. In March 1957, a Chillicothe Cartage truck went off the bridge approach and into the canal while hauling a trailer of flammable liquids.

This Corps of Engineers photo from March 11, 1957, documents the Chillicothe Cartage truck wreck at Bridge #45. It also provides details about the design of the bridges on the Feeder Canal. Illinois and Mississippi (Hennepin) Canal, "Photographic Files," Record Series 497.037, Illinois State Archives.

Today, there is a large parking lot, boat ramp, and several information signs to the west of the canal, and a small parking lot to the east. Because of this, the trail in this area is often busy on weekends and during good weather. Heading south, the trail passes the Floyd and Evelyn Royer bench, through some heavy woods, and then through a right-of-way that is heavily tree-lined. The trail is still paved in this area.

At Bridge #45 is a typical canal park with automobile parking, benches, information signs, and other facilities. Because of its location on Illinois Highway 40, it is often very busy. Photo by Barton Jennings.

2.5 UNION DRAINAGE DITCH – Look for the concrete spillway and flush duct on the east bank of the Hennepin Canal. This ditch passes under the canal and flows to the northwest, eventually entering the Rock River.

Heading south, there is another Rock River Development Authority (RRDA) and Jedi Amusement bench, this time with "amusement" misspelled as "amusment."

Feeder Canal

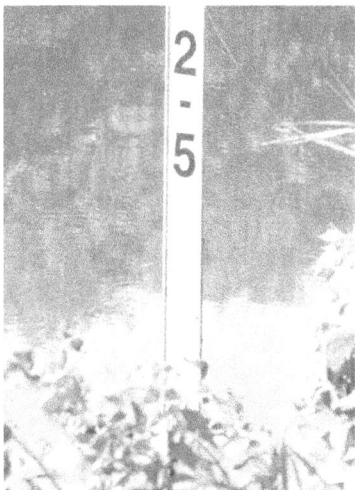

The north end of the Feeder Canal is marked with yellow mileposts like this one at the Union Drainage Ditch. Photo by Barton Jennings.

2.8   BRIDGE #45A – The canal passes under Interstate 88 just west of Exit 41. Interstate 88 is mostly a toll road, managed by the Illinois State Toll Highway Authority. The road is promoted as the Chicago to Kansas City Expressway, Illinois Highway 110, and is marked with special "CKC" signs.

This road began as Illinois Highway 190, and then Illinois Highway 5, stretching from Interstate 80 near Silvis, Illinois, to I-290 and I-294 in Hillside, near Chicago. By the 1980s, Illinois 5 was built to Interstate Highway standards, but was still a state highway. The National Maximum Speed Law (NMSL) enacted in 1974 restricted speeds on roads, but allowed 65 mph on rural Interstate Highways. To raise the speed limit on this road, the Illinois Department of Transportation and Illinois State Toll Highway Authority petitioned the American Association of State Highway and Transportation Officials to make the highway an Interstate, which was done in 1987.

Heading south, the Hennepin Canal right-of-way is lined with trees as the canal passes through field after field, generally growing corn or soybeans. The canal turns to the west-southwest just south of I-88.

3.6 **BRIDGE #46** – Bridges #46 through #50 were identical when the canal was built. They were all 98-foot steel Pratt truss bridges, installed in June 1907. The American Bridge Company produced them. However, they have all been replaced by earthen fills and culverts.

The canal is heading southwest at this location, and north-south Buell Road crosses the canal on a high fill. The Hennepin Canal Parkway Trail passes through the fill using a large culvert underpass, and the waterway passes through in a twelve-foot culvert, a standard for the canal today.

This is the south end of the paved urban trail. South of here, the trail is a mix of small stone and dirt. Heading south, the canal flows through farmland, but north of here the surroundings are more urban, with some new suburbs. Because of the number of local residents using the trail north of here, there is a picnic table and the Homer and Lois Ellis bench. There is also a parking lot along the trail at the north end of the Buell Road fill. Buell Road connects directly to the residential areas on the west side of Rock Falls, located several miles to the north, and a large residential area about a mile to the south.

4.9 **BRIDGE #47** – Riverdale Road is another north-south road which crosses the canal using a high fill. There is a small parking lot to the north. Just to the west of the bridge, the canal turns back to the south.

Feeder Canal

This bridge was originally a 98-foot Pratt truss span. It had a 16-foot-wide concrete deck, larger than the Pratt truss spans built on the eastern end of the canal due to the newer highway standards in effect at the time of its construction.

Riverdale Road crosses over the canal trail and its identification sign is mounted on the highway's guard rail above the trail's culvert. Photo by Barton Jennings.

5.1   CULVERT #2 – This is a concrete spillway on the east bank of the canal, designed to release flood waters into a small channelized stream that flows under the canal and then northwest to the Rock River. These flush ducts or spillways were not an initial design for the canal, but were soon included as the experience of operating the Milan Section was used to make design changes for the rest of the canal. These flush ducts could be used to flush debris out of the culverts below the canal, and were built with either a lift gate or sluice gate to control the water flow.

Just south of this culvert is a 700-foot long turnout, with the widened canal channel cut to the east. When built, there were not many turnouts or turning basins on the Feeder Canal, but when grain traffic began to move, the Corps of Engineers added some of these design features to the route. Heading on south, the canal continues to turn until it is heading south.

Many of the features of the Hennepin Canal are slowly disappearing or becoming invisible as time passes. This flush basin is a good example as trees and brush slowly cover the spillway. Photo by Barton Jennings.

5.5   BRIDGE #48 – Another fill across the canal carries Knief Road. A small parking lot is available on the east bank. The Hennepin Canal Parkway Trail again passes through the fill using a large culvert. There are several small farms and a number of houses to the east, and this area has developed as a series of rural subdivisions for people who work in nearby cities.

Just north of Knief Road is the Trisha M. Reitzel bench, which provides a nice shady spot to sit on warm afternoons. Heading south, the three miles to the next bridge is one of the longer stretches of the canal without public access.

Feeder Canal

6.0 MAGELLAN PETROLEUM PIPELINE – Look for the opening in the woods and the pipeline warning signs on both sides of the canal. This pipeline handles finished petroleum products like gasoline and diesel fuels. The east end of the canal is at several petroleum refiners in the Chicago area.

7.3 SPILLWAY – Look for the fenced spillway and flush duct on the west bank of the Hennepin Canal, next to the trail. This spillway, which still has its steel Tainter Gate, sends water into a drainage canal to the east which connects with Coon Creek. Just north of this spillway, the canal makes a small turn to the south-southwest. The woods are thick in this area, covering all of the canal's property, and there is plenty of afternoon shade.

Old and New. At Milepost 8.2, several old telephone poles still stand as the canal passes under a modern electrical transmission line. Photo by Barton Jennings.

8.5 BRIDGE #49 – The canal has turned to the south-southwest and Ridge Road crosses it at an angle, using a large fill. Water passes through the fill using a large culvert, while the trail crosses the north end of the fill at grade. There are parking areas on both sides of the canal. Ridge Road runs north-south and serves as the boundary between Montmorency Township to the east, and Hume Township to the west.

Large steel culverts like this one at Bridge #49 were used on many of the new fills on the Feeder Canal to allow water to flow through the system. They are large enough for small boats and recreational craft to move through them. Photo by Barton Jennings.

This bridge was, like Bridge #47, originally a 98-foot Pratt truss span. It had a 16-foot-wide concrete deck, larger than the Pratt truss spans built on the eastern end of the canal due to the newer highway standards in effect at the time of its construction. The book *History of Whiteside County*, written by Davis in 1907, described these bridges. It stated that the "common roads through Montmorency and Hume cross the feeder of the Hennepin canal by

Feeder Canal

means of high steel bridges, approached by long embankments. They are visible afar, and make graceful landmarks."

Just east of the canal is Coon Creek, whose own channel closely follows the Hennepin Canal in this area. Coon Creek forms from a series of small farm creeks to the northwest.

8.9 **BRIDGE #50** – Illinois Highway 172, Star Road, bridges across the Hennepin Canal and trail, using a modern beam and concrete bridge. This was originally the southern-most 98-foot Pratt truss span bridge built on the Feeder Canal. Illinois 172 is part of the Ronald Reagan Trail, but is only a dozen miles long, connecting Illinois 40 and Illinois 92 via Tampico. There is a parking lot north of the bridge on the west side of the canal, where there are also toilets.

Bridge #50 is still a bridge, although the original Pratt truss span has been replaced. On this summer day, park employees were working to repair some flood damaged trail under the bridge. Photo by Barton Jennings.

There is some conflict about when the first grain moved on the canal. Some reports state that the Sterling, Dixon & Rock Falls Packet Company started moving grain in early 1909 from this area. Others state that the first grain shipment on the Illinois & Mississippi Canal was loaded and shipped from here in early October 1909. The move was reportedly made from the Smith-Hippen elevator using their own fleet of boats, moving about 10,000 bushels of corn and 3000 bushels of oats. In November, the steamer *Niagara* and the barge *Red Wing* moved 12,000 bushels of oats and corn to Pekin, reportedly to be moved further east by rail. According to the Corps of Engineers, this and other elevators were built on canal property, initially leased for five dollars an acre per year. Note the moon-shaped boat turning basin cut out of the east bank not far south of Bridge #50. This basin was built when the grain elevator opened and was not part of the canal's original plan.

Smith-Hippen Elevator

Records of the Corps of Engineers state that a Smith-Hippen wooden grain elevator once stood here on the east bank, just south of Bridge #50. As with most of the elevators along the canal, the ownership changed, with the Turner-Hudnut Company acquiring Smith-Hippen in 1927. A May 1, 1934, lease showed that Turner-Hudnut was still running the elevator. By 1939, Turner-Hudnut was acquired by W. W. Dewey & Sons, Inc., and a May 1939 lease of the property was made in the Dewey name.

An interesting feature of this business is that grain, especially corn, dominated the freight move-

Feeder Canal

ments on the Hennepin Canal for decades, and most of it moved off of the Feeder Canal and not the main channel. For example, in 1929, the year of the highest tonnage ever moved on the canal, grain made up 99% of the eastbound tonnage, while gravel was 99% of the westbound tonnage.

Not far south of here, the canal again turns to the south. This location is at the border between Hume Township and Tampico Township.

9.9 COON CREEK – Coon Creek, which has been closely following the Hennepin Canal to the east since north of Bridge #49, passes under the canal and heads west. Eventually, it enters the Rock River at Prophetstown, Illinois, the location of Prophetstown State Park. Coon Creek also has the name County Ditch #1. The culvert features a drain system for overflow canal waters on the east bank.

On the east bank of the canal is another flush basin and spillway. Many of the culverts under the feeder canal in this area feature a flush basin. Photo by Barton Jennings.

10.3 SOUTH FORK DITCH – This drainage canal drains the fields to the east, passes under the Hennepin Canal, and then flows to the west into Coon Creek. There is a flush basin drain system for overflow canal waters on the east bank.

11.7 BRANCH DITCH – This is another drainage ditch that drains the land to the east. It flows under the canal here and then heads northwest to flow into Coon Creek. The spillway culvert on the east bank features a drain system for overflow canal waters. Not far north of the Branch Ditch, the canal is located on an elevated fill above the surrounding farmland.

12.0 BRIDGE #51 – Fargo Road crosses the Hennepin Canal using a low fill, and the trail crosses the roadway at grade. There is a small parking area on the west side of the canal, north of Fargo Road. Next to the parking lot is the Lori (Boostrom) Marcom bench.

Bridges #51 through #64 were all manufactured by the American Bridge Company's Toledo Plant in 1906, under contract with Wallace Marshall. They were all 75-foot Warren lattice pony truss spans with two 21-foot I-beam approach spans. This was the most common bridge type built on the Feeder Canal, but Bridge #51 was one with a rare concrete deck (only five were built that way). A pony truss has no top like a normal through truss bridge, and the sides are connected only below the bridge deck. The Warren truss consists of a top and bottom longitudinal member connected by angled cross-members. From the side, the bridge looks like a number of triangles all connected together. The design was patented in 1848 by its designers James Warren and Willoughby Theobald Monzani.

Bridges #51 through #64 were some of the last bridges designed and built on the canal, with most being installed in June 1907. This was due to the change in road designs that was occurring during the early 1900s. The Corps of Engineers faced many legal challenges, and they had to change their designs several times. Two of the changes required included the roadway width and the approach grade to the bridges. One of the results was a lowering of the bridges, which then created problems for boat traffic on the canal. Some of these bridges had to be raised so that grain could move on the Feeder Canal.

Just south of Bridge #51 is an NGL pipeline, operated by Enterprise Products. NGL products are Natural Gas Liquids such as ethane, propane, normal butane, isobutane and natural gasoline, and are used for manufacturing by the petrochemical industry, by refineries in the production of motor gasoline, and by industrial and residential consumers as fuel.

12.5 **SPILLWAY** – A concrete spillway and flush basin are on the east bank of the canal. Water flows into a small drainage canal that follows the canal to the east and passes under the feeder canal at this location.

Hennepin Canal Parkway: History Through the Miles

The spillway and flush basin at Milepost 12.5 still feature the original steel gate and the chain that was once used to raise and lower it, quite unique for the canal. Photo by Barton Jennings.

13.0   BRIDGE #52 – The canal is crossed by a large fill that carries Hahnaman Road, also known as County Road 12. The Hennepin Canal Parkway Trail passes through the west end of the fill near a parking area. The original bridge was a 75-foot-long Warren pony truss span with two 21-foot I-beam approach spans and a concrete deck.

This crossing of the canal was an important one as Hahnaman Road crossed much of the county and connected a number of small communities to Tampico. Not far to the west of the canal was the Maple Hill School, located on the southeast corner of Hahnaman and Luther Roads. The school building still stands and is used as a home.

The *Tampico Tornado* newspaper had a number of reports about the construction of the Feeder Canal. Several of them were about the railroad that the Corps of Engineers built as part of the construction project. The May 24, 1902, issue stated that the "nar-

Feeder Canal

row gage railroad along the tow path of the canal was completed this week as far as the railroad bridge east of here. This makes a continuous railroad line from Rock Falls to Tampico, but as it does not carry passengers or freight....the road is used exclusively to haul crushed rock to riprap the banks." The railroad didn't last long as an article in the December 11, 1903, issue stated that the tracks had been removed that week, brought to Tampico, and shipped to the "company headquarters."

13.4 **RAILROAD BRIDGE #8** – Above the canal and trail is an abandoned through plate girder bridge that was once part of the Chicago, Burlington & Quincy Railroad (CB&Q). It was built for the Corps of Engineers by the King Bridge Company of Cleveland, Ohio, as a part of the canal project. The bridge was sometimes referred to as the Hennepin Feeder Canal CB&Q Bridge #2. The length of the bridge is 100 feet and it crosses the canal at a slight angle. Just to the south of the bridge the Hennepin Canal makes an S-curve to the west.

This rail line started as a planned route from Joliet to the Mississippi River. The planning used several names, including the Illinois Grand Trunk; the Camanche, Albany & Mendota Rail Road; and the Joliet & Terre Haute Railroad. However, none of these built any track. A second Illinois Grand Trunk was incorporated on February 28, 1867, using the assets of the earlier railroads. Some construction took place, and the CB&Q leased the railroad during October 1870. A line from Mendota to Prophetstown, both in Illinois, opened on May 14, 1871. Over the next several years, the railroad was expanded. The route generally stayed rural in nature, although it had a connection to the CB&Q mainline at Mendota. Burlington Northern abandoned the line from Mendota to Tampico and on to Prophetstown in 1985. Little remains of the railroad except the bridge, a grade at the Rock River Lumber & Grain facility immediately to the west, and a wide path through Tampico.

Looking at this photo of Railroad Bridge #8, taken in 1936, it is hard to imagine that it is the same bridge that stands abandoned today. When the canal was in operation, the right-of-way was kept clean and mowed. Today, this area is in the middle of woods and this photo would be impossible to take. Illinois and Mississippi (Hennepin) Canal, "Photographic Files," Record Series 497.037, Illinois State Archives.

Feeder Canal

Railroad Bridge #8 was last used in 1985, and the vegetation has grown up so much around it that it is hard to see from almost any angle. Photo by Barton Jennings.

Tampico

Less than two miles to the northwest is Tampico, the birthplace of President Ronald Reagan, born on February 6, 1911. Before the surrounding area was drained, this was a slough. The first white settlers arrived in 1852, and the Tampico Township was created in 1861. In that year, John W. Glassburn bought 160 acres of land in the area. The railroad arrived in 1871, creating a small population boost. The Tampico post office was established the same year on September 1st. In response, the CB&Q built a station on Glassburn's farm in 1872 and Glassburn platted his entire farm as Tampico, with the community officially organized as a village on July 1, 1872. The weekly *Tampico Tornado* newspaper was established with some humor on May 4, 1876.

The town had a rough start, burning in 1872, 1874, and 1876. Much of the town was also destroyed by a tornado in 1874, which helped set some of the fires. However, Tampico survived and became a farm center for the area. Tampico was also a livestock center for the railroad. The railroad company had a large stockyard here, giving one street the name Pig Alley.

The Tampico Farmer Shipping Association reported that in 1928, $253,201.32 was paid to the owners of livestock shipped from Tampico. In 1928, the railroad handled 10,034 hogs, 378 head of cattle, 532 calves and 174 sheep, requiring 153 railroad stock cars to handle the moves, about the average number of shipments for the seven previous years. Unfortunately for the canal, none of this freight moved by water.

The railroad is no longer in service or even exists at Tampico, but the town still serves surrounding farmers with a post office, banks, stores and more. Today, the downtown area is the Tampico Main Street Historic District. Included in this historic district are two apartments that the Reagan family occupied in the early 1900s. The population of Tampico is approximately 800.

Tampico and the Hennepin Canal

There was a great deal of debate about whether the canal would help or hurt Tampico during the planning and construction of the canal. For example, there were many who believed that a new East Tampico would develop alongside the "raging canal" where all of the business would move, leaving just residences, schools, and churches at the current Tampico. Many others felt that the canal would be a failure and that Tampico would not be helped or harmed.

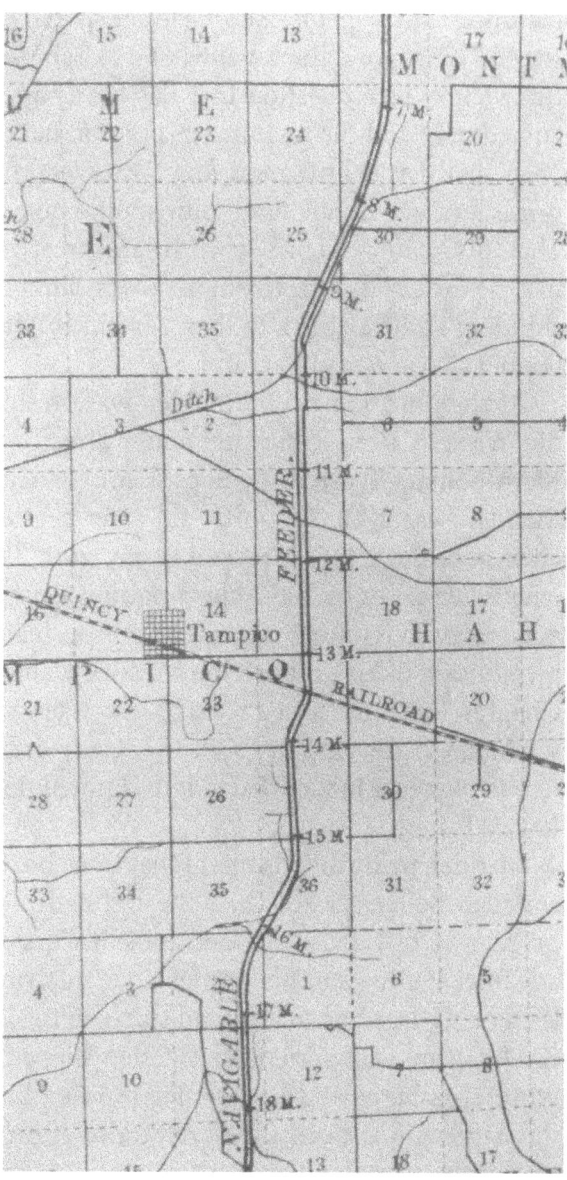

Feeder Canal Map – Tampico Area. Illinois and Mississippi (Hennepin) Canal, "Canal Route Plat Files," Record Series 497.008, Illinois State Archives.

The *Tampico Tornado* newspaper was a big supporter of the canal and reported regularly on its planning and benefits. The October 4, 1907, issue stated "What good the canal will be to Tampico and this vicinity is a question that has been much discussed here and the unanimous opinion has always been that it was little more than a useless ditch to cause farmers trouble and help spoil arable lands. That this opinion is entirely wrong and great benefits may be expected comes from no less an authority on shipping and freight rates than Martin B. Madden, the big Chicago manufacturer."

At the time, Martin B. Madden was president of the Western Stone Company and a director of the Metropolitan Trust & Savings Bank of Chicago. Madden was a big supporter of water service and later became a U.S. Representative from Illinois, where he served on the Appropriations Committee and supported canal and river improvements. In recognition of his support, the Madden Dam on the Chagres River in the Panama Canal water system was named after him in 1935. The reservoir behind it was named Madden Lake, but is now known as Lake Alajuela.

Madden made the statement that canal boats gave shippers better service than the railroads. A firm proponent of canals, Madden took his first job at age fifteen as a water boy in the stone quarries, and then on a barge line that hauled stone on the Illinois & Michigan Canal. In 1871, Madden slipped while tying up a barge and had his leg crushed between the barge and the canal bank. Because of the damage, his leg was amputated at the knee. To prevent a lawsuit, the firm employed Madden as a clerk. He quickly advanced in the stone industry and served as president of the Quarry Owners' Association of the United States, vice president and director of the Builders and Traders' Exchange of Chicago, and as a member of the Chicago City Council during the late 1800s. During his entire career, he was a supporter of water transportation.

During the early 1900s, Tampico was used as a center for construction on the Feeder Canal. Many workers lived in Tampico during the construction, and the rail terminal was often used to bring in materials and supplies. However, when the construction ended, the workers and construction activity left Tampico. With the established elevators on the railroad, a grain terminal was not built on the canal near Tampico, and an East Tampico never materialized.

Tampico and Ronald Reagan

Ronald Reagan, the 40th President of the United States, was born on February 6, 1911, in a second-floor apartment in the Graham Building, located at 111 South Main in Tampico. The building was built in 1896 for G. W. Stauffer and the first floor was used as a tavern until 1915, when it became a bakery. The bakery lasted until First National Bank occupied the building in 1919, which stayed there until 1931.

Jack and Nelle Reagan moved into the apartment on October 1, 1906, while Jack Reagan worked at H. C. Pitney Variety Store, located across Main Street. On May 5, 1911, the family moved to a nearby house at 104 Glassburn Street, today marked with a sign proclaiming it to be the "Ronald Reagan Boyhood Home." The Pitney store closed in 1914 and the Reagan family moved about to nearby cities like Chicago, Galesburg and Monmouth. They returned to Tampico in 1919 when the store reopened, but then moved to Dixon, Illinois, on December 6, 1920, when the store closed again. Because of this, both Tampico and Dixon claim to be the boyhood home of Ronald Reagan. Today, the Main Street apartment has been restored and is available for tours. The downstairs has been restored as the First National Bank, since many of its features remained.

This sign stands alongside the highway entering Tampico, proudly showing a connection between the town and Ronald Reagan, the 40th President of the United States. Photo by Barton Jennings.

14.0 BRIDGE #53 – Jersey Road crosses the canal on a low fill, which the trail crosses at grade. There is a small parking area on the west bank. Jersey Road is located at the south end of a canal S-curve. The original bridge was a 75-foot-long Warren pony truss span with two 21-foot I-beam approach spans and a concrete deck. Just over a mile to the west is Illinois Highway 172, providing good access to this point.

Feeder Canal

The May 31, 1907, issue of the *Tampico Tornado* reported on the opening of several bridges over the canal. The bridges were described as having had their approaches cut down, making them less steep and easier to cross. The approaches were also macadamized, a paving process created by Scottish engineer John Loudon McAdam around 1820. The paving process features compacted layers of single-sized crushed stone, held together by stone dust or another binder such as oil or tar.

The newspaper referred to the two bridges just opened as the Darling and Burke crossings. In 1912, Peter Burke owned the land on the east side of the canal between Jersey Road and Hurd Road. Property maps show that his house was located on today's Jersey Road, where the farmhouse still sits to the east of the canal.

In 1903, Wilford L. Darling lived a mile east of Tampico in Section 24 between Hahnaman Road and Jersey Road. Darling acquired his farm in 1897, and soon served on the school board. The canal passes through the middle of Section 24, and apparently close to the Darling home on Hahnaman Road.

14.3 **KINDER MORGAN PIPELINE** – Look for the signs on the adjacent embankments warning about the underground natural gas pipelines. These underground pipelines supply natural gas for homes and industries to the areas around Chicago, and further to the north.

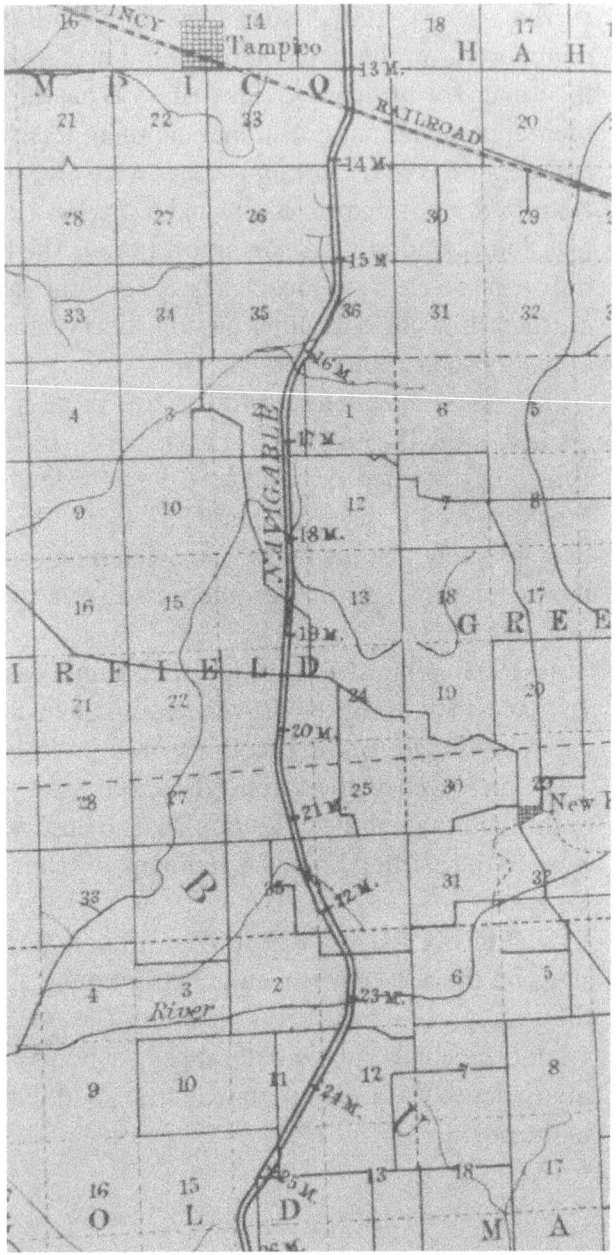

Feeder Canal Map – Tampico South. Illinois and Mississippi (Hennepin) Canal, "Canal Route Plat Files," Record Series 497.008, Illinois State Archives.

Feeder Canal

15.0 BRIDGE #54 – Hurd Road, named for the Hurd family, crosses the canal on a low fill, which the trail crosses at grade. There is a small parking area on the west bank. The original bridge was a 75-foot-long Warren pony truss span with two 21-foot I-beam approach spans and a concrete deck. Just south of this bridge, the canal makes another S-curve to the southwest.

Many of the highway fills on the Feeder Canal are low, so the trail crosses them at grade. Because of this, expect to see a number of gates that are designed to prevent vehicles from using the trail, such as this one at Bridge #54. Photo by Barton Jennings.

In this area are a number of spoil embankments, extra material from the construction and dredging of the canal. While dirt was needed elsewhere for canal construction, the cost of moving it from this area was too great, and the dirt was simply piled along the canal's right-of-way.

15.5 ONEOK NORTH SYSTEM PIPELINE – This pipeline is easy to find thanks to the large "Do Not Anchor or Dredge" sign on the east bank of the canal.

The company reports that the "pipeline transports NGL purity products and various refined products, including unleaded gasoline and diesel fuel throughout the Midwest markets, particularly near Chicago, Illinois." NGL products are Natural Gas Liquids such as ethane, propane, normal butane, isobutane and natural gasoline, and are used for manufacturing by the petrochemical industry, by refineries in the production of motor gasoline, and by industrial and residential consumers as fuel.

16.0 **FAIRFIELD DITCH #1** – This drainage canal passes under the Hennepin Canal here. Fairfield Ditch #1 forms to the northeast and drains a number of fields, moving the water south to the Green River. The culvert features a drain system for overflow canal waters on the east bank.

This ditch is one of the few homes in Illinois of the endangered blacknose shiner and weed shiner. The blacknose shiner is a species of minnow that requires very clear water and moderate amounts of vegetation. They are noted for their black nose that turns into a black stripe along their body, and they are typically just 2-3 inches long. The weed shiner is smaller at 1-2 inches long, and is generally located in small-to-moderate sized streams of slow-to-moderate flow. The name weed shiner is an incorrect description of the minnow as they are prevalent in both vegetated and non-vegetated waterways.

16.1 **BRIDGE #55** – Osage Road, also known as County Road 3000 North, crosses the canal on what is known as Bridge #55. Here, it also serves as the county line between Whiteside County to the north, and Bureau County to the south. **Whiteside Coun-**

Feeder Canal

ty was created from parts of Jo Davies and Henry counties in 1836. The county, which borders on the Mississippi River, was named for General Samuel Whiteside, an Illinois officer in the War of 1812 and the Black Hawk War. The county seat is Morrison, and the current population is approximately 60,000. Whiteside County includes the birthplace of President Ronald Reagan – Tampico.

Bureau County was organized out of Putnam County in 1837 with its county seat at Princeton. It was named for Michel or Pierre de Beuro, French Creoles, who ran a trading post from 1776 until 1790 near where Big Bureau Creek empties into the Illinois River. The southern part of Bureau County includes part of the Military Tract, established in May 1812, to provide bounty lands as payment to volunteer soldiers who participated in the War of 1812. The land was surveyed in 1815-1816 and opened to settlement. At the time, the land was a mix of forest and wild prairie. Today, major parts of the county are planted in corn or soybeans and the county's population is less than 40,000.

Like most roads in this area, Osage Road crosses the Hennepin Canal on a low fill. Osage Road also uses the name 3000 North Avenue. The original bridge was a 75-foot-long Warren pony truss span with two 21-foot I-beam approach spans, with a plank deck that was sixteen feet wide.

16.2 TRANSCONTINENTAL CABLE CROSSING – Look for the AT&T warning signs, mounted on tall wooden poles. This line heads west from the Chicago area and provides connections across the country.

17.2 BRIDGE #56 – County Road 2900 North crosses the canal using a modern concrete bridge. Also known as Illinois Highway 92, there is a parking lot, boat ramp, and toilet on the west side of the canal alongside the Hennepin Canal Parkway Trail. As found at most major access points, there are also three signs that explain the canal's history and engineering. At one time there was an overseer's house here, built by the Corps of Engineers. It was a two-storied frame house with eight rooms on a foundation measuring 24 feet wide and 30 feet long.

There are plenty of signs at Bridge #56, including those that deal with boating and fishing regulations, and those that explain the history of the canal. Photo by Barton Jennings.

As the canal started regular operations, the Corps of Engineers started using generic structures. One of these was a Blaw-Knox Company steel garage, built here as a storage building for the overseer's house. Blaw-Knox started as two separate companies, each working with steel shapes and forms. Jacob B. Blaw of Philadelphia, Pennsylvania, had patented a

Feeder Canal

re-useable steel form for constructing concrete sewers and tunnel linings. The Blaw Collapsible Steel Centering Company was created in 1906, and became the Blaw Steel Centering Company, or Blaw Steel Construction Company (records conflict on the name) in 1911. Meanwhile, the Knox Pressed and Welded Steel Company was created in 1909 to make pressed and welded steel for the manufacture of water-cooled equipment for open hearth furnaces and for other high temperature applications.

On July 6, 1917, the two firms merged to create The Blaw-Knox Company. As advertised, if a project or product required large metal components, Blaw-Knox was often involved. Among their products were prefabricated buildings of all sizes, from large factories and warehouses to small temporary portable housing and offices for contractors. The firm also designed railroad freight houses, gasoline stations, garages, watchman's houses, and other such buildings. The Corps of Engineers bought several of their metal structures, including the Handy House 1928 (a 14'x22'x8' garage structure) and Garage Model #23, a building designed in 1929.

At one time, on the east side of the canal and south of the bridge was a Smith-Hippen Company grain elevator. This elevator was apparently similar to the one at Mile 20 on the Feeder Canal, as the lot was the same size (600 feet by 110 feet). The earliest contract was dated May 1, 1909, and contracts lasted through 1927, when Turner-Hudnut bought the firm.

As the canal aged and technology improved, changes in how things were done reduced the need for staffing. Originally, canal inspectors walked or boated the route, taking a full day to inspect their typical six-mile territory. However, photos from 1936 show tire tracks on the towpath on the west side of the Feeder Canal. The photo also shows that there was no towpath on the east side of the Feeder Canal around Bridge #56.

This Corps of Engineers photo from April 1936 shows a typical bridge on the lower part of the Feeder Canal, a 75-foot-long Warren pony truss span with two 21-foot I-beam approach spans. Illinois and Mississippi (Hennepin) Canal, "Photographic Files," Record Series 497.037, Illinois State Archives.

Technology was also impacting the use of roadways and bridges, and heavier and larger trucks were becoming an issue. There was pressure to make the bridges larger and with more weight capacity. The Corps was still responsible for the maintenance and repair of these bridges, and accidents were an issue for them. For example, on August 4, 1955, a truck drove through the railing of the east approach span of Bridge #56 and landed in the canal.

Bridge #56 marks a divide in the canal trail. North of here to Bridge #46 at Milepost 3.6, the trail is generally grassy with some small stone. South of here, the trail is generally paved. The trail continues to be

Feeder Canal

on the west bank and the canal is lined by a thin row of trees as it passes through open farmland.

The trail is often at a higher elevation than the surrounding fields. This provides views such as this one of a neighboring farm. Note the traditional gambrel roof design on the barns, used by the Corps of Engineers for many of its canal houses. Photo by Barton Jennings.

17.9 FAIRFIELD UNION SPECIAL DITCH – Look for the fence alongside the parkway trail, and the spillway and flush duct on the east bank of the canal. This drainage ditch starts in farmland to the east, flows west under the Hennepin Canal, and then to the southwest where it eventually flows into the Green River. This is one of the few places in Illinois where the endangered weed shiner is still known to exist.

18.6 BRIDGE #57 – County Road 425 East crosses the canal on an angled fill. The Hennepin Canal Parkway Trail passes through the west end of the fill using a large culvert. The original bridge was a 75-foot-long Warren pony truss span with two 21-foot I-beam approach spans, with a plank deck that was sixteen feet wide. This was the most common design used on the Feeder Canal.

To the southeast is a low, wooded hill standing about fifty feet above the surrounding farmland. It helps to create a small wooded area alongside the canal. However, heading south, the east bank is lightly treed, while the west bank still features a row of trees about fifty feet thick, providing nice afternoon shade.

On the lower part of the Feeder Canal, there are a number of private homes and camps, many with their own boat docks. This one is located not far south of Bridge #57. Photo by Barton Jennings.

19.3 DRAINAGE CANAL – Look for the fencing alongside the parkway trail. This protects those using the trail from falling into the drainage canal, which moves water from this area westward to the Fairfield Union Special Ditch. The culvert under the canal has been rebuilt, and it features a concrete block headwall.

Feeder Canal

It is often easy to tell that the trail alongside the Feeder Canal has less foot and bike traffic than the Main Channel trail. Things like the grass growing in the trail and narrow paths around gates clearly show the difference. This photo looks northbound at Mile 19. Photo by Barton Jennings.

19.5 BRIDGE #58 – The canal is crossed by another low fill, this one carrying Backbone Road, earlier known as Old Indian Trail. The original bridge was a 75-foot-long Warren pony truss span with two 21-foot I-beam approach spans, and a wooden plank deck that was sixteen feet wide. The trail crosses the road at grade, so watch for traffic.

Just south of here near Mile 20 was a very unique Corps of Engineers building, a concrete patrolman's house. It was the only employee house that was built of concrete. However, it was built to the common design of two stories with a gambrel roof over seven rooms, measuring 22 feet by 28 feet. Thirty employee houses were built to this design, but none others of concrete. The concrete foundation of this unique house can still be found in the woods on a raised embankment.

20.0 SMITH-HIPPEN ELEVATOR – On the west bank, there was another Smith-Hippen elevator, built by 1910. The need to serve the new elevators caused the Corps of Engineers to make a number of improvements along the Feeder Canal. The first project was to raise the lower five bridges, changing them from the twelve-foot clearance back to the originally planned seventeen feet. This allowed larger towboats to move on the Feeder Canal south of this elevator. During the winter of 1911-12, the canal water level was lowered so turning basins could be built at the grain elevators. This allowed towboats and barges to be turned as needed at each elevator. The local turning basin can be found by looking for the moon-shaped cutout in the east bank, with the canal 130 feet wide instead of its normal 90 feet. It should be noted that the Corps of Engineers paid for all of these improvements, and received only $5 an acre per year for the land that the elevators sat on, a real bargain for the grain companies.

According to the *List of Leases Granted by the Secretary of War During the Calendar Year 1915*, the Smith-Hippen Company obtained two leases of canal property on December 1, 1915. One was a short six-month lease at the cost of $2.50 a month, while another was a five-year lease for $5 per year. Both were simply described as being a "tract of land comprised within the right of way for the Illinois & Mississippi Canal," with no further details provided by the report.

Feeder Canal

However, copies of the leases available in the Illinois State Archives add information about the location. First, the lease for the property was initially effective on May 1, 1909, and was good for five years, as most leases along the canal seemed to be. The next piece of information from the lease was that the property was 600 feet along the canal, and then 110 feet deep, providing plenty of room for the grain elevator. The Smith-Hippen lease for the 1.5 acres was renewed on May 1, 1914, with the new rate of $10 per year. By the May 1, 1929, lease, the rate was $31 per year for the property.

During 1927, Smith-Hippen was acquired by the Turner-Hudnut Company. Turner-Hudnut continued the leases of the Smith-Hippen Company. By 1939, Turner-Hudnut was acquired by W. W. Dewey & Sons, Inc. According to a 1946 Corps of Engineers report, the W. W. Dewey Grain Company had an elevator next to the Turner-Hudnut elevator in Pekin, Illinois. Both firms had been listed as Peoria grain merchants since at least the early 1920s.

The Corps of Engineers believed in fences, and made several different types of fence posts. These larger posts were used for gates, indicating that a house or office once stood here. Photo by Barton Jennings.

In the area around Mile 20, there are a number of foundations and fence posts that remain from the many structures that once stood here. This foundation can be found on a slight rise in the woods to the west of the trail. Photo by Barton Jennings.

In this area, the canal makes a slight turn to the south-southeast.

20.6 CORPS OF ENGINEERS HOUSE COMPLEX – At the south end of the curve, and just north of the turnout cut into the east bank, was a typical employee housing complex, located on the west bank of the canal. It included, from the north, a house, a barn, and then an ice house. The ice house was still standing in 1940. However, today this area is heavily wooded.

Feeder Canal

On April 1, 1940, the Corps of Engineers documented their ice house at Mile 20. Note the disassembled ramps used to move ice in and out of the building. Illinois and Mississippi (Hennepin) Canal, "Photographic Files," Record Series 497.037, Illinois State Archives.

20.7 OLD INDIAN BOUNDARY LINE – There is nothing on the ground, but an overhead electrical power line does mark this important location. The line was described as "beginning in La Salle County, at a point on the Fox River, about seventeen miles above its mouth, and thence running west through the northern parts of La Salle, Bureau, Henry and Rock Island counties to the Mississippi River." Following its creation in 1816, tracts of land in the area that were granted by U.S. patents were described as being south or north of this line. The lands south were surveyed in 1821, the lands north in 1833 and 1842. Many maps still show "The Indian Boundary Line" or "The Old Indian Boundary Line", and the line has an interesting history that was described in the April 1935 issue of the *Journal of the Illinois State Historical Society* in the article "The Indian Boundary Line under the Treaty of August 24, 1816," by Charles G. Davis.

The basic version of the story is that many area tribes fought on the side of the British during The War of 1812, and the Treaty of August 24, 1816, signed in St. Louis, established this line to divide land between Indians and whites. Further fighting and treaties led to changes in the line and the eventual removal of the tribes, but the line became a legal reference point for many land surveys. The Old Indian Boundary Line actually has some relationship to the canal, as some sources state that the line was created in such a way that a canal route between Lake Michigan and the Illinois River became possible.

21.2 BRIDGE #59 – This is County Road 2500 North, also shown as County Road 9. It crosses the canal using a high fill that the trail passes through on the west end, although the trail also has connections up to the roadway. This route was an important early road. To the east where County Road 32 comes in from the north was once the Fairfield Church and a small number of houses. To the west about one mile, where 400 East Street runs north-south, was Johnson School. The school was built on land donated by William G. Johnson, thus its name. Nothing remains of either building.

County Road 2500 North stretches across the county, connecting with a number of roads and communities. However, there is very limited parking at this location.

Feeder Canal

On the south end of the Feeder Canal, milepost signs no longer exist in the waterway, and the traditional green signs are used to label locations, such as this one at Bridge #59. Photo by Barton Jennings.

21.5 HUNT SLOUGH – This waterway, another once-wandering slough that has been channelized to drain area fields, passes under the Feeder Canal using two modern corrugated culverts, and is easily seen from the trail. Hunt Slough flows west, joins with another canal, and then flows into the Green River. Look for the large culvert that flows under the Feeder Canal.

Hunt Slough was likely named for George Hunt, who arrived in Bureau County in 1846, acquiring 80 acres in today's Gold Township. George Hunt is generally recognized as one of the earliest pioneers of the area, and cleared land and farmed here until his death. Maps from 1892 show farms east of here operated by Charles D. Hunt and George C. Hunt, sons of George Hunt.

Not far south of Hunt Slough, the canal passes through some wooded land with pine trees, unique for much of the canal's path. There are several small clearings to the west, one used as a dump pile for canal debris such as broken fence posts and poles. Several larger-than-normal fence posts show that this area once housed another canal facility.

22.6 BRIDGE #60 – County Road 2370 North crosses the canal here on a low fill. The original bridge was a 75-foot-long Warren pony truss span with two 21-foot I-beam approach spans, and a plank deck that was sixteen feet wide. There is limited parking here due to guardrails and canal access roads. The canal turns back to the south as it passes under Bridge #60.

There are a number of houses and trailers on the west side of the Feeder Canal in this area, especially south of Bridge #60. This is part of Lee's Recreational Campground, mostly a summer vacation facility. However, some of the houses are used year round. With direct access to the canal, several have their own docks on the water.

Overseer's House

At one time there was an office, overseer's house and a barn at Mile 22.8, built by the Corps of Engineers. To the north was an office, with a foundation that measured 18'x40'. The foundation can still be seen next to the trail, and several concrete bollards (often called snubbing posts by the Corps of Engineers) and other canal items, now considered to be trash, have been dumped inside. Further south was one of the last three overseer's houses left on the property when the canal was added to the National Register of Historic Places. As described, the house was a "two-storied frame house with eight rooms on a foundation twenty-four feet wide and thirty feet long." There were a total of thirteen of these overseer's houses built by the Corps of Engineers.

The foundation of one of the Corps of Engineers structures still exists not far south of Bridge #60. Also in this area are several concrete sidewalks and fence posts that indicate how busy this location once was. Photo by Barton Jennings.

At the south end of the current houses are several interesting features from the canal's early days. There is an extension of the canal fencing to the trail, and a concrete sidewalk is located on the north side of the fence. To the south of this fence is a small pile of concrete bollards, removed from alongside the canal. These bollards were used to tie up barges and boats that were used on the canal.

South of this fence is an open area, and then the remains of another fence, that probably once surrounded this area. Besides a house for workers, many of these locations also featured a warehouse, barn, and other structures. Gardens and livestock were also often kept by the employees. All of these structures were here at one time, spread alongside the canal.

23.1 AQUEDUCT #9 – This five-span concrete trough on concrete piers aqueduct crosses the Green River, giving it the name of the Green River Aqueduct. The Modern Steel Structural Company of Waukesha, Wisconsin, was involved with its construction, and the aqueduct was built in 1904 and is of the same design as the others on the Hennepin Canal system. The *Tampico Tornado* newspaper, in its December 9, 1904, issue, had an article entitled "Green River Aqueduct Is Completed." The article stated that the aqueduct was "one of the largest concrete structures ever undertaken in Northwestern Illinois" and "has just been completed." The newspaper article also stated that 3820 barrels of cement were used to build the aqueduct.

Aqueduct #9 can easily be photographed from the shore of the Green River, where a bit of time can be taken to fish, swim or even use the swing ropes that someone has installed. Photo by Barton Jennings.

Feeder Canal

When Henry and several surrounding counties were drained, the Green River was straightened and channelized as a part of the work, and many early maps show it as the Green River Ditch. The river flows to the west and enters the Rock River south of Colona. The main channel of the Hennepin Canal follows the Green River in that direction.

On the aqueduct was a set of emergency gates that could shut off the water flow should the canal suffer a break on the feeder, main route, or on this aqueduct. These gates used a Desfontaines Gate, a design created by M. Desfontaines, the chief engineer of the Marne-Rhine Canal in France. This design of gate is like one side of a barrel, and when water flows the gate is on the bottom of the water channel. To close the gate, it is revolved on a horizontal axis and rested on a concrete pedestal, blocking the flow of water. Only a single gate was needed, as it extended across the entire aqueduct. However, there were gates on each end of the aqueduct because of the fear of losing the aqueduct to flooding. A feature of the aqueduct was that when a gate was closed, outlets would open and water could pour into the Green River. Look for the notches in the ends of the aqueduct where the gates would rest when closed.

This fear was justified. In 1909, the southeast corner of the aqueduct was lost three different times, requiring the hiring of hundreds of temporary workers. The first failure was during the night of May 16-17, 1909. After basic repairs were made, the area failed again on June 24, 1909, with Corps of Engineers employees watching. Repairs were again made, but high water on July 13th led to the third failure in two months. The canal was reopened on July 23, 1909.

Aqueduct #9 still exists and the trail crosses it on the west side. Photo by Barton Jennings.

The Hennepin Canal Parkway Trail crosses the Green River on the west side of the aqueduct. The canal turns to the southwest at the south end of the aqueduct. From here to mile 24.4, the trail generally passes through thick woods, with wildlife quite common.

23.4 BRIDGE #61 – County Road 2285 North curves across the canal on a fill at this location. Like the majority of the bridges on the Feeder Canal, the original bridge was a 75-foot-long Warren pony truss span with two 21-foot I-beam approach spans, and a plank deck that was sixteen feet wide.

The trail crosses County Road 2285 North at grade, and guard rails and canal access roads leave little to no area parking. Heading south, there is a flooded hardwood swamp to the west that is often full of various types of waterfowl, deer, squirrels, and other wildlife.

Just south of Bridge #61, look for the concrete mooring bollard alongside the canal. There were once hundreds, if not thousands of these bollards, installed to allow barges to tie up for loading/unloading while awaiting their turn through a lock or aqueduct, or while parking at night. While many remain as part of the concrete locks, most of those scattered alongside the canal like this one have been removed for safety purposes, and to make mowing the canal right-of-way easier. What is hard to tell is that the bollard actually goes about four feet down, providing enormous strength to hold any barge or boat in place. There are several piles of these bollards alongside the canal where they have been placed after their removal.

Almost hidden in the brush alongside the Feeder Canal is this concrete bollard, also known as a snubbing post by the Corps of Engineers. They were used by boats to tie themselves to the banks. This is one of the few concrete bollards that still remain, as most have been removed for safety reasons. Photo by Barton Jennings.

Every once in a while, something unusual pops up along the Hennepin Canal. During early Spring 2019, these two instruments were found hanging from a tree at Milepost 23.5. There must certainly be a good story somewhere which explains them. Photo by Barton Jennings.

24.4 GOLD TOWNSHIP ELEVATOR COMPANY – In 1915, the Secretary of War leased "a tract of land within right of way of the Illinois and Mississippi Canal, Ill., containing 1.03 acres more or less" to the Gold Township Elevator Company. The term of the lease for the 500'x90' tract was for five years starting on January 1, 1915, and the lease payment was $5 per year. Located on the west bank of the canal, this elevator company was organized on January 9, 1915, by a number of Gold Township farmers and businessmen to promote the local economy. Gold Township was named for the large amount of fish and game in the area, something the area's earliest settlers felt was as "good as gold."

A September 1916 report by the Secretary of State of Illinois stated that the company had capital stock of $2800, and the headquarters was shown to be

Feeder Canal

Sheffield. The incorporation records show that three farmers with major land holdings just west of here – Herman Gray, M. C. Roe, and A. E. DeMange – as well as businessman F. G. Boyden, were the main parties responsible for the elevator's organization. F. G. Boyden once owned the *Bureau County Times*, and later the *Sheffield Times* newspapers. The Boyden family ran several general stores and banks in towns across a several county area.

By 1923, M. C. Roe was shown as the company's president, and J. W. Gish as company secretary. Various reports show that M. C. Roe had leased a great deal of land out to other farmers, but little else is known about the elevator company, except the last lease with Gold Township Elevator seemed to have been written January 1, 1930. However, there was a lease dated January 1, 1935, with Turner-Hudnut, for the same property. No remains of the elevator can be found alongside the canal, and a home with several livestock sheds now stands in its place.

Heading south to Bridge #62, the trail is right next to, but above, County Road 410 East. County Road 425 East is alongside the canal to the east. Because of this, there are few trees alongside the canal and trail, creating some great views of the area farmland.

25.4 BRIDGE #62 – County Road 410 East Street follows the canal on the west side and then crosses the canal on a high fill at this location. A large culvert is used by the Hennepin Canal Parkway Trail to pass through the west end of the fill. There is a limited amount of parking to the east near a traditional farm complex, but don't block the access gates. The original bridge was a 75-foot-long Warren pony truss span with two 21-foot I-beam approach spans. The bridge had a plank deck that was sixteen feet wide.

Just to the south, the canal turns back to the south and then makes an S-curve to the southwest, eventually again heading due south at Bridge #63. Throughout this area, the right-of-way is lined with concrete fence posts and sections of the telephone line are still marked by concrete telephone poles.

On the east side of the canal south of Mile 26 are several docks and a number of cabins and houses at what is known as Rogue's Roost. The Corps of Engineers once had a house and barn in this area.

There are a number of places along the Feeder Canal where the telephone poles still stand. The telephone poles manufactured by the Corps of Engineers used a concrete pole with a wood cross-piece, as clearly shown by the remains of this pole at Milepost 25.8. Photo by Barton Jennings.

Feeder Canal

27.0 BRIDGE #63 – County Road 2000 North crosses the Feeder Canal here on a high fill. The trail passes through the west end of the fill, and the canal uses a similar corrugated culvert. The original Bridge #63 was a 75-foot-long Warren pony truss span with two 21-foot I-beam approach spans, and a plank deck that was sixteen feet wide. The highway guard rails prevent much parking here.

Not far north and south of this bridge are several original culverts that pass under the canal. The one just north of Bridge #63 consists of a single steel culvert, with its ends protected by stonework. To the south, near a protection fence, is a culvert consisting of two steel pipes, also protected by stonework.

Culverts like this could be found all over the canal. Most have been replaced with modern corrugated culverts, but this one still has its original steel pipes and concrete block headwall. Photo by Barton Jennings.

27.4 BRIDGE #64 – The location of the last bridge on the Feeder Canal is now a fill that carries County Road 39, 1945 North Avenue. As with most of the other original bridges on the Feeder Canal, this was once a 75-foot-long Warren pony truss span with two 21-foot I-beam approach spans, and a plank deck that was sixteen feet wide. The trail crosses County Road 39 at grade. There is parking, a boat ramp, and toilets to the north of the bridge on the west shore. Watch for the many ground squirrels that have taken over the area.

The area around Bridge #64 is popular with a colony of thirteen-lined ground squirrels, noted for 13 stripes down their backs. The stripes alternate between solid white and dark with white dots. This type of ground squirrel lives in short grasslands and weedy areas, eating grasses, weeds, seeds, crops, earthworms and insects. Photo by Barton Jennings.

The parking lot was once the site of a patrolman's house, with a barn to the north. Reports from the early years of the canal stated that the rent for the house was $10/month. This house featured a living room, kitchen, dining room and bedroom on the first floor. The second floor had two bedrooms, a closet, and a small room for a bathroom that was not installed.

Feeder Canal

Bridge #64 is a popular spot on the Feeder Canal because of this boat ramp, which provides access to the entire Feeder Canal and much of the Main Channel of the canal. Photo by Barton Jennings.

28.3 HICKORY CREEK – Look for the fencing alongside the canal, designed to keep bikers and hikers from falling into the stream. Hickory Creek forms to the east, and then flows west and under the Hennepin Canal. It then turns to the northwest and eventually flows into the Green River. The canal turns to the south-southeast here to head to the Feeder Junction.

On the east bank of the Feeder Canal not far south of Hickory Creek is the Lazy T Campground. The campground has historically featured both RV and tent camping, but is now signed as being for members only. The campground features a dock on the canal for fishing and boating, and most of the 28 sites in the campground are located within 100 feet of the Hennepin Canal.

This was another area of the canal that suffered a break, this one in 1935. The emergency gate at the Green River Aqueduct was used to quickly protect the canal from a total loss of water, and area farms from major flooding.

Hennepin Canal Parkway: History Through the Miles

This small boat dock at Milepost 28.8 on the Feeder Canal belongs to the Lazy T Campground, a private camp on the eastern shore. Photo by Barton Jennings.

29.3 FEEDER JUNCTION – The Feeder Canal flows into the main channel of the Hennepin Canal from the north, forming a large Y-shaped basin. The trail joins with the main channel trail to the west at the 350 East Street crossing at what would be Feeder Canal Milepost 29.6.

A number of concrete telephone poles can be found along the trail, and through the woods to the west.

29.6 TRAIL JUNCTION – The Feeder Canal route of the Hennepin Canal Parkway Trail follows the west side of the basin and joins with the main channel trail at the 350 East Street crossing of the main canal channel (Bridge #18A), at Milepost 28.3 of the Main Channel of the Hennepin Canal.

Feeder Canal

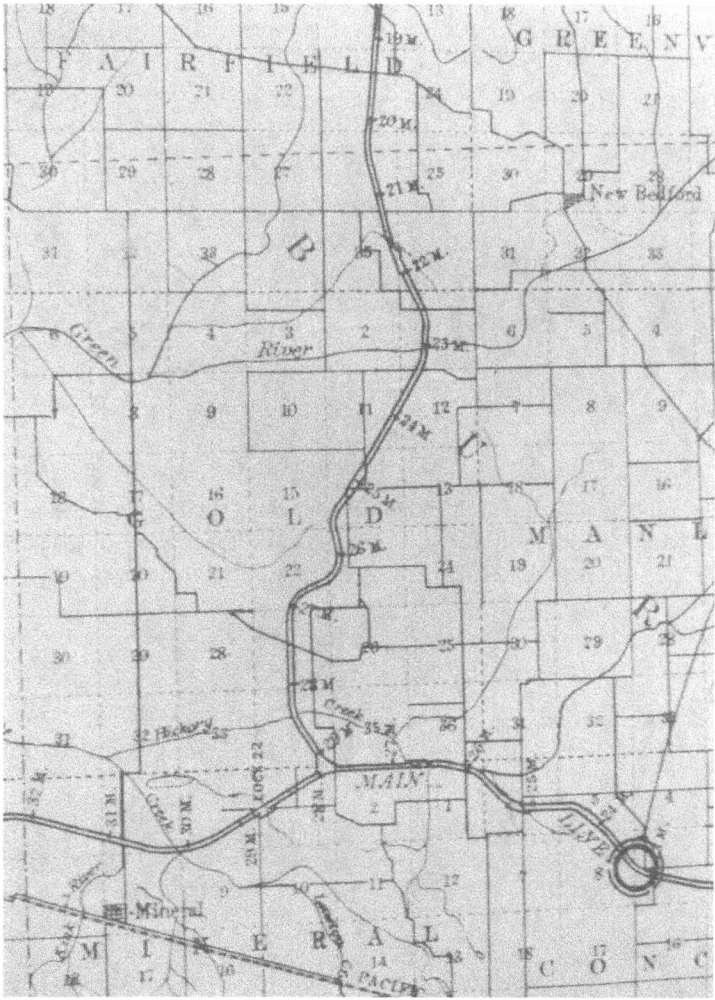

Feeder Canal Map – Feeder Junction North. Illinois and Mississippi (Hennepin) Canal, "Canal Route Plat Files," Record Series 497.008, Illinois State Archives.

This sign marks the south end of the trail along the Feeder Canal, and provides directions to the Hennepin Canal Visitor's Center. The sign is located just north of Bridge #18A. Photo by Barton Jennings.

About the Author

For more than four decades, Barton Jennings has been involved with the transportation industry, including rail, motor carriers, and water. During this time, he has had the pleasure to meet many professionals in the field, and has had access to many of the records of their transportation companies. This experience led to an interest in all transportation operations, especially those with a unique history like the Hennepin Canal.

Bart has a basement with several rooms full of books, timetables and other documents about numerous transportation companies and routes – important research items from a time long before today's internet. Today, Bart Jennings, after years working in the railroad industry, is a professor of supply chain management and teaches transportation operations. He also does research and writes about the history of transportation companies. It is hoped that you enjoy your adventure with the Hennepin Canal and that this book is of assistance in some ways – *Hennepin Canal Parkway: History Through the Miles*.

Hennepin Canal Parkway: History Through the Miles

The author takes a minute to lean against a telephone pole along the Feeder Canal on a pleasant summer afternoon. Photo by Sarah Jennings.

www.ingramcontent.com/pod-product-compliance
Lightning Source LLC
Chambersburg PA
CBHW052008070526
44584CB00016B/1664